THE POLITICS
OF PROTECTION

The U.S. Secret Service
in the Terrorist Age

Philip H. Melanson

PRAEGER SPECIAL STUDIES • PRAEGER SCIENTIFIC

New York • Philadelphia • Eastbourne, UK
Toronto • Hong Kong • Tokyo • Sydney

Library of Congress Cataloging in Publication Data

Melanson, Philip H.
    The politics of protection.

    Bibliography: p.
    Includes index.
    1. United States. Secret Service. I. Title.
HV7961.M44 1984   363.2'8   84-11606
ISBN 0-03-070737-4 (alk. paper)

to Jess and Brett

Published in 1984 by Praeger Publishers
CBS Educational and Professional Publishing
a Division of CBS Inc.
521 Fifth Avenue, New York, NY 10175 USA

© 1984 by Praeger Publishers

456789 052 987654321

Printed in the United States of America
on acid-free paper

ACKNOWLEDGMENTS

I am very grateful to those who in various ways helped me to undertake and complete this project. Excellent research papers from Nancy Gendron and Kevin O'Reilly in the fall of 1981 provided the intellectual stimulus to begin research. My friend and colleague Dr. Lauriston R. King, now at Texas A&M University, read and commented on first-draft material. A grant from the Southeastern Massachusetts University Research Committee in 1983 funded some of the research conducted in Washington, D.C. Liz Tucker, the secretary of the political science department at Southeastern Massachusetts University, typed the large quantity of correspondence required by my research. My research assistants, Robert F. Hoaglund and Joan Smith, worked on various phases of research and manuscript preparation. My largest debt is to my wife Judith who edited and typed the manuscript and provided insight and encouragement throughout all phases of the project.

CONTENTS

INTRODUCTION

The United States Secret Service is one of the most interesting of federal agencies. Its agents and its protective work are witnessed by millions of Americans who watch the president's activities on television or who turn out to see presidential candidates. Unlike FBI and IRS agents whose work is rarely witnessed by a mass audience, Secret Service guards do much of their work in full public view. Despite the public visibility and notoriety of its protective mission, the Secret Service has remained in the shadows of the federal bureaucracy, receiving practically no attention from scholars and very sporadic attention from journalists, mostly during presidential election years or immediately following an assassination attempt.

There are several reasons for this neglect. First, the Secret Service is, by federal standards, a fairly reclusive organization in terms of public relations outreach. It is also a highly secretive agency. Unlike the most secretive federal organizations — CIA, FBI, National Security Agency — which are involved in intelligence gathering, espionage and/or counterespionage, the legitimacy of the Secret Service's secrecy cloak derives from its protective mission, from the claim that the security of protectees will be compromised if the Secret Service reveals too much about its methods and operations. Unlike the CIA and FBI, which have come under heavy criticism during the past 15 years concerning alleged abuses of secrecy, the Secret Service's secrecy, though not nearly as extensive as that of some other agencies, has been subjected to only minor criticism from the press, public, and politicians.

The legitimacy of the Service's secrecy cloak has remained intact for a variety of reasons. One contributing factor is that the organization has escaped the major debacles that have severely tarnished the reputations of the FBI and CIA — the FBI's vendetta against Dr. Martin Luther King, Jr.; the CIA's illegal domestic spying and its relationship to Watergate intrigue. The Secret Service has an excellent organizational reputation among political leaders, the press, and the public. And it has so far been spared any show-and-tell exposés by its former employees, exposés of the kind that have created such embarrassment for the CIA, FBI, and the IRS. The only books written by former Secret Service agents have been so laudatory that they might have been produced by the Secret Service's Office of Public Affairs, though they were not.

The comparative lack of attention given to the Secret Service by scholars studying the federal bureaucracy (and by others who might analyze it from the same rich variety of perspectives that have been applied to the CIA, FBI, and to a lesser extent, IRS) is a result of the Service's relatively small size compared with the FBI and CIA and also results from the dearth of existing data. The Secret Service has not been subjected to lengthy Congressional probes or to extensive Freedom of Information Act (FOIA) litigation that might generate a rich data base about its operation, even in spite of its policies of secrecy. The hundreds of thousands of pages of declassified documents that provide insights to researchers about the workings of FBI and CIA do not exist regarding the Secret Service. There is no Secret Service FOIA reading room where researchers can go to study agency records. The closest thing to it is a newspaper-clippings file maintained by the Service's Office of Public Affairs in Washington, D.C.

The Secret Service did provide data, via interviews, correspondence and telephone calls to its Office of Public Affairs, under the direction of Secret Service Assistant Director Robert R. Snow. The Treasury Department also provided some documentation relating to Secret Service mission and organization, through the office of Richard W. Terry, Special Assistant to the Secretary of the Treasury. In addition to the literature on the American Presidency and to print and elctronic media, the author reviewed previously declassified documents held by FBI, CIA and the National Archives, dealing with American political assassination cases and with domestic intelligence gathering. These files yielded several thousand pages of documents written by or about the Secret Service. This data provided invaluable information concerning the workings of the organization (especially given the absence of such data at Secret Service itself).

The Secret Service is a paradoxical agency — very visible, yet highly secretive; highly professional and merit-based, yet frequently dominated by the political arena in which it operates; a complex, dual-purpose organization with a series of missions and a variety of occupational specializations, but an organization that is stereotyped in the public perception as an elite group of clean-cut, well-dressed men who guard political leaders.

This study is the first major analysis of the U.S. Secret Service in 16 years (by other than a former agent). It seeks to provide a clear and complete portrait of this small but complex federal agency about which little is known in comparison with other agencies.

In addition, this is a study with a decidedly political focus. It will view the Secret Service in terms of its interactions with the American political process and political culture as well as in terms of federal bureaucratic politics. Because of the organization's protective mission, any analysis of the Secret Service must also deal with what political scientist James W. Clarke has called "the darker side of politics" — the specter of political assassination and violence. Assassinations have had a profound impact upon our political system during the past two decades beginning with the assassination of John F. Kennedy.

Because of the Secret Service's mission of protecting political leaders as they perform their political roles, an analysis of the organization provides a unique window into the American political process.

1
PROTECTING MONEY, SECRETS, THEN PRESIDENTS

It should not be concluded that important events in the evolution of governmental programs take place prior to the time when the birth of a new agency is legitimatized by legislative enactment. On the contrary, existing agencies are undergoing a continual process of adaptation and change that may so transform them over a span of years as to make them into almost new organizations.

Herbert A. Simon

Like people, organizations are influenced throughout their lifetime by the conditions of their birth and the experiences of their formative years. The organizational evolution of the United States Secret Service is a colorful one--a checkered history of false starts, reorganizations, changed missions, and political intrigue. Many people probably imagine that the Secret Service evolved in linear fashion, that it was created to protect presidents and still performs this basic mission (though, like baseball players, agents' attire has changed markedly from the nineteenth century to the present). In fact, however, the organization which is now known to the public almost exclusively for its protective mission had no such mission at all for the first three decades of its existence. Along the way to becoming the United States' premier protective agency, the Secret Service actually became the country's predominant espionage agency (though only for a brief interlude).

But there is one mission that the Secret Service has performed consistently from its creation in 1865 until the present. Organizations are usually created in response to a particular problem, and the Service was created to protect something that our system may value even more than

1

the lives of its political leaders—money. The presidential protection mission emerged much later in the organization's history and was a Congressional afterthought.

There were two false starts in the formation of what is now the U.S. Secret Service. During the Civil War, Allan Pinkerton, who had founded the United States' first financially successful private detective agency by making a profit on solving crimes, was working on a criminal case in Baltimore when he claimed to have discovered, inadvertently, a plot to assassinate president-elect Abraham Lincoln (in 1861). Pinkerton reported the plot and Lincoln changed his itinerary and avoided harm.[1] Impressed with Pinkerton's skills at intelligence gathering (and, no doubt, with his reputation as a crime solver), Lincoln and General George B. McClellan held a series of meetings with him. The result was that Pinkerton was allowed to organize a government agency called the Secret Service. He headed it and ran it as a spy agency, sending some of his agents to penetrate the Confederacy and gather intelligence while others formed counterespionage networks in the north. Pinkerton was soon removed from his post: his star fell with that of his friend and patron General McClellan, who was fired as head of the Union Army. Still, an organization called the Secret Service had been established, albeit informally, and was functioning as an intelligence apparatus.

After several months of confusion following Pinkerton's departure, LaFayette C. Baker took over as head of the fledgling organization. Baker, who had participated in a vigilante movement in San Francisco in 1856 (one aimed at Irish immigrants), had risen to the rank of Brigadier General in the Union Army by virtue of his daring espionage work against the Confederacy. The swashbuckling Baker appeared to run the Secret Service as if it too were a vigilante organization. His agents became notorious for disregarding constitutional rights. They made arrests without due process and conducted searches without warrants.[2]

Then, on April 14, 1865, while Baker was still in charge of the Secret Service, Abraham Lincoln became the first U.S. president to be assassinated. The Service had no protective mission at the time. Lincoln's bodyguard for the evening performance at Ford's theater was a Washington, D.C. policeman. The policeman was supposed to secure the corridor that led to the President's box; but he wandered from his post, leaving John Wilkes Booth free to come within a few feet of Lincoln and inflict a mortal head wound at close range.

After Lincoln's death, the Secret Service became so politicized that it was abolished by Lincoln's successor, Andrew Johnson. Johnson discovered

that Secret Service Director Baker had established his own espionage network inside the Johnson White House.[3] Rather than be spied upon, President Johnson simply disbanded the organization. Baker later provided
testimony against Johnson during Johnson's impeachment trial. Baker
was also accused of forging letters to incriminate Johnson. Ironically, the
Secret Service organization which met its demise under Baker would be
reborn with the primary task of catching counterfeiters and forgers.

The organization that would ultimately become the modern Secret
Service was officially created in 1865.[4] This time, it was not created to spy
but to save the U.S. currency system from collapse. It has been estimated
that during the Civil War, one-third of all currency in circulation was
counterfeit. There were about 1600 state banks, each designing and printing its own money. With several thousand varieties of genuine currency in
existence, it was very difficult to spot counterfeit bills. The solution arrived at by Congress was to set up a national currency system. In 1863 Congress created the national banking system and issued the first "United
States notes," a set of bills in denominations ranging from one dollar to
one thousand dollars. Yet the new national system, while making it easier
to detect counterfeit money, did not, by itself, stop counterfeiting. State
and local enforcement of the new system proved ineffective and counterfeiting continued to rise. The new national system needed national-level
enforcement in order to succeed.

On the very afternoon of the day he was assassinated, one of
Lincoln's last meetings was with Secretary of the Treasury William P. Mc-
Cullough, who described the severity of the counterfeiting problem to the
president. McCullough suggested: "We should have a regular permanent
force whose job it will be to put these counterfeiters out of business." Lincoln agreed.[5] But that evening, he was assassinated; the formation of the
modern Secret Service would be delayed for months by the subsequent
political chaos and intrigue, which climaxed in the disbandment of the
Secret Service by President Johnson.

Finally, on July 5, 1865, the Secret Service Division of the Treasury
Department* was established under the Directorship of William P.
Wood, formerly the keeper of the Capitol Prison. Wood was told: "Your
main objective is to restore public confidence in the money of the coun-
try."[6] A squad of ten "operatives" was sworn in collectively along with
Wood. Soon the Service hired additional operatives and even employed

---

*The predecessor Secret Service organization had been located within the War Department.

several exconvicts who had an intimate knowledge of counterfeiting techniques.

Business was brisk. During its first four years of operation, the Service arrested more than two hundred counterfeiters per year. As would become typical of its evolution, it began to broaden its activities into other investigative areas as problems arose—smuggling, piracy, mail robbery, land fraud. At this point in its history, the Secret Service was in the unique position of being the only general federal law enforcement agency —there was no FBI as yet—and, therefore, its operational horizons seemed limitless.

The budding agency also investigated the law enforcement establishments in areas of Texas, Alabama, and Florida where peonage was common practice. Hoboes and convicts were being sold to plantation owners, mines, and factories to perform hard labor. The Service arrested police and even some judges who were involved in the illegal practice.[7]

In 1867 Congress expanded the Secret Service's mission to "detecting persons perpetrating frauds against the government." Congress envisioned that the Service would use this charge in order to prevent false bounty claims and false claims regarding back pay from the federal government. But the vague Congressional mandate and the Service's unique status as the only federal law enforcement agency caused the organization to become involved in a wide variety of activities.

In Pulaski, Tennessee a group of young men organized a post–Civil War group which they called the Ku Klux Klan.[8] Soon the white robed, hooded Klansmen were terrorizing and assaulting blacks and conducting lynchings. Congress sent a resolution to President Grant condemning the KKK. Grant's attorney general dispatched eight Secret Service operatives to investigate the Klan in North and South Carolina, Alabama, Florida, and Georgia, as well as Tennessee. Over the next three years, the Secret Service arrested several hundred persons involved in Klan activities.

In 1869, Herman C. Whitley became the second Director of the formally established U.S. Secret Service. He is credited with transforming the organization into a centralized, professionalized law enforcement unit—the embryonic beginning of a modern bureaucratic agency. Whitley began by dismissing every one of the operatives hired by his predecessor. He then discontinued the practice of giving operatives a twenty–five-dollar bounty for each successful counterfeiting conviction. He cultivated a working relationship with local police departments, as the FBI would do during the following century.

Whitley moved the organization's headquarters from Washington to New York and expanded the headquarters operation, creating the position of assistant director and hiring four clerks and a messenger. This may have been bureaucratically top heavy since the organization had only twenty operatives in the field; but that was twice as many operatives as it had five years earlier at its founding, and the creation of a viable headquarters that could provide central direction was a landmark development in the Service's evolution.

Whitley used his new headquarters office to institute the compilation of criminal records to aid in investigations. He required daily reports from all operatives (accounting for their time and resources). By 1870 there were 11 field offices throughout the century. Each of the 20 operatives was allowed to employ assistants and to develop their own network of informants. Field offices were required to report all data to headquarters (a practice which, in the modern era, would generate literally tons of documents).

Whitley issued badges to all operatives, but the expensive ($25) shields were paid for by involuntary deductions from the operatives' paychecks. The money was generously returned upon resignation or retirement, if the badge was turned in.

Whitley's five-year stewardship created the foundation for a bureaucratized, centralized, professionalized federal law enforcement agency. However, upon his departure in 1874, the agency fell into political disfavor and underwent hard times. For reasons not historically clear, the Solicitor General's office launched an investigation of the Secret Service. The final report of the investigation recommended that the Service be totally reconstructed and that most of its investigative work be turned over to federal marshals and to the U.S. attorney's office. The number of Secret Service operatives was cut in half (from 20 to 10), which was barely enough to provide one operative for each field office. Stripped of its investigative mission and its personnel by a hostile Treasury Department and an empire-building U.S. attorney's office, the tiny agency floundered.

By 1880, 15 years after its creation, the Secret Service had no public support or clientele and no political support in Congress. That year, Congress cut the Service's budget from $100,000 to $60,000. Moreover, Congress added a rider to the budget appropriation that restricted the Service to performing only one mission—investigating counterfeiting and forging. Congress had become distrustful of the organization. The Service suffered because of the reputations of several of its operatives who allegedly paid little attention to constitutional niceties in their investigative work.[9] Thus the Secret Service had come full circle in only fifteen years: its expanded investigative and law enforcement missions had been cut back to its original, narrow mission of stopping counterfeiters and forgers.

By the early 1890s things had begun to turn around. The Service's annual appropriations were on the rise and its duties were broadened a bit to include the investigation of fraudulent pension claims and of the management of national banks. Then, in 1898, the organization suffered another setback when a routine investigation by the office of the Secretary of the Treasury discovered what was regarded as a blatant misuse of the Service's budget for an activity which it had no authority to engage in—the protection of a president's private home. The Treasury investigation revealed that, on several occasions, two or three Secret Service "operatives" had been assigned to guard President McKinley's vacation retreat in Massachusetts.

In 1981 when the Service was legally authorized to protect presidents, there would be controversy over agents guarding President Ronald Reagan's empty Hollywood home while the Reagans waited for a buyer. But in 1898, the Service had no formal protective mission at all, and the guarding of a president's home was perceived as administratively scandalous. Then Director of the Secret Service William P. Hazen was demoted to field operative because of the shocking "mismanagement."

The Secret Service was pulled from its organizational-political limbo by the Spanish–American War. As in the Civil War, the organization was pressed into espionage duty. It served as the primary intelligence agency for President McKinley's War Department, to the displacement of none other than the Pinkerton Detective Agency. It will be recalled that Allan Pinkerton, the detective agency's founder, headed the Secret Service during its first, short–lived incarnation.

By 1898 the Pinkerton Agency was being run by Allan Pinkerton's two sons, and it had become a powerful nationwide organization— America's leading private detective agency.[10] The Pinkerton family's staunch anti-communism and anti-anarchism coupled with the size of its operation made the firm the leading candidate to receive a contract to perform spy chores during the Spanish American War. Ultimately, however—to the Secret Service's benefit—the firm's tarnished reputation, which included charges of falsifying evidence and bungling criminal cases, caused the McKinley administration to reject the idea of contracting with the Pinkerton Agency.[11] Thus the Secret Service became a domestic intelligence agency run by civilians in the Treasury Department. It worked closely with the departments of State and War in performing counterintelligence functions throughout the war with Spain. The Service's espionage mission was the result not only of the rejection of the Pinkerton firm but also of a close relationship between Secret Service Director John E. Wilke and President McKinley.[12] Wilke was brought into the President's inner circle of wartime advisors; the Secret Service soon became the United States' foremost spy agency.

Its work during the Spanish-American War primarily involved the gathering of military intelligence rather than political intelligence concerning Spain.[13] It also conducted counterespionage activities against Spanish agents and engaged in counterinsurgency against Spanish agents and sympathizers who attempted to destabilize the United States by fomenting political unrest within its borders and who sought to raise money for the Spanish cause from within the U.S.[14] The Service ran a far flung network of operatives that extended to Cuba.[15] It shadowed Spanish agents in Washington, D.C., New York, Florida, Louisiana, and Washington state.[16]

In one case, the Secret Service obtained a letter written by an American citizen to a Spanish diplomat describing U.S. coastal defenses and suggesting how to circumvent them. In its most famous case, the Service exposed Ramon Carranza, a former attaché of the Spanish legation in Washington, D.C., as the spymaster in charge of the entire Spanish espionage network in the United States.

Overall, the Secret Service performed its espionage duties fairly well. It seemed more adept at counterintelligence work than at producing effective intelligence. In the latter area, it was criticized for centralizing information (hoarding it) without properly analyzing it or dispensing it to the military.[17]

By the end of the war, Secret Service Director Wilke had built the organization into what historian Rhodri Jefferys-Jones described as "the pivotal intelligence agency of its day." At this point in its history, the Secret Service could well have evolved to become something like the modern FBI or the CIA, or even a combination of both (performing both domestic and foreign intelligence roles). Instead, it was sidetracked by a variety of factors: political intrigue, bureaucratic rivalries, and by the emergence of a new mission which was to become the organization's hallmark—presidential protection.

Who protected presidents prior to the Secret Service? Often no one did; sometimes, they protected themselves. Andrew Jackson was foremost among the selfprotectors. In 1835 while exiting the Capitol rotunda after attending a funeral service for a Congressman, the unguarded president was approached by Richard Lawrence, who drew a small pistol and fired at the president from only thirteen feet away. The cap went off with a loud report but the powder failed to ignite and the gun misfired. Jackson rushed toward his attacker while brandishing his cane. Lawrence dropped the first gun and pulled out a second: this time, he fired at the President's chest from point blank range.[18] The second gun also misfired. The crowd subdued the assailant.

Previously Jackson had had an encounter in the White House with a former Navy man who had been expelled from the military for allegedly misappropriating funds. The man registered his protest with the president by striking him in the face. Jackson grabbed his trusty cane and chased the intruder out of the mansion.[19]

During the Civil War, President Lincoln walked unescorted through the city of Richmond to inspect the aftermath of the fierce fighting. He took numerous walks and coach rides without any bodyguards.[20] In fact, the first twenty-five of our forty presidents had no formal protection at all, not until the Secret Service was formally authorized to protect President Theodore Roosevelt in 1906. (The Secret Service had performed informal, sporadic protective duties for presidents since 1894.[21])

Secret Service agents had actually been in close proximity to two presidential assassinations before the Service was given authorization for its protective mission. A Secret Service agent wrote in his daily report of July 2, 1881 that he observed some commotion of unknown origin at the railway station in Washington, D.C. and witnessed police taking a man into custody. The man turned out to be Charles Guiteau, who had just assassinated President James A. Garfield.[22]

In 1901 President William McKinley was shot while standing in a reception line greeting visitors to the Pan American Exposition in Buffalo, New York. Three Secret Service agents were present and were standing near the president at the time of the shooting. They had been sent by the director of the Secret Service as a courtesy to the president to help keep the reception line moving and prevent the crowds from overwhelming the chief executive.[23]

Following the assassination of President Garfield in 1881, Congress considered legislation that would make an attack on a president a federal crime, but such a law would not be passed until after the assassination of John F. Kennedy. Congress tried unsuccessfully to pass some kind of protective legislation, but failed. The only existing law on the books was one that made it possible to investigate and prosecute anyone who sent obscene matter to the president.[24] Yet assaulting or assassinating a president was not a federal crime.

The Secret Service began to assume protective duties even in the absence of legislation. In the late 1890s its part-time, informal protection of the president increased to become nearly full-time. In 1894 the Service helped to foil an assassination plot against President Cleveland that was hatched by a group of Colorado gamblers. Word of the plot came to the attention of the White House, which then requested that the Secret Service conduct an investigation. This request came not because the Service had a protective mission but because it was the only federal law enforcement agency of any consequence.[25] The Service investigation revealed that there was, in fact, a threat to the President's life. Both the Secret Service operative who had investigated the plot in Colorado and his hired informant were commissioned as special policemen and assigned to the White House to watch for suspicious persons who might turn out to be the assassins sent by the Western gamblers. This assignment continued for several months until President Cleveland left Washington for his summer vacation.

Following the assassination of President McKinley in 1901, Congress again tried to produce protective legislation. No fewer than seventeen bills were introduced; again none passed.[26] One unsuccessful resolution called for a constitutional amendment that would make presidential assassination an act of treason. A bill making it a federal crime to assault a president died in committee. One measure that had broad support but ultimately failed would have given formal responsibility for presidential protection to the U.S. Army.

While Congress groped for some constitutional or legal formula, President Theodore Roosevelt remained unprotected. The Secretary of the Treasury directed the Secret Service to provide protection, even without a legal authorization. However, Roosevelt was not fretting over the fate of the protective mandate in the Congressional morass. He wrote to his friend Senator Henry Cabot Lodge: "Of course they [the Secret Service] would not be the least use in preventing any assault upon my life. I do not believe there is any danger of such an assault."[27]

Despite Congressional inaction and presidential indifferrence, the first White House protective detail was established by the Secret Service in 1901. It consisted of two full-time agents. Additional agents were provided when Roosevelt traveled.[28] Since the Congress had not appropriated any money for Secret Service protection, the Service was forced to absorb the cost, thus reducing the funds available for pursuing counterfeiters.

The formation of a presidential protection detail without a legal mandate drew sharp criticism from Congress, which also discovered other instances in which Secret Service agents had been used for work in various cabinet departments. Congress formally prohibited Secret Service agents from performing any duties except certain specified ones within the Treasury Department. The White House detail was now illegal.[29] Thus the Congress actually prevented the Service from providing protection to the president while the Congress itself floundered in its search for acceptable protective legislation.

Finally, five years after the assassination of President McKinley, Congress passed a single line of legislation inserted into The Sundry Civil Expenses Act of 1907 (passed in 1906) that legalized the use of appropriated funds "for the protection of the person of the president of the United States."[30] Still, assault on a president was not a federal crime.

Just when the Service obtained authorization for a protective mission, it ran afoul of the Congress, which took punitive action. In 1907 there was a scandal involving false homestead claims that were being used to defraud the federal government of valuable western timberland. Secret Service agents had been loaned to the Justice Department to investigate the case. The agents traced the conspiracy-to-defraud to an Oregon senator and congressman, who were prosecuted. Congress reacted by tacking on a rider to the 1909 appropriations bill that made it impossible for Secret Service agents to be paid by funds from any other government agency (as the Justice Department had done in investigating the western land fraud). President Roosevelt was incensed by Congress' action which, in effect, denied federal agencies the use of the government's best law enforcement agents. He wrote:[31]

> The chief argument in favor of this provision was that the Congressmen did not want to be investigated by the Secret Service men. . . . I do not believe that it is in the public interest to protect criminals in any branch of the public service.

Roosevelt used his executive authority to transfer permanently eight Secret Service agents to the Justice Department so that it could continue criminal investigations.[32] In the long run, this had a much greater impact upon the evolution of the Secret Service than did the political fallout from the homestead scandal, for these eight agents became the nucleus for the formation of the FBI, which was founded in 1908.

During the decade following Congressional authorization of a protective mission (1906), that mission was solidified and expanded.[33] In 1908 the Service began to protect presidents-elect when it assumed responsibility for guarding William Howard Taft after his victory. In 1913 Congress gave the Service a more protracted protective authority. The 1906 authorization had granted only temporary authority. Yet, even this new authority had to be renewed annually until 1951 when Congress finally made it permanent.

In 1917 Congress passed a law making it a crime to threaten a president by mail or any other means. This first threat statute, passed in response to an increased volume of hate mail arriving at the Wilson White House, expanded the Service's investigative and protective roles. In that same year, Congress for the first time authorized the Service to protect the president's immediate family. The White House detail more than doubled, from two to five agents.

Even a burgeoning protective mission did not prevent the Service from again becoming involved in the activity that had long preceded protection—espionage. As it had done during the Civil War and the Spanish-American War, the organization assumed intelligence duties in World War I, working closely with the State Department in both intelligence gathering and counterespionage.[34] Before America entered the war, President Wilson directed the Service to investigate German violations of U.S. neutrality, particularly sabotage against American factories that manufactured supplies used by the allies. The Service set up a counterespionage unit at its New York field office and staffed it with eleven agents.

This unit's most celebrated case involved the briefcase of Dr. Heinrich Alpert. The Service had an associate of Alpert's under surveillance because he was the publisher of a pro-German newspaper called "The Fatherland." The publisher met with Alpert on a trolley, then departed. The Secret Service agent who was now watching Alpert noticed that as the doctor rushed out of the trolley to avoid missing his stop, he forgot his briefcase. The agent grabbed it and departed by another exit.[35] The combination of Alpert's thoughtlessness and the agent's quick thinking yielded an intelligence bonanza. Alpert turned out to be the chief fiscal agent for Germany's American spy operations. An account book revealed that he had received $27 million in German funds with which to attempt to cut off the flow of American supplies to the allies by causing strikes and logistical problems within American industry. He also used the money to purchase newspapers and publishing companies with which to launch a propaganda blitz aimed at preventing America from entering the war. Agents also found Alpert's plan for the military occupation of the United States, the first phase of which called for 85,000 German troops to land in New York City and seal the city off from the rest of the country until it surrendered because of starvation.

Throughout this period of vastly increased protective responsibilities and a resumption of espionage activities, the Secret Service continued to perform its original function of combating counterfeiters and forgers. In 1917 alone, agents chalked up 1,038 counterfeiting convictions and seized $283,706 in phony bills and coins. They also investigated the counterfeiting of internal revenue stamps used for liquor and pursued investigations of federal pension fraud.

World War I was to be the Secret Service's last major foray into intelligence work. During World War II, it would seize the files of hundreds of Japanese business firms, protect Japanese property confiscated in America, and conduct background investigations on Japanese aliens. But it would not assume a prominent intelligence role as it had done in three previous wars. Between the two world wars, the FBI and military intelligence would grow and would expand their intelligence functions until the Secret Service, which had been the predominant intelligence agency at the turn of the century, would be out of the intelligence business by the early 1940s.

In 1922, the Secret Service became involved in the investigation of another scandal even greater than the 1907 homestead-fraud case—Teapot Dome. This time, however, the trail led not to congressmen but to the Harding White House. Harding's Secretary of the Interior, Albert Fall, had illegally leased the federally owned Teapot Dome oil fields to a private oil company. The lease was awarded secretly and thus there was no competitive bidding. A Senate investigation of the leasing resulted in a Congressional resolution that appropriated funds to investigate the affair (funds for lawyers, clerks, and investigators). Four Secret Service agents were assigned to the case and conducted a three-year investigation, obtaining evidence that ultimately led to the conviction of the Secretary of the Interior and that crippled the political-administrative effectiveness of the Harding administration. The president's protectors had become the investigative arm of those prosecuting his administration. The Congress, which had taken action to sharply curtail the Secret Service's ability to carry out such investigations when congressmen were the target, was not hesitant to authorize the Secret Service to investigate the Harding White House. This time, unlike the previous case, the Service escaped organizationally unscathed from its investigative involvement in high-level scandal.

In 1930 an organizational change was made that would significantly augment Secret Service personnel and duties. The Service was placed in charge of the White House police, which would eventually become the Secret Service uniformed division.[36] Washington, D.C. metropolitan police had been protecting the White House grounds since 1864 when four were assigned during the Civil War. Prior to 1864, D.C. police had general responsibility for protecting persons and property within the city but gave no special attention to the White House or the president. When the Civil War ended, the police detail was reduced from four officers to three; and they were assigned to protect only the mansion, not the president.

In 1895, during the Grover Cleveland's second term in office, Mrs. Cleveland became alarmed at the number of threatening letters arriving at the White House. She persuaded the president to increase the police detail. It went from three to 27 officers. Over the next decade, the number gradually increased to over 50. Even when the Secret Service protective mission was given formal Congressional authorization in 1906, the Service still had no control over the White House police who functioned completely independently.

In 1922 President Harding executed a kind of coup d'état against the White House police unit. Fearing the presence of a large police contingent over which he had no control concerning personnel or activities, Harding persuaded Congress to create a new police organization—the White House Police Force. This new unit was no longer under the control of the Washington, D.C. police department but was instead under the direct authority of the president, to whom Congress delegated supervisory responsibility. Harding placed the police force under the command of one of his military aides. Personnel for the new unit were "handpicked" by the Harding administration from Washington D.C. police and from the U.S. Parks Department.[37]

The Secret Service took control of the White House Police Force in 1930. Congress granted the authority at President Hoover's request. Hoover was dissatisfied with the police force's performance. A benign intruder (a curious citizen) had wandered into Hoover's dining room one evening, past police guards. Hoover called in the head of the Secret Service's White House detail and demanded an explanation. The president was told that the problem was that the Service had no control over the police force, a situation which Hoover remedied.[38] The Secret Service had achieved complete control over White House protection.

But in the late 1920s and early 1930s, the Secret Service faced a formidable organizational challenge to its protective, investigative, and intelligence roles. No longer was it in the unique position of being the only general law enforcement agency within the federal government as it had been for so many decades. Nor was it any longer the most respected and skilled among such agencies. The FBI had grown rapidly during the 1920s. By the mid-1930s it had become the most famous, best equipped, and largest federal law enforcement agency, thanks in no small measure to the political skills of its young director, J. Edgar Hoover, who took over the Bureau in 1924 at the age of twenty-nine.

Because of the combined effect of the Bureau's ascendance and the Congress' restrictions on the Secret Service's investigative role, the FBI had become the federal government's investigative agency of choice, a position long held by the Service. Moreover, Hoover's Bureau even made forays into the Service's protective-mission turf. In 1929, there was no Congressional authorization to protect vice-presidents. But there had been no formal authority to protect presidents-elect when the Service simply assumed the responsibility in 1908. When Herbert Hoover's vice-president, Charles Curtis, wanted protection, it was the FBI who provided it from 1929 to 1933.

Then, in 1938, the Secret Service was finally frozen out of the intelligence business. President Franklin D. Roosevelt called for a review of the espionage establishment. His administration developed a plan granting exclusive control over domestic intelligence to a troika of agencies—the FBI, military intelligence (MID) and ONI (Office of Naval Intelligence). Roosevelt sent a confidential directive to all federal agencies instructing that the troika would have exclusive responsibility over "the investigation of all espionage, counterespionage, and sabotage matters."[39] The Secret Service was out. Its long history of chasing spies and saboteurs during three wars was at an end.

Having lost its intelligence role, the Service was also confronted with a challenge to its protective role from the empire-building J. Edgar Hoover, who had a close working relationship with FDR. According to Frank Donner, Hoover was encouraged by Roosevelt "to run the Bureau as an adjunct of the White House."[40] FDR came to view the FBI "as his eyes and ears" and used Hoover's men to spy on presidential aides and to plug press leaks in the White House by using wiretaps. In addition, FBI agents became a second protective detail in the Roosevelt White House and were used "to supplement the Secret Service's more routine duties." The Secret Service must have worried that with a foot in the protective-mission door, Hoover's Bureau might eventually displace the Service in presidential protection as it had in espionage, but this was not the case. The FBI's protective activities turned out to be a temporary by-product of FDR's special relationship with the Bureau.

In 1940, the Secret Service escaped organizational disaster when a proposed relocation did not come about. The proposal was to transfer the Secret Service from the Treasury Department, where it had been since its creation, to the Justice Department—the home of the FBI. There, the Service would, no doubt, have been even further eclipsed by the Bureau, if not gobbled up by it.[41]

Although its espionage role had ended and its general investigative role had declined drastically, the Secret Service went on to expand its duties in the missions left to it—protection and combating counterfeiting and forgery.* In these areas of endeavor, presidents would not hesitate to delegate new duties as problems arose. During World War II, the Service, which in past wars had protected America's secrets, was charged with protecting its national treasures, such as the original Declaration of Independence and the Constitution. It relocated them out of Washington, D.C. and guarded them until the war ended.[42]

In 1962 the Service was assigned to protect a visiting masterpiece—the Mona Lisa. In 1964 when the government began to print food stamps, the Service was given responsibility for investigating forgery cases involving the stamps.

Throughout its 120-year history, the U.S. Secret Service has had sixteen directors, serving an average of 7.5 years. The longest tenure was that of William H. Moran, 1917-38; the shortest, James J. Malony, 1947-48. Along the way, the organization that was created to save the currency would evolve from America's premier spy agency to its premier protective agency.

NOTES

1. Rhodri Jeffreys-Jones, *American Intelligence* (New York: The Free Press, 1977), p. 13.

---

* The expansion of the protective mission in the modern era is described in the next chapter.

2. *Ibid.*, pp. 13–14.

3. *Ibid.*

4. The basic events of the organization's evolution are described in "Excerpts From the History of the United States Secret Service, 1865–1975," Treasury Department, U.S. Secret Service.

5. *Ibid.*, p. 8.

6. Harry Neal, *The Secret Service in Action* (New York: Elsevier-Nelson, 1980), pp. 66–67.

7. *Ibid.*

8. *Ibid.*

9. Jeffreys-Jones, *American Intelligence*, p. 34.

10. *Ibid.*, p. 18.

11. *Ibid.*, p. 18.

12. *Ibid.*, p. 3.

13. *Ibid.*, p. 18.

14. *Ibid.*, p. 30.

15. *Ibid.*, p. 18.

16. Neal, *Secret Service in Action*, p. 68.

17. Jeffreys-Jones, *American Intelligence*, p. 18.

18. James B. Kirkham *et al.* (eds.), *Assassinations and Political Violence* (New York: Bantam, 1970), Kerner Commission Report, p. 61.

19. *Ibid.*

20. David W. Lima, "The Lincoln Assassination," paper presented at Seminar on Political Assassinations, Southeastern Massachusetts University, Dec., 1981, Dr. Philip H. Melanson, pp. 12–14.

21. Secret Service, *Training Manual*, 1954, 133 pages, Warren Commission files, National Archives, Washington D.C., file #22, "Records Relating to the Protection of the President 1954 and 1963–4."

22. Secret Service, "Excerpts from History of Secret Service, 1865–1975," p. 12.

23. *Ibid.*, p. 15.

24. Secret Service, *Training Manual*, p. 35.

25. *Ibid.*, p. 9.

26. Secret Service, "Excerpts from History of Secret Service, 1865–1975," p. 16.

27. Warren Commission document, from file #22 (see cite 21 above), folder-A, "Brief History of Presidental Protection," U.S. Secret Service, 1964, p. 12.

28. *Ibid.*

29. Secret Service, *Training Manual*, p. 35.

30. Secret Service, "Excerpts from History of Secret Service, 1865–1975," p. 17.

31. *Ibid.*, p. 18.

32. Neal, *Secret Service In Action*, pp. 74–76.

33. Warren Commission document "Brief History of Presidential Protection," p. 14.

34. Jeffreys-Jones, *American Intelligence*, p. 58.

35. Secret Service, "Excerpts from History of Secret Service, 1865–1975," p. 19.

36. Secret Service, *Training Manual*, p. 37.

37. Secret Service, "Excerpts from History of Secret Service, 1865–1975," p. 22.

38. *Ibid.*, p. 23.

39. Frank Donner, *The Age of Surveillance* (New York: Vintage Books, 1981), pp. 56–57.

40. *Ibid.*, p. 96.

41. Warren Commission document, "Brief History of Presidential Protection," p. 19.

42. Secret Service, "The Secret Service Story," Washington, D.C. (pamphlet published by the Secret Service).

2

THE MODERN SECRET SERVICE: AN ORGANIZATIONAL PORTRAIT

The Secret Service used to be much more secret than it is to-day.

U. S. News & World Report, Oct. 2, 1978

The United States Secret Service is an organization of 36,000 people existing within the Treasury Department, which also houses the Internal Revenue Service (IRS), Customs, and the Bureau of Alcohol, Tobacco and Firearms (ATF). Titularly, the Secretary of the Treasury oversees the Secret Service and its sister agencies, but the Director of Secret Service has extensive autonomy and actually runs the organization. Within the Treasury Department, one of the assistant Secretaries of the Treasury is assigned administrative oversight of Secret Service, but this is more a liaison function than an involvement in day-to-day operation. The Service assigns an administrator to the assistant secretary's office to serve as liaison with the Treasury Department.[1]

The director of Secret Service is not a political appointee from out-side the organization, nor is he selected from the larger Treasury Depart-ment. He is instead chosen by the Secretary of the Treasury from the ranks of career agents (subject to the approval of the Civil Service Com-mission). The present Director is John R. Simpson who, after serving as an agent in the field, headed the Service's protective operations office before becoming director. Under the director are five assistant directors, each overseeing a distinct functional area, a separate office, within the Service: investigation, protective operations, inspection, administration, protective research. The modern Secret Service has a complex internal structure for such a relatively small federal agency, primarily a result of the scope and diversity of its duties. (See organizational chart.)[2]

The Office of Investigations has line authority over the Service's 63 field offices (61 in the U.S., two abroad). These offices spend most of their time on counterfeiting and forgery cases, but they also do protective work when the need arises. The Washington D.C. field office is an exception. By virtue of its location, it does more protective work than any other office. In a more typical field office such as Boston, there are approximately 30 agents assigned, and they usually pursue nearly 4,000 forgery and counterfeit cases a year, an activity which consumes most of their time.[3] Forgery investigations and arrests are more frequent than those involving counterfeiting.

Some field offices (besides Washington, D.C.) will become heavily involved in protective work to an atypical degree because of their location. The Los Angeles field office will continue to do a great deal of protective work as long as Mr. Reagan is president and visits his Santa Barbara ranch.

At the Secret Service's Washington headquarters, the Office of Investigation's forgery division reviews forgery cases (treasury checks, government bonds, food stamps) and assigns them to field offices for investigation. It also performs handwriting analysis and helps the field offices to present evidence in the courtroom. Another subdivision of the Office of Investigation is the Special Investigation and Security Divsion. It has experts who analyze questioned documents to determine if they are forgeries. It analyzes fingerprints and conducts forensic analyses. It also conducts security surveys to determine whether security is adequate at selected government buildings.

The Office of Protective Research's Forensic Services Division has about 15 employees—clerks, laboratory personnel. It does crime-related research and analysis and has polygraph experts who administer and interpret lie detector tests.

Another task performed by the Office of Investigations is to conduct background checks on government employees. Perhaps surprisingly, this office does not investigate assassination attempts or successful assassinations of political leaders or assaults on political leaders. The Secret Service investigates threats, but it is the FBI that has investigative responsibility after the incident has occurred. It is the Bureau that determines whether an assassination incident was a conspiracy.[4]

The Secret Service and the FBI have entered into a formal agreement—a "delineation agreement," which is common among federal

UNITED STATES SECRET SERVICE
Organization Chart

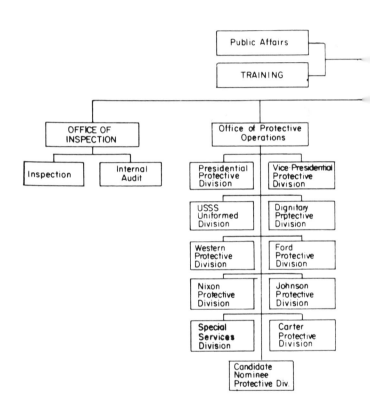

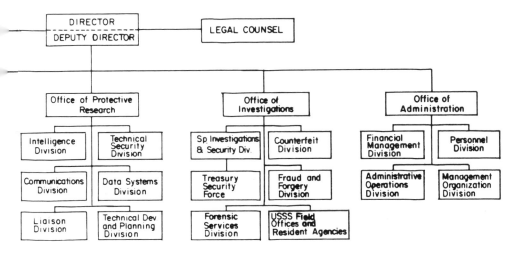

agencies. The agreement specifies that the Service has responsibility for assuming control over the scene of an assassination or assault only until a "logical and coordinated transition of control of the investigation can be delegated to the FBI." In essence, the Service is supposed to hold suspects at the scene and preserve evidence until the Bureau can take over. The agreement further specifies that the Service must give the Bureau immediate access to all evidence and investigative materials. However, all of the activities covered by the agreement are secondary to the Secret Service's primary responsibility, which has priority over the pursuit of suspects or the preservation of evidence—the safety of the protectee.

The Office of Investigations also contains the Treasury Security Force, a small unit of 80 to 100 officers. This unit provides 24-hour protection for the main Treasury Building and the Treasury Annex, both located near the White House, and for the grounds surrounding these mammoth stone buildings.

Officers of the Treasury Security Force have special powers of arrest in connection with crimes or violations of law occurring within these buildings or on their grounds. The officers' primary task is to control access to the buildings. Except for the public tour of the exhibit hall located in the basement of the Treasury Building, access is limited to employees or persons with valid visitor's badges. Security Force guards stand at the doors to the buildings and at small guard shacks near the gates that guard the vehicular entrances; they also patrol the roof of the Treasury Building, which overlooks the White House. They have the authority to search the belongings of persons entering the buildings.

The Treasury Department occupies other buildings in Washington in addition to the main building and the annex—Secret Service headquarters, for example. These other locations are not protected by the Treasury Security Force but by the landlords or the occupants. Secret Service headquarters is housed in a privately owned office building and is protected by regular Secret Service personnel.

The Service's Office of Protective Operations contains the Uniformed Division, a unit of 900 officers that guards the White House and foreign missions within the Washington area. This division will be discussed in more detail later in this chapter. Also, the Uniformed Division has provided security for United Nations missions (located in New York) of several Middle East countries because of increased threats of terrorism. This protection has been provided on a semipermanent basis for the past decade and costs over $750,000 per year.[5]

The Office of Protective Operations also contains the protective details—one of which is organized into a division for each protectee: a division for President Reagan, one for former President Carter, one for Lady Bird Johnson. Thus the number of such divisions depends upon the number of protectees—former presidents, widowed first ladies, and so forth—who are alive at any given time.

The Secret Service's penchant for intricate organizational structure (rooted partly in the organization's complex nature) is epitomized by the subdividing of the presidential Protective Division into three distinct units: Support and Logistics, Operations, Training and Special Programs. The Operational subunit is broken down even further into three separate entities—one for presidential protection, one for protection of the first lady and presidential family, one for transportation.[6]

The Candidate/Nominee Protective Division is a recent creation. It was formed because of the Service's recognition that the length and complexity of the presidential nominating process demanded full-time attention. This division has only a handful of agents and a small administrative staff, but it provides an ongoing function of administrative coordination for candidate protection.[7] As the need arises, agents are borrowed from field offices to form protective details. Previous to the creation of this skeletal division, the candidate-protection function had no permanent staff and was entirely *ad hoc*.

The Dignitary Protective Division, which protects visiting foreign leaders, is, like the Candidate/Nominee Division, a skeleton operation. Its only permanent personnel are a detail leader and assistant leader. Unlike other protective details, except the Candidate/Nominee Division, the agents who staff the dignitary division are field-office personnel who are assigned on a temporary basis, as dignitaries visit and the need arises.

The Office of Protective Research, which works very closely with the Office of Protective Operations described above, is the nerve center of the protective mission. It is responsible for collecting, analyzing, storing, and disseminating vital data gathered by the Service itself or provided to it by other federal agencies. There are files on over 40,000 U.S. citizens who, for one reason or another, have come to the Service's attention. There is data on threats against political leaders and on the *modi operandi* of terrorist groups. This office compiles and maintains the "watch list" of 400 persons considered dangerous to protectees. There is even an in-house research psychologist who works on the identification of dangerous persons.

The Office of Protective Research's Technical Security Division conducts manual and electronic surveys to make sure that each environment is safe for the president—no surveillance devices in the Oval Office, no poison in the food, or deadly bacteria in the air. This division has its own researchers to perform environmental analyses and its own research engineers. It uses this staff to provide technical support and expertise for the Service's investigative as well as protective work. It also manufactures and issues the passes and credentials that afford access to the White House and the Executive Office Building.

The Technical Development and Planning Division of the Office of Protective Research conducts long-range analyses in various areas of Secret Service endeavor (a kind of in-house think tank). It maintains extensive contact with private industry to keep abreast of the latest technological developments. This division installed the security system for the Capitol building—a system that has 110 TV surveillance cameras, numerous x-ray scanners, and sensors that are distributed throughout the building and grounds (including the 3.5 miles of heat and water pipes that run under the Capitol grounds).[8] The entire system is keyed in to a control center within the Capitol. This division has installed a similar system in the White House.

The Office of Protective Research's Communications Division installs and maintains all of the various radio, telephone, teletype, and cryptographic (coding and decoding) equipment used by the Service. It has its own communications personnel who are in direct contact with Washington, D.C. police and with the National Crime Reporting Center.

The Office of Protective Research's Liaison Division was created because of a recommendation by the Warren Commission, which felt that the Secret Service of 1963 did not maintain sufficient contact with state, local, and federal agencies and was therefore not receiving enough of the kind of data it needed to perform its protective mission effectively. Although the primary purpose of the Liaison Division was to increase the Service's ability to gather intelligence, the Treasury Department's report on the attempted assassination of President Reagan in 1981 criticized the division's alleged passivity:

> Insofar as the Liaison Division is involved in intelligence support, the process is largely ad hoc. Liaison agents operate in an informal manner and, by and large, take their intelligence support roles to be passive ones, responding to Intelligence Division requests rather than generating more and better intelligence and sources.[9]

The Secret Service's Office of Administration has four divisions and performs management-analysis and administrative-housekeeping functions in such areas as personnel, budgeting, and purchasing. The fifth office, the Office of Inspection, conducts internal audits and serves a function similar to that of the internal affairs office of major police departments, conducting investigations of employees when conditions warrant.

In addition to the five major offices that are under the Director of Secret Service, the Director has staff units that work very closely with his office: public affairs, training, legal counsel. Public affairs deals with the press, Congress, and the public. It issues brochures, talks with reporters and researchers, and maintains a clipping file of articles written about the Secret Service collected from newspapers throughout the country.

The Director's training office gives specialized courses to agents (courses in both protective and investigative work) and trains the Treasury Security Force and the Uniformed Division as well. It also trains clerical and administrative personnel. Within the training office is a specialized in-house reference library.

The legal counsel provides legal advice to the Director and works for the Secret Service, but reports directly to the Treasury Department's General Counsel. The Service's legal counsel keeps the organization informed about changes in the law and about Supreme Court rulings that relate to the detention and arrest of suspects and the rights of the accused. Secret Service agents make as many as 1,200 arrests a year (most of them involving forgery); its conviction rate for cases going to trial is 98.8—a statistic aided by agents' familiarity with required constitutional procedures. Counsel also works with the Director in drafting new legislation and amendments to existing laws which will then be submitted to Congress.

In 1982, Congress passed a law making it a crime to threaten candidates or officials. Previously, laws made it illegal to threaten presidents, presidents-elect, vice-presidents, and vice-presidents-elect, punishable by a $1,000 fine, up to five years in jail, or both. Before the 1982 law, there were only vague, indirect statutes relating to threats against presidential candidates or other officials besides those mentioned above. With this new law, the Service can prosecute a threat against a candidate or congressman with the same legal tools used for presidential threats: the protective mission now has a more solid legal foundation.

One proposed reorganization within the Treasury Department that would have had a profound impact on the Secret Service was the 1982 legislation that would have abolished the Service's sister agency the

Bureau of Alcohol, Tobacco and Firearms (ATF). ATF's main function is to enforce laws regarding firearms, explosives, liquor, and tobacco, but it was the enforcement of firearms laws that earned the Bureau the enmity of the very powerful National Rifle Association (NRA). Pushed by the NRA, the Reagan administration introduced a bill to eliminate ATF. Despite a personal plea to congressmen by White House advisor Edwin Meese and despite hard work by Reagan's close friend Senator Paul Laxalt (R, Nevada), the bill died in committee in the Senate.[10]

Had ATF met its demise, most of its agents would have been transferred to Secret Service. The NRA, which originally backed the idea, reversed its position on abolishing ATF when it began to fear that the Secret Service would inherit ATF functions and would use its superior intelligence-gathering system and renowned investigative talents to enforce the gun laws more strictly than ATF ever could. Senator John Dingell (D, Michigan) had another concern: he feared that the large infusion of ATF agents would dilute the quality of the Service, which he regarded as a superior organization. Other senators worried that if the Secret Service took over ATF functions, it would become politicized and have to battle the NRA over gun control, to the detriment of the protective mission.

Secret Service headquarters is located at 1800 G Street in Washington, D.C., in a private building owned by a bank. The Service's co-tenant is the National Science Foundation. The headquarters offices are handsomely appointed but somewhat crowded by federal standards, especially for clerical workers.

The Service has offices in seven other locations in Washington. The presidential and vice-presidential details work out of the castle-like Old Executive Office Building located next to the White House. There is a training office on L Street. Secret Service would very much prefer to consolidate all of its scattered offices at 1800 G Street[11] for sound logistical reasons as well as for reasons of organizational pride. After all, the FBI dwells in the huge, modern J. Edgar Hoover Building located on Pennsylvania Avenue.

Secret Service headquarters befits a secretive agency. There is little public access and no public tour available. In contrast, the FBI allows large groups to be guided through the Hoover Building so that the Bureau can show off its facilities and tout its history. There is even a life-sized replica of J. Edgar Hoover's office, preserved behind glass and faithful in every detail.

The Secret Service has only a small, pleasantly-decorated briefing room adjoining the Public Affairs Office where, by appointment only, visitors in very small groups can see an automatic slide show with taped audio and can ask questions of an agent spokesperson from Public Affairs. The only historical exhibits are two revolvers displayed under glass—one used by Sara Jane Moore to shoot at President Ford in 1975; the other used by one of the Puerto Rican nationalists who attacked Blair House in 1950 trying to assassinate President Truman and killing Secret Service uniformed officer Leslie Coffelt. There are some small displays dealing with counterfeiting. Compared to the FBI, which offers a long tour of its laboratories and training facilities and which displays hundreds of weapons and artifacts from famous criminal cases, the Secret Service shows little to the public.

In the basement of the Treasury Building across from the White House is Treasury Theater, where the public can view films and exhibits depicting the work of the Treasury Department's various agencies. Unless the visitor has a keen eye, he or she may think that the Secret Service had been transferred to the Defense Department. It has only a small exhibit which is dwarfed by the colorful displays of coins, bills, and minting equipment. The four films shown are about IRS, Customs, the U.S. Mint, and "keys to the Treasury." The U.S. Secret Service likes to keep a low profile.

At Secret Service headquarters, the knowledgeable visitor cannot help but be impressed with how very seriously security is taken. As a researcher who had done work at FBI and CIA on numerous occasions, I was surprised to discover that the Secret Service consistently scrutinizes a visitor's identification and checks personal possessions more slowly and carefully then either of the other agencies.

THE UNIFORMED DIVISION

What is now the Secret Service Uniformed Division began in 1930 when the Service took over supervision of the police unit that protected the White House. Before 1930 this unit was under the jurisdiction of the Washington, D.C. Police Department. Although the Uniformed Division is a subdivision of the Service's Office of Protective Operations it is practically an organization within an organization and deserves special attention. In 1970 this unit, which was then known as the White House Police Force, was reconstituted as the Executive Protection Service, with expanded duties and increased personnel. At that time, it was given responsibility for protecting foreign diplomatic missions in the D.C. area. In

1977, the name was again changed to the United States Secret Service Uniformed Division—its present title.[12]

The Uniformed Division's protective responsibilities overlap with those of the protective details staffed by regular Secret Service agents. The Division protects: the president and immediate family (primarily at the White House), the vice-president and immediate family, the White House grounds, foreign missions, buildings in which presidential offices are located (the Old Executive Office Building, for example), and the official Washington residence of the vice-president.

The Division's protective responsibilities extend around the clock. Even when foreign ambassadors are traveling away from their Washington, D.C. embassies, those buildings are protected twenty-four hours a day. As is the case with regular Secret Service agents, presidents can assign the Uniformed Division personnel to protect any foreign diplomatic mission whenever they perceive it to be necessary, whether it be a Japanese mission in San Francisco or a Saudi Arabian mission in New York. Since 1973, the Division has, at presidential request, protected several United Nations missions in New York belonging to Middle Eastern countries, on a more-or-less permanent basis. In 1975 President Ford vetoed a bill passed by Congress that would have placed the burden for such protection on the local government of cities outside of Washington in which such missions were located.

One of the Uniformed Division's main activities is to police the White House tours. Over two million visitors come each year, and they queue up in lines that extend halfway around the mansion. Keeping the lines orderly and directing traffic around the White House while guarding the mansion's extensive grounds and its numerous gates and guardhouses requires a large contingent of uniformed officers.

The Uniformed Division executes its protective duties through a network of foot and vehicular patrols. Light-weight motorcycles are used to patrol the streets around the White House. There are fixed guard posts (at White House gates and at embassies), and there are also canine teams.

The canine unit, a subdivision of the Uniformed Division, consists of a dozen teams of extensively trained officers and dogs.[13] Although the dogs undergo training in attack and in scouting—training similar to that given to police dogs—the dogs' primary training, and primary use, is in explosive detection.

It takes thirteen weeks to train a team (dogs and handlers). First there is a four-week session at Lackland Air Force Base in Texas where dogs and handlers are monitored for compatibility so that they can ultimately perform as a well-integrated team. Then there is a nine-week session at Andrews Air Force Base in Maryland where explosive detection is emphasized. The dogs are taught to sniff out all kinds of explosive substances, snarl at them and sit in front in them. Canine teams are given frequent refresher courses after basic training.

Fixed guard duty can be both boring and hazardous for uniformed officers. An eight-hour stint standing near the gate of a foreign embassy can be very tedious and very uncomfortable during Washington's sultry summer heat. Yet, officers must remain alert because burglaries and bombings do occur. In 1980, the Yugoslavian Embassy was bombed.

The responsibility for guarding foreign missions was given to the Uniformed Division in 1970 (when it was called the Executive Protection Service) because of a rising concern among foreign diplomats about possible terrorist attacks. In the late 1960s and early 1970s, Washington, D.C. police were inundated with requests from foreign ambassadors wanting increased protection[14] because of what State Department Security Officer William P. De Coury called an "upsurge of terrorism around the world."[15] In 1970-71, there had also been a couple of incidents of non-terrorist crime on Embassy Row: one embassy was robbed; an ambassador was mugged.[16]

The Washington police did not have the personnel to respond to the demands for increased protection. Congress believed that the safety of foreign representatives was a federal responsibility. Thus the Uniformed Division was given the task of protecting the approximately 2,500 foreign diplomats living and working in the D.C. area in numerous residences and office buildings.

The Uniformed Officers have a narrowly defined law-enforcement role when protecting foreign missions. If they see a burglary taking place a block away from their post, they must remain where they are and radio to the D.C. police or to a Uniformed Division patrol car, which will then proceed to the scene of the crime. Even if such help is too far away to stop the robbery, the Uniformed officer must not leave the post. If there is a political demonstration at an embassy, it is D.C. police and U.S. Park Police who arrest unruly demonstrators in the streets. The Uniformed officers' main task is to protect the embassy, and they would make an arrest only if a demonstrator tried to enter the embassy.[17]

The Uniformed Division's attire provides a sharp contrast to the tailored business suits worn by regular agents. The uniforms are a cross between police and military dress—distinctive black pants with bright gold striping, white shirts with gold trim, gold and blue badges, name tags that include the officer's home state, highly polished black shoes, police-type hats, shoulder chevrons indicating rank. Whereas regular agents' revolvers are carefully concealed under their specially tailored suits, uniformed officers wear theirs in hip holsters. Uniformed personnel also carry radios and nightsticks.

It was the Uniformed Division (then called the Executive Protection Service) that was the focus of President Nixon's attempt to add luster to the already imperial presidency by dressing his uniformed guards in lavish costumes. To the Uniformed Division's embarrassment, the Nixon White House outfitted the uniformed officers in chocolate brown costumes with white tunics draped with gold braid, topped with sharply sloping hats. The new outfits looked like they might have been borrowed from the Vatican or from a sixteenth-century French palace. As soon as Mr. Nixon left office, the uniforms were quickly packed away, where the Secret Service hopes that they will stay.[18]

Even with less ostentatious uniforms, the Uniformed Division has its critics. It has been suggested that the Division's protection of foreign missions is really an expensive subsidy to foreign governments. Critics point out that uniformed personnel provide more than protection: they also perform other chores such as unsnarling traffic jams after big parties at the embassies — all paid for by American taxpayers.

Washington reporter Howie Kurtz, an investigator for columnist Jack Anderson, views even the protective duties performed by the Uniformed Division as a misappropriation of scarce resources.[19]

> The inescapable irony is that the nation's taxpayers, many of whom live in high-crime areas without adequate police protection, are paying over $17 million a year to support a special police force in the one area of the nation's capital that need it the least.

The Uniformed Division points with pride to the relative absence of crime on Embassy Row as evidence of its effectiveness. Kurtz sees it as evidence that the whole operation is a waste of time and money because the diplomats do not need such protection.

COUNTERFEITING AND FORGERY

As a dual-mission organization involved in both protection and in-vestigation, the Secret Service's primary investigative tasks relate to counterfeiting and forgery, activities that generate a combined total of 220,000 cases a year (most involving forgery). Counterfeiting is still a very real problem, though fortunately, not as severe as it was during the Civil War when nearly one-third of all money in circulation was phony.

Modern counterfeiters use sophisticated techniques. Plates for printing bills are made by etching with acid rather than engraving by hand; photocopying devices are used to turn out large numbers of bills rapidly.[20] This puts increased pressure on the Service to act quickly, before huge amounts of phony bills get into circulation.

Of all its duties, catching counterfeiters is the one that depends most upon public cooperation, and the Service actively cultivates public support for this mission. Quick recognition of phony money and prompt reporting by citizens enables the Service to zero in on the counterfeiters more rapidly, before more money is circulated and more people are financially victimized.

The Service's public relations efforts, meager as they are in comparison with some federal agencies, emphasize public education and participation in stopping counterfeiters. Its glossy brochure "Know Your Money" is the largest, most ambitious one it publishes. The brochure has blowups of bills with instructions on how to detect counterfeit money by scrutinizing the presidential portrait, the serial number, and the paper. The usually reclusive, publicity-shy Service even awards U.S. savings bonds (real, not phony) to citizens whose alert reporting helps nab counterfeiters, and it presents these awards with as much press coverage as possible.

According to the Service, the modern counterfeiter is usually someone with expertise in photography and/or printing. Phony bills are usually wholesaled to some group or criminal organization which will attempt to pass them. The counterfeiter typically gets ten to 50 percent of the face value.[21]

Secret Service laboratories analyze phony bills for fingerprints and also trace the materials used in making them. Special chemicals that react to traces of human perspiration are used to detect latent prints on bills, bonds, and checks.[22] In 1981 alone, agents seized $44 million in counterfeit money; over $39 million of it was captured before it went into circulation.

Agents frequently work undercover in attempting to find counterfeiting operations before the money hits the streets. Agents sometimes pose as underworld buyers, purchasing large blocks of counterfeit money, stock certificates, or bonds. Such purchases usually involve large amounts of cash. In one case, a counterfeiter offered an undercover agent $5 million in phony Treasury notes for the price of $450,000.[23] Agents will also set up ongoing "fencing" operations so that they can make contact with a number of counterfeiting rings.

In a single month (May 1982), Secret Service counterfeit cases included: a bust in Atlanta that netted $6.5 million and three counterfeiters; $100,000 in phony bills seized in Atlantic City; $20,000 seized in Orlando, Florida (the result of a tip from a citizen); $3 million and six counterfeiters arrested in Naples, Florida.

Forgery is the second major area of the Service's money mission. Each year an estimated $20 million is lost because of forged bonds and checks. Blank checks or bonds stolen from mail boxes or banks are cashed with forged signatures. In a single year, the Secret Service will investigate approximately 135,000 cases involving forged government checks (the federal government issues $800 million in checks yearly).[24] In one case, a postal clerk swiped 600 blank government checks and sold them. But the Service claims that many forgers operate in groups with divisions of criminal labor—some operatives will steal checks; others, forge signatures.

As with counterfeiting, the Service believes that public alertness is the key to prevention. It publishes a pamphlet entitled "Know Your Endorser," which encourages people to check carefully the endorser's identification and to watch for obvious clues, such as a woman in her twenties cashing a social security check.

Within its Office of Investigations, the Service has "questioned documents examiners," experts who determine whether signatures on bonds, checks, and letters are real, as well as whether the document is otherwise counterfeit. In a single year these analysts are usually called upon to work with 60,000 documents relating to approximately 3,500 criminal cases.[25]

THE PROTECTIVE MISSION

This is the Secret Service's most publicized, best-known activity. In the modern era, the protective mission has greatly expanded since its formal inception in 1906. The original "threat" legislation passed in 1917, which made it a crime to threaten a president via the mails or in any other manner, was extended to include presidents-elect, vice-presidents and vice-presidents-elect (in 1962); it was extended again in 1982 to include presidential candidates and public officials. Following the assassination of John F. Kennedy, 36 bills were introduced into Congress, all seeking to make assassination of a president a federal crime. Finally, in 1965, Congress passed one of these: the bill makes it a federal crime to assassinate, assault, or kidnap the president, vice-president, president-elect, vice-president-elect, or the next in line for succession to the presidency if the person be other than the vice-president, as in the case in which the vice-presidency is vacant and the Speaker of the House of Representatives is next in line until the vice-presidency is filled.

Also in 1965, additional legislation was passed to extend protection to former presidents and their wives, and to widows of former presidents until their remarriage or death. This bill also provides protection for children of former presidents until they reach the age of sixteen. In 1968, responding to the assassination of Robert F. Kennedy while he campaigned for the presidential nomination (June 1968), Congress granted protection to major presidential and vice-presidential candidates. Ten received protection in 1968; thirteen in 1972.

In 1971 Congress enacted a law that gave the Service a permanent protective mission for visiting representatives of foreign governments and for official U.S. representatives on foreign visits. There are usually between 100 and 150 foreign representatives who visit the United States each year. They stay for periods of a few days to several weeks, and some of them travel extensively within the United States during their stay. Depending upon the number of visiting dignitaries and their itineraries, this responsibility often puts a real strain on the Service's personnel resources.

In 1976, Congress extended protection to include the wives of presidential and vice-presidential nominees for a period not to exceed sixty days after the nominating convention.

Any of the persons defined by law as eligible to receive protection may decline it. Presidential candidates are asked by the Service to sign an official waiver of protection if they wish to refuse it. Normally, the total number of protectees at a given time is about 30, but this number increases greatly during a presidential election year.

The protective mission was made less predictable for the Service when Congress added a catchall phrase to its 1971 legislation. The statute allows Secret Service protection to be granted ''at the direction of the president.'' This has resulted in a mixed bag of assignments over the years—protection of foreign missions to the United States located outside of Washington, D.C.; President Carter ordering protection for Ted Kennedy before he became a legally qualified presidential candidate; President Reagan providing protection to his three top White House aides (James Baker, Edwin Meese, Michael Deaver).

The protection of presidential candidates is one of the largest single extensions of the protective mission in terms of the increased number of protectees and in terms of the increased number of protectees and in terms of the frenzied itinerary of a campaign. It is much more demanding for the Secret Service, in terms of the number of agents needed and the amount of protective research required, to protect a presidential candidate who travels constantly than to protect the widow of a former president who stays home most of the time. Under the guidelines used by the Secret Service for the 1980 presidential race, a candidate was eligible for protection only when he or she had qualified for federal matching funds by raising $100,000 garnered from at least 20 states and had also raised total funds of $900,000. Alternatively, a candidate could qualify for protection by receiving ten percent of the vote in two consecutive primaries.[26]

The 1980 guidelines were stricter than those used previously, requiring only that a candidate raise $100,000 from twenty states. The additional requirement of raising a total of $900,000 made it more difficult to qualify. Nearly 200 persons filed with the Federal Elections Commission the basic documents for declaring a presidential candidacy, but less than a dozen went on to qualify for federal matching funds. Of those who qualified for protection, five refused it, including perennial candidate Harold Stassen. In addition to President Carter, six candidates qualified for, and accepted, Secret Service protection: Republicans Reagan, Bush, Baker and Crane, Democrat Kennedy, independent candidate Anderson.

The guidelines were drafted for the Service by the Advisory Committee for presidential and vice-presidential protection, which is composed, by law, of the Senate majority leader, the Speaker of the House, the minority leaders of the House and Senate, and a fifth member chosen by the other four. For the 1984 presidential election, the committee adopted essentially similar guidelines, but made it even more difficult to qualify for Secret Service protection by increasing the requirement for total funds raised form $900,000 to $1.5 million.

The 1980 guidelines also stated that even those candidates who qualified early on in the campaign must wait until January 11, 1980 to begin receiving protection; but the guidelines left a very large loophole as did the 1984 guidelines, by further stating that if a candidate who had qualified wanted protection before that date, he or she could get it simply by asking for it. Ronald Reagan began receiving protection in November of 1979. Regardless of what that advisory committee's guidelines state, the incumbent president can grant protection to any politician or candidate at any time, as President Carter did for Ted Kennedy before Kennedy had qualified.

For candidates who do receive protection, the Secret Service has its own guidelines as to what its responsibilities entail. It does much more than stand guard around a candidate. In addition to "providing protection 24 hours a day, seven days a week," the Service will:[27]

- handle all security problems and police contacts
- provide security extending to the candidate's food, letters, packages, luggage, cars, and residences
- handle all outside inquiries directed to the staff regarding Secret Service duties and functions
- normally provide a Special Agent to facilitate access by traveling press

The dramatic expansion of the protective mission in the modern era is a result not only of the increased number of legally-mandated protectees but also to the pace of modern politics. Presidents and candidates travel much more now than in past decades. Theodore Roosevelt was the first U.S. president to travel outside the country while in office. Both the modern presidential office and the modern presidential campaign involve extensive travel which greatly increases the scope of protective work. As late as World War II, the White House detail consisted of only 16 agents; now there are 70.

Although it is a relatively small federal agency, the modern Secret Service has a very complex organizational structure in terms of the number and diversity of its divisions and subdivisions. Although it is true that modern bureaucracies appear to have an innate tendency toward proliferation and compartmentalization, the Secret Service's intricate structure accurately reflects the complexity and diversity of its responsibilities. It is a dual-mission organization (protection and investigation of counterfeiting and forgery) with overlapping yet distinct activities for each basic mission, and with increasingly varied and numerous responsibilities that have grown out of these two basic missions. The organization that once consisted of a dozen plainclothes operatives and a director now includes handwriting experts, intelligence analysts, psychologists, uniformed officers, and canine teams.

NOTES

1. Interview with Special Agent Mary Ann Gordon, Secret Service Office of Public Affairs, Washington, D.C., Oct. 26, 1982.

2. "Management Review on the Performance of the U.S. Department of the Treasury in Connection with the March 30, 1981 Assassination Attempt on President Ronald Reagan," Dept. of the Treasury, August 1981, 101 pages, at p. 15. Hereafter cited as "Treasury Department Management Review." This report is the primary source for the following descriptions of Secret Service offices and subdivisions.

3. Kevin A. O'Reilly, "Presidential Protection," paper presented at Seminar in Political Assassination and Violence, Southeastern Massachusetts University, Professor Philip H. Melanson, Dec., 1981. O'Reilly interview with Special Agent Charles W. Collins, head of the Service's Boston field office.

4. Interview with Secret Service Director of Public Affairs Robert Snow, Secret Service Office of Public Affairs, Wash., D.C., March 15, 1983; description of delineation agreement from "Treasury Dept. Management Review," p. 68.

5. Howie Kurtz, "Executive Protection Racket," *The Washington Monthly*, Oct., 1978, pp. 47–50, at p. 49.

6. "Treasury Dept. Management Review," p. 53.

7. Interview with Special Agent Mary Ann Gordon.

8. Harry Neal, *The Secret Service in Action* (New York: Elsevier-Nelson, 1980), p. 136.

9. "Treasury Dept. Management Rept.," p. 38.

10. Tim Reiterman, "NRA Backs Out—And Gun Agency Survives Reagan Ax," San Francisco *Sunday Examiner and Chronicle*, April 25, 1982.

11. Interview with Secret Service Director of Public Affairs Robert Snow.

12. U.S. Secret Service (pamphlet), "The United States Secret Service Uniformed Division," Washington, D.C..

13. Neal, *Secret Service in Action*, pp. 129–33.

14. A. O. Sulzberger, Jr., "Secret Service Uniformed Division Stays Close to Capitol Diplomats," New York *Times*, June 10, 1980.

15. Howie Kurtz, "Executive Protection Racket," *The Washington Monthly*, Oct., 1978, pp. 47–50, at p. 49.

16. *Ibid.*, p. 50.

17. *Ibid.*, pp. 49–50.

18. *Ibid.*, pp. 48–50.

19. *Ibid.*, pp. p. 47.

20. Neal, *Secret Service in Action*, p. 48.

21. U.S. Secret Service (pamphlet), "Use of Illustrations of Obligations and Securities of the United States and Foreign Governments," Washington, D.C.

22. Neal, *The Secret Service in Action*, pp. 16–17.

23. *Ibid.*, p. 39.

24. *Ibid.*, p. 134.

25. *Ibid.*, p. 62.

26. "Secret Service Tightens Guides on Protecting Presidential Candidates," *Wall Street Journal*, Oct. 30, 1979, p. 4.

27. U.S. Secret Service (pamphlet), "Election Year 1980," Washington, D.C., designed for presidential and vice-presidential staffs.

3

A FEW GOOD MEN
(AND A VERY FEW WOMEN)

Special Agents must qualify to perform both protective and investigative assignments since the needs of the Secret Service are such that it is impractical to have agents specialize in only one area.

Secret Service recruitment brochure

By the standards of the leviathan federal bureaucracy, the United States Secret Service is a very small organization. It consists of approximately 1,800 special agents, 900 members of the uniformed division, 80 to 100 people on the Treasury Security Force and over 32,000 personnel of other kinds (clerical, data processing, laboratory personnel)—a total of 36,000 employees.[1] The Treasury Department as a whole (in which Secret Service exists) has 110,500 employees; the entire federal bureaurcracy has 2.85 million.[2] The Pentagon has twice as many public relations officers as the Secret Service has special agents (1,800). The Interior Department has twice as many employees as the Secret Service.

In terms of fiscal resources, the Service's annual budget is $180 million per year.[3] This is a relatively small chunk of the Treasury Department budget of $65.6 billion. Some subdivisions of the departments of Energy and Agriculture and of the Environmental Protection Agency have budgets measured in billions of dollars; the Service spends only one-fifth of a billion dollars.

Are these resource levels adequate for effective protection? Like the old Peace Corps recruitment advertisement, the answer depends on whether the viewer thinks the glass is half full or half empty. The Service thinks it is half empty.

The organization's resources have grown impressively in the past two decades. Its budget has risen faster than inflation: from a mere $8 million in 1963 to $27 million in 1970, to $98 million in 1975, to its present level of $180 million. The Secret Service of the early 1960s had only 350 special agents and 170 uniformed officers, compared with today's 1,800 agents and 900 uniformed officers. The White House detail which protected President Kennedy had 36 agents; the one protecting President Reagan has nearly twice that many.[4]

At face value, this surge of resources would appear to satisfy even the most ardent of bureaucratic empire builders. The bad news for the Service is that its protective mission has expanded very rapidly during the same two decades. In the Service's view, the increased scope of its duties has outstripped the growth of its resources. During the Kennedy presidency, it protected only the president and immediate family, vice-president, and former presidents. Since then, its mission has been broadened to include foreign diplomats stationed in embassies in the United States, presidential and vice-presidential candidates, spouses and children of former presidents, and visiting foreign dignitaries.

Much of this increased workload is very unpredictable in nature so that rational budgeting becomes difficult if not impossible. Whereas the cost of protecting the president and family can be estimated with ballpark accuracy, there is no way that the Service can predict how many presidential candidates there will be in an election year. Protecting a single candidate can easily cost $300,000 a month and can require 30 agents. And this is only the tip of the iceberg: protective research and field-office work also increase with each additional protectee, as the number of incidents, cases, or threats to be checked out multiplies.

The money and personnel needed to protect former presidents depends upon their life-styles and activities as well as their number. In 1980 it cost $30 million to protect former presidents and their families. Within the last two years, former President Ford has had an urge to travel, raising the cost of his protection by approximately $2 million per year. Mr. Nixon stayed in seclusion for the first two years after his resignation but then began globetrotting (to China and, in 1982, to four Eastern European countries), which vastly increased the protective resources required.

In 1983 Secret Service Public Affairs Director Robert Snow told the author that ''it's easier to manage criminals than protectees,'' meaning that the Service can predict its money and personnel needs for dealing with forgers and counterfeiters more easily than it can for its protective mission. Snow said that the Service is in constant contact with the staffs of ex-presidents who inform the Service about travel plans. The problem, according to Snow, is that ex-presidents do not always plan their agendas very far ahead of time.

Nor can the Service predict the cost of protecting visiting foreign dignitaries. For several years the number of dignitaries was fairly stable—80 to 90 per year. In 1977 it suddenly bulged to 150, doubling the cost.

To meet these unpredictable demands, the Service is forced to live hand-to-mouth, constantly asking the Congress for supplemental funds and frequently borrowing personnel from other Treasury Department agencies (Customs Bureau, Internal Revenue Service, and the Bureau of Alcohol, Tobacco and Firearms). It also borrows personnel from the National Parks Service of the Department of the Interior to help with work in Washington, D.C.—especially with controlling the White House tour line. Sometimes, during a presidential campaign year, there are more non-Secret Service Treasury Department personnel doing protective work than there are Secret Service agents.[5]

The Secret Service's budget is reviewed by the Treasury Department and by the Office of Management and Budget (OMB) before it goes to Congress. The Treasury review usually results in a cutting of the Service's requests, but a time-honored Treasury gag rule (typical of many federal agencies) prevents the Secret Service from appealing directly to Congress for a larger budget.[6]

The need to borrow personnel from other Treasury agencies has significant implications for the quality of protection. As professional and diligent as these ''second stringers'' may be, the fact remains that they are not Secret Service agents: their training and work experience are not the same, and they are given protective assignments only sporadically. Although these Other Treasury Personnel (OTP) are ''retrained'' for protective work or are given refresher courses, and although many OTPs may have worked with Secret Service agents many times in the past,[7] they are still not full-time security personnel.

The personnel shortage affects working conditions. The average shift for White House agents is eight hours, and there are three eight-hour shifts per day. For many kinds of work, an eight-hour shift is appropriate, but, depending on what the protectee is doing, eight hours can be too long a stint for agents to be able to maintain the unblinking concentration required for effective protection. There is a great deal of difference between an eight-hour shift when the president is asleep and one in which he hosts a breakfast for businessmen at the White House, meets with a foreign ambassador, and then goes out to attend a luncheon.

The fatigue and stress on agents is severe. Said Agent Clint Hill, who retired in 1975 as head of the White House detail at the age of 43, "a lot of the agents are getting tired." Hill claimed that some were discovered by doctors to manifest the same type of fatigue experienced by soldiers in combat.[8]

Dr. Frank Ochberg, a psychiatrist from the University of Michigan who studied agent stress, found that the job's travel requirements made it difficult to maintain a normal family life and social life. "It gets so they [agents] can never invite people for dinner because they might have to leave at the last moment," Ochberg observed. The daughter of one agent told him sarcastically that she doubted if her father would be at her wedding.[9] Even so, the divorce rate among agents is no higher than that of the general population.

The Secret Service has an in-house psychologist to counsel agents about stress and about the problems it can create, such as alcoholism. As part of an ongoing program of stress evaluation, agents are given physical exams yearly and agility tests every six months. But, according to the Secret Service, self-awareness is the key: agents are taught to discern warning signs of severe stress manifested by themselves or their colleagues.[10]

For the men and women of the Service's Uniformed Division, there is a different kind of stress. Standing fixed guard duty for eight hours is boring and has a numbing effect on alertness. Although reducing protective shifts to five or six hours would reduce stress in all kinds of protective work, the increased cost of additional personnel would necessitate a hefty increase in the Service's budget.

In addition to money and personnel, technical expertise is another important organizational resource. As with personnel, the Service often borrows from other agencies. Traditionally, though secretively, the Service has received training and equipment from the CIA. For example, it was revealed in 1976 during the hearings of the House Intelligence Committee that the CIA manufactured the color-coded lapel pins worn by agents as an unobtrusive identity badge. The Service has also requested such things as "technical countermeasures equipment" (antibugging devices) and has received "briefing/training" of a classified nature from the CIA.[11]

One of the few declassified CIA documents dealing with aid to the Service indicates that in 1973 alone, the Service was provided with such equipment as: 6 portable X-ray units; 1 frequency counter; Mohawk printer; motor drive; receiver; transmitter; 1 [item deleted].

The CIA's vast expertise in sophisticated technologies of surveillance, countersurveillance, bomb-detection and espionage is a crucial resource that the Service cannot generate on its own. Yet it is the Secret Service that is responsible for making sure that every room entered by the president is free of eavesdropping devices and explosives. Although the precise nature and extent of Secret Service dependence upon CIA remains top secret, it is surely important given the Service's limitations of personnel and resources.

That the Secret Service can use all the free technical assistance it can get became embarrassingly clear in 1978 when Congress provided a special appropriation of four million dollars for the purpose of developing "audio countermeasure equipment." In the absence of such equipment, it seems that the average ham radio operator could easily monitor the often top-secret transmissions of the United States' premier protective organization.[12]

Despite the stress and the problems of resources, Secret Service employment seems to be perceived as good work, if you can get it. The Service claims that applications have remained high and turnover is low, especially for the job of agent. Thus the Service can afford to pick only the most qualified applicants.[13]

Applicants for positions within the Uniformed Divison must have a high school diploma or equivalent, or one year of experience as a police officer in a city with a population of at least 500,000. They must pass a written test and then undergo an interview. In addition, all hireres are required to have a valid driver's license, must demonstrate a willingness to work weekend shifts, and must qualify for a top-secret clearance via an extensive background investigation.

Applicants for the position of special agent (Secret Service agent) must be between 21 and 35 years old. The average age of the 1,800 agents is 34.[14] Applicants must have one of the following:

1. a bachelors degree
2. three years working experience of which two years is in criminal investigation
3. a comparable combination of experience and education

College preparation can be in any field. Many agents were former lawyers or teachers. Candidates for special agent must pass a comprehensive physical exam and must meet certain standards of weight-in-proportion-to-height (have you ever seen a conspicuously portly agent guarding the president?). Vision must be 20/30 in each eye, correctable to 20/20.

Applicants must pass the Treasury Enforcement Agent Exam, which is not specific to Secret Service work and which is also taken by applicants for Customs, IRS, and Alcohol, Tobacco and Firearms. Those who pass are put on a waiting list, and those with the highest scores are eventually invited to an in-depth interview where they are judged for: "personal appearance, bearing, and manner; ability to speak logically and effectively; ability to adapt easily to a variety of situations."[15]

The next step is a special agent training course at the Federal Law Enforcement Facility in Brunswick, Georgia, then on to more specialized training at the Secret Service's facility in Maryland. A rookie agent begins by working in one of the Service's 63 field offices and, eventually, he or she may go on to full-time protective work, perhaps even to guarding the president.

All agents undergo rigorous security checks before being appointed. Their character, honesty, and "loyalty to the United States" are scrutinized. All appointees receive a top-secret clearance.

The Service is also very concerned about the appearance and demeanor of agents, especially those on the White House detail who often operate under the media spotlight. Although they will remain anonymous, agents will be seen by millions of Americans. Neither the Service nor the president wants any odd-looking, mean-looking, or scruffy types spoiling the president's image or that of the Service.

Agents have a clean-cut appearance and dress conservatively. Their suits are specially tailored to conceal their pistols and automatic weapons. Except for the radio transmitters in their ears, they look like business executives.

It is indicative of the kind of young men that the Service prefers to recruit that its one outreach program, designed in part to aid recruitment, involves the Eagle Scouts. What better source of clean-cut, loyal young men? Although the Service has more paper-qualified applicants than it needs, and although it is notoriously reclusive and publicity shy, it created the Law Enforcement Assistance Award in 1972, given annually to an Explorer Scout who has helped some law-enforcement agency by preventing a crime or helping to catch a suspect. Each spring the Service hosts a one-day seminar for the presidents of Explorer posts around the country, complete with a tour of the highly secretive Maryland facility. There, scouts can watch agents being trained.

Starting salaries for Secret Service agents are not high by federal standards—a base pay of approximately $25,000 a year plus overtime. Agents are civil service employees and usually begin at GS 5, 6 or 7, depending on education and experience; they typically rise to GS 12 or 13 fairly rapidly.[16] After six to eight years work, agents usually earn $35,000 to $40,000 per year.* They are eligible for retirement at age 50, with 20 years of service. The average age of agents in protective work tends to be younger than that of supervisory personnel. The average retirement age for the organization as a whole is 55. Turnover is only 3.8 percent annually.

Any of the Service's 1,800 special agents can aspire to one day be the Director of the organization. Unlike many federal agencies, the Director is not an outside political appointee but is chosen from within the organization. Most Directors have served on-the-line performing difficult protective assigments. Director H. Stuart Knight, for example, served in the vice-presidential protective detail in Caracas in 1958 and was outside Mr. Nixon's limousine repelling assaults by angry demonstrators.

Another aspiration of many agents is to be among the select group of 70 who, at any given time, draw assignment to the White House detail—the all-star team of protective duty. As we shall see in chapter eight, original assignment to presidential protection may be strictly according to merit and experience, as the Service claims, but the effectiveness and tenure of an agent depends on a variety of factors, including how his personality and operating style mesh with those of the president and/or White House staff.

Women can now aspire to be special agents. The Uniformed Division has long had women officers. Anyone taking the White House tour will find that one-third to one-half of the uniformed guards stationed at the White House gates, around the grounds, and inside the mansion are women. Many clerical jobs have long been filled by women. But it was not until 1971 that the first female special agents were appointed—four of them. Today there are approximately 30 women agents out of a total of 1,800—hardly the quintessence of affirmative action.

---

* The Secret Service Uniformed Division has its own pension and salary structure. Starting salaries are about $14,000 per year.

Moreover, it was not until 1978, during the Carter adminstration, that the first woman agent was assigned to the White House detail on a permanent basis. Previously, women had been given only temporary assignments. In 1978, one woman was assigned to Vice-President Mondale's detail and one, Special Agent Mary Ann Gordon, was assigned to the Carter detail.

In a 1982 interview with the author, Ms. Gordon, who now works in the Service's Division of Public Affairs in Washington, described her landmark appointment as "a matter of timing."[17] Part of the "timing" involved the Carter adminstration's emphasis on affirmative action. But Ms. Gordon's appointment has not resulted in an influx of women into the ranks of special agents. The number of women remains conspicuously small in comparison to the proportion of women involved in other kinds of Secret Service work, including protective work performed by the Uniformed Division.

The training of special agents is intense during the first year of their appointment which is a probationary year. Agents receive both formal instruction and on-the-job training during this year. The degree to which the first-year job experience involves protective work or investigative work (counterfeit and forgery cases) depends upon the Service's personnel needs at the time.[18]

All agents take 16 weeks of formal instruction—eight weeks at the Treasury Department's Federal Law Enforcement Training Center in Georgia; another eight weeks at the Secret Service's Maryland training facility. The quality of training has improved markedly in the past two decades and is now much more extensive and sophisticated. Several of the agents who guarded President Kennedy could not even recognize the sound of gunfire in Dealy Plaza, Dallas. Agents in Kennedy's motorcade mistook the rifle fire for a motorcycle backfire, or firecrackers, or the blowout of a tire. Texas politicians with hunting experience (Governor John Connally, Senator Ralph Yarborough) immediately recognized the sound as gunfire, but the agents had practiced with firearms only on a firing range while wearing earmuffs and had not been trained to recognize the sound of gunfire under natural conditions.[19] In addition, Kennedy's Secret Service driver had had no special training in evasive driving.

Apart from the improved quality, there are two factors that have always influenced the substance and effectiveness of Secret Service training. First part of the training process seeks to develop combat-ready skills and instant reflexes to be used in actual situations, such as an assassination attempt. But these situations occur only once every few years or once in a decade. To use a military analogy, agents must be trained to be combat-ready within a split second for situations that, fortunately, occur too infrequently to provide much actual experience.

Second, Secret Service training is dual purpose. All agents do both investigative (counterfeit and forgery cases) and protective work and are trained for both. A typical career pattern for an agent would be to spend the first three to four years, after the probationary year, in one or more of the Service's field offices.*[20] Then, if the organizational needs and agent skills permit, the agent may enter full-time protective work. Tours of duty in protective work are from a minimum of three years to as many as five or six years. Afterward, the agent is transferred back to a field office. Unlike the first field-office assignment, the agent has some choice of location. Agents can then "bid" (apply for) an administrative post.

Limiting protective duty to a three-to-five year span helps reduce stress and prevent agent burnout. The Service's Public Affairs Director, Robert Snow, told the author that the dual-mission career pattern has benefited the Service. "We find that it works well. Protective agents are better, sharper because of their investigative training."[21]

Snow also claimed that even when working in a field office, half of an agent's time is spent in "protective work." While this may be literally true, "protective work" in the field offices primarily involves protective intelligence gathering and case work—checking out threats or monitoring dangerous persons—rather than guarding a protectee (providing direct on-the-line protection).

The skills and knowledge needed to discern a phony Treasury bond or bust a ring of counterfeiters are quite different from those needed to repel an assassination attempt. True, both are law-enforcement functions, as the Service is fond of pointing out. But the relationship of the two kinds of work is such that it would be equally accurate for a young man who worked in both stage lighting and adagio dancing to point out that both relate to the theater.

The training of agents is relatively short and quite intense. It surely does not maximize the effectiveness of the protective mission when half or more of the training received is not directly related to that mission. The Secret Service points out that protective training is continuous

---

* The Service prefers to assign each agent to two successive field offices, one large and one small, but the cost and logistics of such a policy make it difficult to implement, even though it provides a broader exposure to the organization.

throughout an agent's career: Agents involved in protective work take refresher courses periodically and learn about relevant changes in the law and about new protective techniques.[22] But this does not obviate the dual nature of the basic, most important training received by agents. The Service claims that "it is impractical to have agents specialize in only one area,"[23] given the Service's dual mission and scarce resources, but it could prove very practical for the effectiveness of protection.

At the Treasury Law Enforcement Center in Georgia, which trains all Treasury agents and not just Secret Service agents, the curriculum covers:[24]

Ethics and Conduct for Investigators
Organized Crime
Orientation of Federal Law-Enforcement Agencies
Orientation on Contraband Narcotics
Civil Rights
Conduct and Testifying in Court
Conspiracy
Constitutional Law and Rules of Evidence
Federal Court Procedure
Preparation for Trials
Searches and Seizures
Arrest Techniques
Bombs and Explosives
Surveillance Techniques (including the use of electronic devices)
Undercover Operations
Firearms Training (including night shooting)

The protective-mission relevance of most of the above topics is limited, at best.

It is at the Service's Beltsville, Maryland facility that agents receive their specialized training for protective duty. The eight-week course covers both investigative and protective work. The curriculum includes general training that is not specific to either investigative or protective work — classes in history of the organization, in how to write reports.

The investigative training is extensive. Agents learn how to find fingerprints on government checks and bonds. They study methods of forgery and counterfeiting, which includes learning about the paper and metal used to make currency. They visit the paper mill in Massachusetts that produces most of the paper used for bills.[25] They visit the Bureau of

Engraving and Printing in Washington, D.C. There are practical exercises and simulations — questioning a suspect (played by an instructor), conducting handwriting and typewriting analyses to catch forgers. Then there is a simulated raid on a counterfeiting operation. Instructors set up a complete operation, including equipment, so that agents can raid it, search it, make arrests, and gather evidence.

Investigative training also includes learning how to conduct a stakeout of a suspected counterfeiting operation, including how to take photographs that will be useful in court if an arrest can be made. Arrest techniques, such as how to handcuff a suspect, are practiced. The Service will not reveal how much of the eight weeks of training is consumed by investigative training and how much is left for protective training. But it is clear from the depth and scope of investigative training received that it consumes a major chunk of the available time.

Some of the training received in Maryland is relevant to both protective and investigative work — care and use of firearms, karate, wrestling, boxing. There is a "ten-minute medicine" course in which agents learn how to keep a heart-attack victim or an injured or wounded person alive for the ten critical minutes until professional help arrives. Cardiopulmonary resusitation (CPR) is taught — this alone takes a full day — as are techniques for controlling bleeding and for treating shock and bullet wounds. Even a basic knowledge of firefighting is provided.

All of this is, of course, potentially useful to protectees. Since 1973 agents have saved 35 lives (most have not been protectees). When the president and his family are at a secluded retreat, agent's life-saving skills could be crucial in case of emergency.

Last, but not least, there is training in protective methods and procedures, conducted in the classroom and via practical exercises. Topics covered include protective research (intelligence gathering), bomb detection and disposal, methods and techniques of counterterrorism. There is a mini-course given by psychiatrists on distinctions between normal and abnormal behavior to help agents in detecting potential assassins. Agents are taught how to fall from a moving limousine without getting hurt.

Firearms training is extensive and, unlike the previous training at the Treasury's Georgia facility, focuses specifically on the special problems of protective work. Trainees learn how to shoot in the dark, with and without a flashlight, and how to shoot from inside a limousine at both moving and stationary targets. The "running-man" course involves shooting at a target while it is running through a crowd of innocent bystanders.[26] There is training in the use of submachine guns and shotguns. All this, even though agents rarely use their weapons and are taught that their first priority is to cover the protectee rather than return fire.

The Service's Beltsville, Maryland facility is one of the most sophisticated firearms training centers in the country. It is used by all federal law enforcement agencies except the FBI, which has its own modern practice range in the J. Edgar Hoover building. Beltsville has several firing ranges. The indoor ranges can host 24 shooters at one time, each having a control booth that can simulate daytime or nighttime conditions. One outdoor range is for rifles; another for pistols.

Agents study movies of assassinations and attempted assassinations — the Zapruder film of President Kennedy's assassination, tapes of the two attempts on President Ford. They also study numerous assassination cases, both foreign and domestic, and analyze each one — Robert F. Kennedy, President Park of South Korea, George Wallace, Martin Luther King, Jr., Malcolm X, Jack Ruby's murder of Oswald, Mrs. Ferdinand Marcos (the wife of the Philippine president).[27]

There are driver-training courses — how to drive an armored limousine and a follow-up car, evasive steering, handling blowouts, controlled braking. Techniques are learned on a track at Beltsville, then it is out into the nearby cities and suburbs of Maryland for practice under real traffic conditions. Trainees are carefully supervised by instructors, but there is no sign atop the limousine announcing — student driver.

Simulation and instant replay are primary training methods. Agents practice at escorting a make-believe president through crowds and in and out of vehicles, during which spontaneous, simulated attacks or medical emergencies occur. Agents' reaction times are clocked. Execution of emergency procedures is videotaped and played back, then discussed by students and instructors.

Beltsville is a sprawling facility encompassing 420 acres. It has administrative offices, a cafeteria, student lounges, ammunition and firearms storage rooms, a canine training area (where dogs learn to sniff out bombs), an armorer's workshop, locker rooms, classrooms, and firing ranges. But the pride of Beltsville are its two massive mock-ups—"Hogan's Alley" and the White House.

Hogan's Alley looks much like a Hollywood back lot. There is a street and a facade of several buildings approximately one city block in length. On foot and in passing "motorcades," agents sharpen their protective skills. A computer-controlled program presents an array of stimuli. Cutout figures pop up without warning — in windows, in doorways, along the street. The figures are moveable and bullet-sensitive; some (the assassins) have an audio "shooting" capacity. The figures appear for different lengths of time and carry a variety of objects—briefcases, umbrellas, guns. The agent's task is to quickly determine which figures are assassins and which are innocent bystanders and to react accordingly without guning down an ordinary citizen whom the wily computer has programmed to appear suddenly in a second-story window holding what looks like a gun but is only an umbrella. The simulations are complex and demanding: a cutout of a woman pushing a baby carriage may move in front of a figure who begins "firing" at the presidential limousine.[28]

In April of 1982 the Service announced its plans to build the ultimate mock-up—the White House and vicinity.[29] The $1.6 million project is part of a planned ten-year expansion program that will ultimately extend Beltsville's mock-ups to include an entire minicity complete with a shopping mall and numerous streets. The White House facade alone is slated to cost almost $400,000, and there will also be mock-ups of Blair House and Lafayette Park, which is located across the street from the White House. The buildings will consist only of facades, no interiors. Said Agent James Boyle:

> Most of our agents work there [in and around the White House] at one time or another on temporary or permanent assignment. Each of those environments have their idiosyncracies, and that's what we want our people to be familiar with.[30]

Secret Service agents used to be taken to the actual area for training—to the White House and to Lafayette Park. "It's not feasible to run them through there," said one Secret Service instructor.[31]

The mock White House lacks realism in some respects. There is no Oval Office for agents to train in. On the other hand, trainees can conduct exercises at the Beltsville White House which would be impractical in the real setting, such as engaging in a simulated firefight with terrorists on the "south lawn" then chasing them down "Pennsylvania Avenue.'"

Secret Service training is highly sophisticated in its technology and techniques and very ambitious in its scope. Still, eight weeks is not long, considering the dual-purpose nature of the training—investigative and protective. Some protective skills, such as falling off of a moving limousine without getting hurt, can be mastered in a short time; others—such as scanning a crowd to watch for quick movements while looking for the faces of individuals known to be dangerous while simultaneously maintaining a specified proximity to the protectee—must be developed more slowly and require extended practice. Moreover, the nature of the potential threats faced by agents has changed in recent years, as international terrorism has expanded and the technology of assassination has become frighteningly effective. This means that there is even more ground to cover during the portion of the eight weeks devoted to protective training.

NOTES

1. Interview with Special Agent Mary Ann Gordon, October 26, 1982, Secret Service headquarters in Washington D.C.; interview with Secret Service Director of Public Affairs Robert Snow, March 15, 1983, Secret Service headquarters in Washington D.C..

2. David G. Saffell, *The Politics of American National Government* (Cambridge, Mass.: Winthrop 1982), p. 361.

3. Figures are for fiscal 1982, from Carl T. Rowan and David M. Mazie, "Shield Against Assassins: The Secret Service," *Readers Digest*, April 1982, pp. 141-42.

4. Warren Commission document 1052, letter from Secret Service Director James Rankin to Commission General Counsel J. Lee Rankin, June 8, 1964.

5. Kevin A. O'Reilly, "Presidential Protection," paper presented at Seminar in Political Assassinations and Violence, Southeastern Massachusetts University, Professor Philip H. Melanson, Dec. 1981. O'Reilly interview with Special Agent Charles Collins, head of the Service's Boston field office.

6. Snow interview (note 1).

7. *Ibid.*

8. Mike Wallace interview of agent Clint Hill, Dec. 1975. Grolier Educational Corporation: Vital History Casettes, Encyclopedia Americana—CBS News Audio Resource Library, tape #2, side A.

9. "Guarding the President—A Rugged Job," *U.S. News & World Report*, Dec. 10, 1979, p. 63.

10. This description comes from the interview with Robert Snow.

11. CIA memo of June 5, 1973, "Secret Service Request," from CIA's 362-page domestic police training file.

12. "Guarding the President: The Job Gets Tougher," *U.S. News & World Report*, Oct. 2, 1978, pp. 76-79.

13. Interview with Mary Ann Gordon.

14. *Ibid.*

15. U.S. Secret Service, "Special Agent," Washington, D.C. (pamphlet).

16. *Ibid.*

17. Interview with Mary Ann Gordon.

18. *Ibid.*

19. Letter from Secret Service to Warren Commission June 29, 1964 in Warren Commission file "Records Relating to the Protection of the President."

20. Interview with Robert Snow. The Service prefers to assign each agent to two successive field offices, one large and one small, but the cost and logistics of such a policy make it difficult to implement, though it provides a broader exposure to the organization.

21. Interview with Robert Snow.

22. *Ibid.*

23. U.S. Secret Service, "Special Agent."

24. Harry Neal, *The Secret Service in Action* (New York: Elsevier-Nelson, 1980), p. 113.

25. *Ibid.*, p. 113–15.

26. *Ibid.*, p. 116.

27. *Ibid.*, p. 118.

28. *Ibid.*, pp. 115–16.

29. Loretta Tofani, "A Totally Up Front White House," Boston *Globe*, April 8, 1982, pp. 1 and 10.

30. *Ibid.*

31. *Ibid.*

4

AGENTS
IN
ACTION

Every practical precaution and safeguard should be taken to **prevent** *the actual perpetration of an attack, because:*

(a) There is seldom any assurance that an attack can be suppressed before its objective has been reached, and

(b) Even if the president escapes unharmed, the cost in other lives, injuries or property damage is usually very great before the attacker is subdued.

Secret Service training manual

Long before the United States Secret Service was created or had a protective mission, the problem of political assassination was present in the American political system. In 1835 Richard Lawrence tried to assassinate President Andrew Jackson as he exited the Capitol building. Lawrence tried twice to shoot the president, using two different pistols. Both miraculously misfired. In 1865 Abraham Lincoln became the first American president to be assassinated while in office, shot by John Wilkes Booth. Booth entered the president's box at Ford's Theatre and inflicted a mortal head wound. In 1881 President James A. Garfield was assassinated by Charles J. Guiteau as the president waited for a train in the Washington, D.C. station. President William McKinley was killed by Leon Czolgas in 1901 while standing in a receiving line at the Pan American Exposition in Buffalo.

The next known attempted assassination of a national political leader occurred in 1912. Although the Secret Service had been formally authorized to protect presidents in 1906, and although Theodore Roosevelt, McKinley's successor, was the first president to be formally protected by the Service, the Service was not authorized to protect presidential candidates until 1968. So in 1912 when then presidential candidate Theodore Roosevelt was wounded while campaigning to regain the White House, he was not a Secret Service protectee.

Roosevelt was campaigning in Milwaukee and was exiting his hotel en route to give a speech when John N. Shrank shot him in the chest from six feet away. The bullet probably would have killed the former president if it was not for the fact that it struck his metal glasses case, then was slowed by the 50-page speech that Roosevelt had double-folded in his breast pocket. This may be the only instance in history in which the political system unquestionably benefited from a very long speech. The bullet still managed to penetrate several inches into Roosevelt's chest, fracturing his rib. Seeing his wound, the former Rough Rider coughed into his hand. Since there was no blood, he insisted on delivering the speech. The Bavarian-born Shrank claimed that President McKinley's ghost had inspired him to prevent Roosevelt from serving another term as president. Five court-appointed psychiatrists determined that Shrank was insane, and he was institutionalized for the remainder of his life.[1]

Over two decades later when the next serious incident occurred, the Service was protecting president-elect Franklin D. Roosevelt. FDR was giving a speech at Bayside Park in Miami when Guisseppe Zangara attempted to assassinate him.[2] Zangara arrived one and a half hours before the speech but was unable to get a front row seat. As the speech ended and the president-elect departed, Zangara stood on a vacated chair and fired, missing the president but wounding Chicago Mayor Anton Cermak, who was standing near Roosevelt's car. Secret Service agents tried to speed away from the scene in order to protect the president but Roosevelt insisted that agents put the wounded Cermak into the car and take him to a hospital. Cermak died. Zangara, who professed a hatred of "the capitalists," was found sane and was electrocuted.

Franklin Roosevelt's long tenure as president was free of assaults, but his successor, Harry Truman, was the target of an assassination attempt by two Puerto Rican nationalists in 1950.[3] Truman was living at Blair House while the White House was being restored. He was upstairs napping in a second-floor bedroom and was guarded by agents and uniformed White House policemen.

The two assailants carefully studied Blair House and its guards and doorways. Then, at 2:20 P.M., Oscar Collazo and Griselio Torresola walked toward Blair House from opposite directions and met at the front entrance, according to their prearranged plan of assassination. Collazo drew an automatic pistol and attempted to shoot White House policeman Donald T. Birdzell, who was guarding the stairs leading up to the front door and who had his back turned to the attackers as he talked with Secret Service Agent Floyd Boring. Collozo's pistol misfired; Birdzell turned and was struck in the leg by Collozo's second shot. Despite his wound, Birdzell rushed into the street to draw the assailants' fire away from the house.

An extended gun battle ensued during which 26 more shots were fired by the combatants (the two attackers and a half dozen agents and White House police). Collazo was wounded; his co-conspirator Torresola was killed in a shoot-out with White House policeman Leslie Coffelt, who was also killed in the same exchange of gunfire. Two other policemen (Downs and Birdzell) were wounded, but they recovered. Inside Blair House, Mr. Truman was protected by additional agents. Agent Stewart Stout heard the shots and rushed to a gun cabinet, retrieved a Thompson submachine gun, and stood in the hallway guarding the stairs and elevator to the second floor.

This was the most savage gun battle in the history of the protective mission. The assailant had hoped to assassinate the president as a means by which to shock the American public and thereby draw attention to the cause of Puerto Rican nationalism, even though President Truman had already sent to Congress a special message recommending that Puerto Rico's status be changed to one of four options, including outright independence. In spite of Truman's expressed sympathy for Puerto Rican self-determination, he was selected as a target because of the shock and visibility the would-be assassins hoped to create.

Collazo was sentenced to death after refusing to allow his lawyers to plead insanity and after the defense failed to convince the jury that Collazo had planned only to demonstrate in front of Blair House but that his deceased accomplice, Torresola, had started the shooting. President Truman commuted the sentence to life in prison.

From 1950 to 1963, there were no direct assaults on presidents until John F. Kennedy was assassinated. (The JFK assassination will be dealt with in detail in Chapter 9.) Dr. Martin Luther King, Jr. was not a Secret Service protectee when he was assassinated in April of 1968; nor was Robert F. Kennedy when he was assassinated in June of 1968. King was not a presidential candidate. Robert Kennedy was, but it was only after his assassination that Congress extended Secret Service protection to presidential candidates.

The wounding of Alabama Governor George Wallace on May 5, 1972 was the only instance to date in which a presidential candidate under

Secret Service protection has been the victim of a shooting. Although Wallace escaped with his life, he was so seriously wounded—one bullet struck his spine—that he was out of politics for several years and remains paralyzed. Wallace was a key figure in presidential politics in 1972. His importance is often glossed over or neglected, possibly because of the strident nature of his political views.

After running as an independent candidate for president in 1968, Wallace was seeking the Democratic nomination in 1972, challenging Democrats Humphrey, Muskie, and McGovern. Wallace was an able and energetic campaigner who had garnered more popular votes along the primary trail than any of his rivals, up until he was shot. However, Wallace did not lead in the number of convention delegates won. His states-rights, law-and-order themes had struck a responsive chord with enough voters to result in stronger-than-expected support in several primaries and victories in others, not only in the deep South but in Florida, Pennsylvania, and Indiana as well. After he was wounded, he won the Michigan primary with 51% of the vote, compared with 27% for McGovern and 16% for Humphrey; in Maryland, he obtained 39% with Humphrey getting 27% and McGovern 22%. Wallace was, indeed, a very strong contender—a cause for alarm if not outright panic within the Democratic Party's liberal establishment. At minimum, if Wallace had not been shot he would have gone to the Democratic nominating convention with a large block of delegates with which to bargain for policy concessions or future appointments. With Wallace out of the race, McGovern attained the nomination and was defeated in a Nixon landslide.

If ever a candidate needed protecting it was George Wallace. His pugnacious style of politics rendered him a galvanizing element, arousing political passions to a degree uncommon in American politics. This had been true since 1963, when, as governor of Alabama, Wallace stood in a schoolhouse door to bar black students, vowing: "Segregation now, segregation tomorrow, segregation forever."[4] His 1972 presidential campaign was no exception. Hecklers, hate mail, and threats plagued the campaign constantly.

Campaigning for the Maryland presidential primary had become increasingly volatile as the race among Humphrey, McGovern, and Wallace heated up. While campaigning, Wallace had remarked to an associate: "Somebody's going to get killed before this primary is over and I hope it's not me."[5] In Hagerstown, Maryland a Wallace speech was disrupted by trouble between black and white youths, to the point where police had to be called in. In Frederick, Maryland a brick thrown by a bystander hit

Wallace in the chest; at the University of Maryland students threw a barrage of popsicles at him; at a Wheaton shopping mall, tomatoes and eggs were hurled.

Wallace had conducted a populist-style campaign in which pressing the flesh was essential, but he was certainly not one of those politicians who disdained protection and resisted it. In fact, he was just the opposite. Although he typically waded into crowds in search of votes, he worried about the danger involved. Partly because it was a tradition in his political campaigns and partly because of his distrust of the federal bureaucracy, Wallace actually had two security forces traveling with him on the primary trail, in addition to the local law enforcement personnel who would be called upon to help in each town or city that he visited. Wallace had both a Secret Service detail and a contingent of plainclothes Alabama state troopers. He also brought along his own 600-pound bulletproof podium, draped in red, white and blue, which he used for all of his speeches.[6] Unfortunately, on the day that he was shot the oppressive heat and humidity caused him to forego his bulletproof vest, because of its heavy insulation.[7]

In comparison to 1968, the Secret Service had tightened its protective procedures in 1972. All passengers on flights taken by a candidate had to go through x-ray checks and all bags and cases were inspected. Local press were required to have credentials. Yet even with stricter security procedures, with two protective units (Secret Service and Alabama troopers), with a bulletproof podium, and with the candidate's recognition of the dangers presented by the increasingly volatile campaign, the worst almost happened. Wallace escaped with his life but not with his presidential candidacy.

The appearance at the Laurel, Maryland shopping center had been vintage Wallace. About 2,000 people had gathered in the parking lot to hear the Governor's standard speech, the Wallace litany—"Send a message to Washington," "the pointy-headed intellectuals who can't park their bicycles straight," the "ultra-false liberals."[8] There was mild heckling but nothing serious by the standards of the Wallace campaign. After 50 minutes, a tired, perspiration-soaked Wallace concluded his speech to thunderous applause. Country singer Billy Grammer and his band plugged their instruments into the amplifiers and began to twang away, as the candidate descended the stairs from the makeshift stage.

When he reached ground level, accompanied by Secret Service agents, the Governor appeared headed for a quick exit, but shouts from the crowd drew him back. "Over here. Over here," shouted several bystanders. Arthur Bremer, Wallace's assailant, was one of them. The candidate responded. He stopped his exit and turned back toward the shouts, shed his suit jacket, rolled up his sleeves, and walked toward the cheering crowd.

Wallace began to move along the rope barrier that separated him from the crowd, shaking hands as he went. He shook hands with Clyde Merryman, an exercise boy at Pimlico Race Track. "You've got my vote," said Merryman. As Wallace started to respond, a blond man plunged forward from the second row of spectators. Arthur Bremer's extended hand fired a .38-caliber bullet into Wallace's midsection from approximately one and a half feet away. Bystanders could feel the sharp heat given off by the explosion.

There were five rapid shots. Wallace was struck by four—one each in his midsection, shoulder, chest, and right arm. He fell backward after the first shot, but four more followed amid screems of terror from the crowd. Even as Bremer was shooting, Secret Service agents and Alabama troopers jammed his arm downward and pounced on him, but not before four of the five shots hit the protectee at close range. Wallace lay bleeding on the pavement. Three others were wounded. Alabama trooper E. C. Dothard was shot in the stomach; Secret Service agent Nicholas Zarvos was hit in the throat; a female Wallace supporter was wounded in the leg. All victims survived.

Police and security men jumped on Bremer, as did bystanders who kicked and punched him as he was pushed to the pavement. People in the crowd shouted "Kill him. Kill him." It took ten security men to pry Bremer from the clutches of the crowd and to drag him to a cruiser, where he was pushed inside very roughly. Bremer was gasping for breath and spitting blood.

Meanwhile, for part of this time, Wallace lay on the pavement bleeding, surrounded by the crowd. His wife Cornelia had been at a restroom in a nearby bank when the shooting occurred; but, shortly after the shots, she rushed to her husband. She dropped to her knees and embraced him, sobbing. Secret Service agents moved her away. She broke loose and ran back to her husband. "I was afraid they'd shoot him again in the head," she said later.[9]

Actually, Mrs. Wallace had a point. The governor lay on the pavement, his body completely exposed for several seconds after the shooting, as security personnel struggled to subdue Bremer. Had there been another assailant intent on finishing Wallace off, there was no Secret Service agent or Alabama trooper covering the governor's body with his own body immediately after the shooting, as Secret Service Agent Rufus Youngblood did with Lyndon Johnson after shots were fired at President Kennedy in Dallas.

Two doctors in the crowd came forward to attend to Wallace. "I feel I can't breathe," the governor whispered. One doctor felt for a pulse but could not find one. Time was running out. First the police, then the Secret Service, radioed for an ambulance. The Laurel rescue squad, an award-winning volunteer ambulance unit, was only four blocks away. The ambulance arrived within three minutes. In the interim, however, the doctors at the scene feared that Wallace would expire. Secret Service agents picked Wallace up and gently placed him into the back of a campaign station wagon for transport to the hospital. Just as they were ready to move out, the ambulance arrived.

The incident was described by the press and Secret Service as proving the impossibility of stopping a determined assassin who is willing to take any risk in order to shoot a political leader. As Assistant Secretary of the Treasury Eugene T. Rossides put it, having more agents around Wallace would have "made absolutely no difference."[10] However, stopping an attack once it starts or trying to prevent it by physically surrounding the protectee are only part of the protective mission. Prevention is also an important part—identifying and neutralizing potential assailants, through a variety job data and techniques, *before* an attack is perpetrated. While it may be true that additional agents could not have prevented Bremer from thrusting his arm forward and shooting the governor, it is at least possible that the presence of additional personnel might have increased the chances of spotting Bremer as a potential danger before the attack materialized. Arthur Bremer, though he was not in the Service's files or on its watch list, was not simply another face in the crowd but a face that appeared with frequency: Bremer had been stalking candidates for some time and was conspicuous in his actions.

It seems that Bremer had originally intended to assassinate President Richard Nixon. After failing to kill Nixon, Bremer reluctantly selected Wallace as a target.[11] President Nixon was in Ottawa, Canada on April 13 and 14, 1972. After the Wallace shooting, Bremer was identified by both American and Canadian authorities as being in the crowd outside the Canadian parliament building when Nixon entered to address a joint session. Bremer is clearly visible in newsfilms of the crowd.

Bremer's diary indicates that he stalked Nixon in Ottawa, driving around the city from one location to another as he shadowed the president.[12] Bremer stayed two nights at a downtown hotel. He had hoped to

stay at the same hotel as the press corps so that he could pick up information about Mr. Nixon's movements, but he was unable to get a room
there. Instead, he drank at the bar of the hotel where the press were staying and hung around the press room that had been set up in this hotel. He
had smuggled two pistols and some amunition across the border into
Canada.[13] Ultimately, he failed to get close enough to Nixon to attempt an
assassination. His diary laments: "Just another god Damn failure."

After the Wallace shooting, federal authorities received what appeared to be credible reports of Bremer's presence at a variety of political
events during 1972. He was seen by two Humphrey workers at a Humphrey rally on April 3. Then, on April 7–8, Bremer went to New York City
and registered at the Waldorf Astoria Hotel where Humphrey was
scheduled to spend the night. Because of a last minute change of plans,
Humphrey did not go to New York.[14] The fall before the May shooting of
Wallace, Bremer was arrested in Milwaukee for carrying a concealed
weapon. The charge was later reduced to disorderly conduct, for which he
paid a $40 fine.[15]

More importantly, Bremer was conspicuously stalking George
Wallace. On May 13, less than two weeks before the shooting, Bremer sat
in his car for nearly the entire day, outside of an armory in Kalamazoo,
Michigan where Wallace was scheduled to speak. A shopkeeper called the
police and Bremer was picked up as a "suspicious person." He told
police that he was waiting for the Wallace speech to start. Satisfied with
his explanation, police released him without searching him for a
weapon.[16]

At a Wheaton, Maryland shopping center earlier on the same day
that Wallace was shot at the Laurel shopping center, Wallace was giving a
speech. A television producer from a Washington, D.C. station, Fred Farrar, noticed Bremer. "That smirk of his was almost spine tingling," said
Farrar, who got 15 seconds of Bremer on film. Farrar also noticed that
after Wallace spoke, Bremer tugged on a policeman's sleeve and asked:
"Could you get George to come down and shake hands with me? I'm a
great fan of his."[17] The policeman simply moved away. Bremer tried the
same tactic with a Secret Service agent, with the same result. Bremer continued to grin, wave, and cheer. Wallace never did descend the stage and
go into the crowd. The hecklers were too loud and hostile. But later that
day at Laurel, Wallace would shake hands and Bremer would be waiting.

CBS cameraman Laurens Pierce remembered Bremer's conspicuous presence at Wallace's Hagarstown, Maryland speech. Pierce
described Bremer as "applauding longer, louder and more vehemently than

anyone else. His zeal could not go unnoticed and my camera recorded it."[18] Pierce also recalled seeing Bremer at a Wallace rally in Michigan and at Wheaton, Maryland the morning of the shooting. At the Wheaton shopping center, Pierce saw Bremer standing in the front row directly in front of Wallace's bulletproof podium. Pierce recognized the blond man as someone he had seen before. He approached Bremer. "I've seen you at other Wallace rally's," Pierce said. "Not me," replied Bremer. "Not me."[19]

Had Arthur Bremer been spotted as a stalker by Secret Service agents or by the Service's Protective Intelligence Section, which sometimes analyzes films of crowds, or if newsmen had reported Bremer to the Service as a suspicious person, the outcome at Laurel, Maryland might have been different. The state of Maryland had passed a new law that banned handguns without permits and allowed police to frisk suspicious persons.[20] Had Bremer been in the Secret Service album—the book of pictures of individuals to be watched for—or had his conspicuous behavior been noticed and followed up on by security personnel, he might have been frisked and his weapon discovered before he had a chance to shoot.

Bremer seemed to have been emersed in suicidal and homocidal fantasies during the months before the assassination attempt. One evening he placed a noose around his neck and scrawled KILLER across his forehead with a felt marker pen. The psychiatric testimony offered at his trial was conflicting as to his sanity, but the jury found him guilty and sentenced him to 63 years in prison.[21]

The next attempted assassination of a Secret Service protectee came on September 5, 1975. "Squeaky" Fromme tried unsuccessfully to assassinate President Gerald Ford.[22] Ford had finished breakfast at the Senator Hotel in Sacramento, California and was en route to the state capitol to meet California Governor Jerry Brown. The president exited the hotel and was shaking hands with the smiling, waving crowd outside. As Ford waved, he noticed a small woman standing to his left, distinguished by her red cape, turban, and childlike persona.

From approximately two feet away from the president, Fromme suddenly reached under her cape and drew a borrowed .45-caliber automatic pistol. Said Ford: "I saw a hand coming up behind several others in the front row, and obviously there was a pistol in that hand."[23] Secret Service Agent Larry Buendorf, who was at Ford's right shoulder, spotted the weapon instantly. He jumped in front of the president, screening him, and grabbed the weapon. Buendorf then muscled the would-be assassin to the ground. According to Buendorf, just as he seized her arm Fromme was attempting to pull back the hammer so as to put a round in the chamber. Fromme blurted: "Oh shit, it didn't go off; it didn't go off. Don't be so rough."[24] Buendorf wrestled the gun from her hand. Other agents surrounded the president and whisked him away.

Four cartridges were found in the clip of the weapon. The only injury produced by the incident was a cut on Agent Buendorf's hand, probably caused by the hammer of the weapon. President Ford, grim-faced and shaken, went on to meet Governor Brown and to deliver his speech on law and order to the California legislature.

Lynette Alice "Squeaky" Fromme was 26 years old and had a bizarre history even before the attempted assassination. She was one of the most devoted followers of Charles M. Manson and was a loyal member of the "Manson family." In 1971 Manson was convicted of the ritualistic murders of actress Sharon Tate and six other persons and was sentenced to life in prison. Fromme was not charged in the murders. She was one of Manson's most vociferous defenders during his seven-month trial.

Two months prior to the attempted assassination, Fromme had sought media attention by issuing a statement claiming that she had received letters from Manson blaming Richard Nixon for his imprisonment. During Manson's murder trial, Mr. Nixon remarked to reporters that Manson was guilty. Fromme's statement also asserted that Manson blamed President Ford for continuing Nixon's policies. Fromme and another Manson family member, Sandra Good, sought to publicize Manson's letters and his comments on Nixon and Ford as a way of focusing attention on Manson's plight, which they believed to be unjust. They had little success, so both women took to wearing red capes to dramatize Manson's case.

Political scientist James W. Clarke, in analyzing Fromme, concludes: "It is questionable whether Fromme intended to kill the president. Her frustration had never been directed specifically at Ford except to acknowledge that he was simply another willing "instrument of the ruling corporate elite."[25] Clarke believes that Fromme was attempting to threaten the president with a weapon in order to gain publicity for Manson's cause. While the Manson family had a personal hatred of Nixon, there was no such feeling for Ford, Clarke concluded.

Fromme attempted to turn her trial into a political statement — a political show-trial much like that of the Chicago Seven. But her efforts were frustrated by U.S. District Court Judge Thomas J. McBride, who removed her from the courtroom after her disruptive outbursts and had her communicate via closed-circuit television. Her defense was based upon the contention that she did not intend to assassinate the president but only to receive publicity for Manson. The jury rejected this claim and gave her a life sentence.

In addition to Ms. Fromme's notoriety as a Manson follower, she had been arrested more than a dozen times on charges ranging from drug possession, to petty theft, to robbery, to murder; but she had been convicted of only minor offenses and had spent only a few months in jail.[26] The murder charge was filed in Stockton, California in 1972, in the death of a 19-year-old woman whose body was found buried under a house in which Ms. Fromme had been living. The charge was subsequently dismissed for lack of evidence.

Fromme had been living in Sacramento where Ford was visiting when she pulled a gun on him. There is no evidence that she had stalked Ford or any other political leader, as Arthur Bremer had done. She was not on the Secret Service watch list of 400 dangerous persons nor was her name among the 47,000 in Secret Service files. Although her history of visible association with persons involved in violent crime, her criminal record, and her public statements about Nixon and Ford might seem to have qualified her for inclusion in Secret Service files, she had made no threats against any protectees, not even veiled threats.

Another question, one not so easily answered as the one concerning her absence from Secret Service files, is how Ms. Fromme managed to get within two to three feet of President Ford while carrying a loaded weapon. Then Secret Service Director of Public Affairs John W. Warner, Jr. refused comment on this matter when asked by the press. There is no simple answer, but the problem would recur in 1981 when John W. Hinckley would get within 15 feet of President Reagan and wound him.

Only two and a half weeks after the Fromme incident, there was another unsuccessful assassination attempt on President Ford.[27] Ford was exiting the St. Francis Hotel in San Francisco. A crowd of 3,000 had gathered to see him. The crowd lined the sidewalks for two to three blocks outside the hotel, and was two to three persons deep behing rope barriers. When Ford came out, the crowd cheered; spectators pushed and shoved to catch a glimpse of the president.

Ford smiled and waved. He walked toward his waiting limousine and was surrounded by agents. He was about to reach out and shake a few hands when a single shot exploded from across the street, approximately 40 feet away. The shot, a .38-caliber exploding bullet, missed the president. It ricocheted off a concrete wall and struck a taxi driver, inflicting a minor wound.

At the sound of the shot Ford appeared stunned. Color drained from his face and he doubled over; his knees appeared to buckle. This caused numerous bystanders to fear that he had been shot. At the sound of gunfire, Secret Service Agents Ron Pontius and Jack Merchant pushed Ford down toward the sidewalk, thus reducing his exposure. Amid screams erupting from the crowd, agents pushed the president into the limousine and onto the floor, covering his body with theirs. The limousine quickly sped away. Ford good-naturedly said to the agents covering him, "Hey, will you guys get off me? You're going to smother me."[28]

The assailant was Sara Jane Moore. She had waited for Ford for more than three hours. The nondescript, 45-year-old woman wore baggy tan pants and a neatly pressed blue raincoat and had stood with her hands in her pockets the entire time, except at the moment of the shooting.[29] Secret Service agents are usually on the lookout for persons standing with their hands thrust into coat pockets, because agents know that such persons might have a weapon concealed and could draw it more quickly if their hands are already inside the pockets instead of outside. Agents sometimes request that bystanders remove their hands from coat pockets for precisely this reason.

Moore drew her .38-caliber revolver and aimed at Ford from the second row of spectators. Bystander Oliver Sepple, a 32-year-old, disabled Vietnam veteran, is generally credited with having deflected the gun as it was fired, thus causing the shot to miss. Although, one policeman at the scene believed that Moore had gotten off an unobstructed shot before Sepple deflected the weapon.*[30] Police pounced on Ms. Moore, knocked her to the ground, and wrestled the gun from her hand. They then picked her up and carried her head first, not unlike a battering ram, into the hotel.

Who was Sara Jane Moore and what were her motives? Among other things, she was a political activist and an FBI informant. When Patricia Hearst was kidnapped by the Symbionese Liberation Army, part of the ransom demanded was that her father, William Randolph Hearst, distribute $2 million worth of free food to the poor. Moore volunteered her skills as an accountant to help administer the food distribution and thereby came to the attention of Mr. Hearst, because of her hard work and efficiency. She soon took on the role of liaison between Mr. Hearst

---

*Even at 40 feet from the president, Moore's 38-caliber pistol could have been deadly. The weapon was potentially accurate from between 75 and 150 feet from the target, if the shooter's aim was adequate.

and the political groups distributing the food. Moore seemed to thrive on the importance and excitement provided by her new role, and she emersed herself in the culture and activities of radical politics in the Bay Area of San Francisco.[31]

By April of 1974, her involvements with local radicals were so extensive that the FBI recruited her to work for them as an informant. In what she described as a role that was "just like a very bad movie script," she was asked by the Bureau to make contact with certain individuals and to provide information on some of her acquaintances.[32]

As with every other assailant who has assassinated or attempted to assassinate a Secret Service protectee since the inception of the protective mission, Sara Jane Moore was not on the Service's watch list or in its files. Nevertheless, she was a very visible figure and was known to both San Francisco police and Secret Service agents.

Two days before she attempted to shoot President Ford, Moore called the police and said that she was considering a "test" of the presidential security system.[33] She told police that she had a gun. The next morning, the day before Ford's arrival, police interviewed her and confiscated her gun, a .44-caliber pistol, along with 13 bullets found in her purse and 100 more found in her car.

According to police inspector Jack O'Shea, Moore had asked police during her telephone call to them: "I'm going to ask you something that will make you recoil in horror: Can you have me arrested?" O'Shea stated that he told her that she could be arrested if she were actually walking around with a concealed weapon.[34] When police went to her home, her gun was unloaded. Police claimed that, under California law, all they could do regarding an unloaded gun was to issue a misdemeanor citation and confiscate the weapon.[35]

In any event, police reported Ms. Moore to the Secret Service and agents interviewed her the night before the president's arrival. The two agents conducting the interview concluded that Moore was "not of sufficient protective importance to warrant surveillance during the president's visit"[36] — a conclusion that demonstrates the virtue of having interviewing agents trained in psychology so that they may be able to render more effective judgments concerning the mental state of interviewees.

The morning of Ford's visit, Moore went out and purchased a .38-caliber revolver. Evidently remembering what police had told her about the conditions under which she could be arrested, and seemingly still ambivalent about whether to go through with an assassination attempt, she proceeded to drive erratically through the city at excessive speed while carrying a loaded gun, possibly hoping that she would be stopped and arrested. She was not.

Moore drove downtown and parked. On her way to the St. Francis Hotel she encountered Carol Pogash, a reporter for the San Francisco *Examiner* whom she had met when she worked for Hearst. According to Pogash, Moore blurted out: "You know the Secret Service visited my house yesterday. They kept me for an hour and questioned me. They could have kept me for 72 hours if they wanted to."[37] Pogash did not take Moore seriously and did not want to encourage her to chatter on, as she was prone to do. Pogash left her.

San Francisco police claimed that the had fulfilled their responsibilities by reporting Ms. Moore to the Secret Service. The Service would not comment to the press concerning its protective-intelligence work relating to this case. Said one policeman: "Someone [at Secret Service] apparently made a mistake in judgement."[38]

As is evidenced by the Moore case, the threshold for direct Secret Service action in cases involving potential threats to the president was, in 1975, quite high, tending toward requiring a direct, specific threat rather than the vague intimations made by Moore. Just five hours before Moore's assassination attempt, Secret Service agents arrested a 24-year-old man at a hotel only two blocks from the St. Francis and charged him with threatening the president.[39] The man had allegedly handed to a St. Francis employee a note containing a threat against President Ford. Sara Jane Moore pleaded guilty to attempted assassination of a president. Like Fromme, she was given a life sentence. Her revolver is displayed in a glass case in Secret Service headquarters in Washington.

There are an unknown number of instances in which the Secret Service must take action, sometimes involving force, in order to prevent an assault on the president from materializing. Because the Service usually does not call in the press and reveal its preventive successes — reveal that conspiracies have been foiled or suspicious individuals incarcerated — we do not know how much of what kind of action is taken in order to stop assassination attempts before they occur. However, one strange and complex incident of this type was revealed by the Service. It involved an alleged plot to assassinate President Nixon.

Nixon was scheduled to visit New Orleans in late August 1973, where he was planning to ride in an open car in a motorcade through the city's French quarter.[40] The Service uncovered what it thought to be an assassination plot and asked Mr. Nixon to cancel his motorcade. Reluctantly, Nixon did cancel and gave the order personally. But in San Clemente, California, where Nixon flew after the cancellation, reporters overheard him say to his secretary, Rosemary Woods: "They called me last night. They cancelled. They'll never cancel another time."[41] A White House spokesman said later that Mr. Nixon was not referring to the motorcade. But tensions between the White House staff and the Service's White House detail were running high that year, culminating in the removal of Agent Robert S. Taylor as head of the detail. Taylor's departure was prompted by a rift between his detail and the Nixon staff concerning political priorities versus protective priorities.

Whatever the political machinations between the White House and the protective detail, the Service took the highly unusual step of announcing that it had uncovered a possible plot to assassinate Mr. Nixon in New Orleans. Moreover, the announcement came *while* efforts to uncover the plot were still ongoing. Possibly the announcement was prompted by the Service's need to defend itself against Mr. Nixon's and/or his staff's ire concerning the cancellation of the motorcade.

Suspicion by authorities that an assassination plot might be developing began in early August (Nixon's visit was scheduled for August 20th). Police received a tip originating in the predominantly black central city area that there would be trouble for Nixon when he visited. Then, three weeks before the visit, a paid informant told police that there had been a meeting of six Black Panthers at which an assassination plot was discussed and a high-powered rifle "changed hands."[42] The informant had not attended the alleged meeting but had heard about it. Police informed both the FBI and Secret Service.

According to New Orleans police, the Service requested that the six Panthers be detained until the president's visit was over, but police refused because the evidence was only uncorroborated hearsay, not solid enough to act on. Police Superintendant Clarence Giarrusso claimed to have told the Service: "If you want them arrested then you arrest them. We have no grounds."[43] Police did agree to place all six men under surveillance and obtained from a federal magistrate the authority to arrest any of the six suspects at the first sign of trouble.

Then, just five days before Nixon's planned arrival, a woman informant told police that she had overheard a black man comment that: "Somebody ought to kill President Nixon. If no one has the guts, I'll do it." The informant identified the man as Edwin Gaudet, a former New Orleans policeman whose background seemed, in the view of authorities, to provide a possible link to the alleged Black Panther plot reported earlier by an informant. Gaudet had quit the police force in 1967 following an off-duty barroom brawl. He had been arrested in 1970 for burning an American flag on the steps of city hall. More important in the Service's view, he had also been arrested that same year for throwing a burning American flag across the hood of Mr. Nixon's limousine when the president was in New Orleans.[44] After the latter incident, Gaudet was sent to the psychiatric ward of Louisiana State Hospital and was later released as an outpatient.

The informant's report about Gaudet coupled with the uncorroborated report of Black Panther assassination plot seemed all the more sinister given two events that occurred the day before Nixon's scheduled arrival. A police uniform and badge were stolen from a parked patrol car. Three and half hours later a police car was stolen. Although police would later discover that these two incidents were unrelated and that neither was related to an assassination plot, Gaudet's status as a black ex-policeman coupled with an allegation of a Black Panther plot led the Service to conclude that a well-planned assassination conspiracy was unfolding.

The day after Mr. Nixon's visit was scrubbed, the Secret Service told the press that there existed a "very serious, very large" conspiracy by "nonmentals."[45] The Service used — and, most likely, coined — the term "nonmental" in order to distinguish this plot from the more common variety of threats posed by deranged individuals.

Secret Service agents pursued Gaudet, who was charged with threatening Nixon's life. Acting on information from Gaudet's father, agents located the suspect at an abandoned commune in the mountains of New Mexico.[46] When police officers attempted to serve him with an arrest warrant, Gaudet fled and fired two shots. He ran into the hills carrying a supply of food. Agent Paul Jones got Gaudet's wife and cousin to talk the fugitive into giving himself up, which he did 20 hours after fleeing.

Two days after Gaudet surrendered to authorities, the woman informant who had identified him as the man who had threatened to kill President Nixon recanted: She was unable to identify Gaudet while she was under oath. The alleged Black Panther plot, reported by another informant, was never corroborated by a second source or by any additional data.

The Service described the threat to Mr. Nixon as broad and intense and insisted that the case had not been blown out of proportion. Yet the flimsy intelligence data concerning a plot turned out to be wrong. While it is certainly prudent for the Secret Service to err on the side of caution in such instances, the question remains as to why the Service publicly announced that it had discovered a plot before it had fully investigated the plot or rounded up the alleged plotters, who might escape and hatch a new conspiracy. In addition, President Nixon was receiving threats against his life at the rate of about 300 per year—nearly one per day.[47] Because of the volume of threat cases, determining which ones demand extensive attention is a crucial judgment for the Service. Its resources are limited; it cannot launch a new, major investigation every day. Since all threats cannot be pursued with equal resources, it is important to be able to determine accurately which protective-intelligence data is worthy of extensive investigation and which is not.

The Secret Service must repel attacks on protectees other than the president. In 1979 while Senator Edward Kennedy was a presidential candidate, a knife-wielding woman entered the reception room outside Kennedy's Senate office in Washington. She was subdued by agents before she got close to the senator, who was working in his inner office. One agent received a minor cut during the scuffle.[48]

Taking action to repel assassination attempts is required only sporadically. There were two attempts on President Ford in 1975, then the wounding of President Reagan six years later. Yet there are law-enforcement actions, required by both the protective and investigative missions, which occur with greater frequency than assassination attempts and which can be equally dangerous for the agents involved.

Since agents must shield protectees from any kind of harm—not simply assassination attempts—they must take action in a wide range of situations, some of which are quite singular. President Carter's daughter Amy attended a pet show hosted by Mrs. Ethel Kennedy at her Hickory Hill estate. One of the performers was Suzy, a 6,000 pound elephant who suddenly took exception to the proceedings and charged toward Amy Carter. As the crowd scattered in panic, Suzy stormed to within 35 feet of the president's daughter and was closing in rapidly. One agent scooped Amy up and handed her over the top of a split-rail fence to an agent on the other side, then the first agent climbed over the fence. The elephant splintered the fence and continued to charge, despite efforts by agents to distract her. Agents managed to scramble past the pachyderm and carry Amy safely inside the Kennedy house.[49]

Secret Service agents and uniformed officers must deal with numerous intrusions and assaults that do not directly place protectees in danger. Such incidents often occur at the White House while the president is safely guarded inside or is traveling. One day during the Carter presidency a man came up to the White House gate and announced that he wanted to protect the president because he had "mastered the art." He then displayed a long knife to the uniformed officers stationed at the gate and told them that he knew how to use it. The officers explained that the president was already protected and told the man that if he would surrender the knife, he would not be charged with carrying a concealed weapon. The man complied.

The very next morning, however, he appeared again. This time he scaled the White House fence and dropped onto the lawn. Two uniformed officers quickly approached him. He drew a hunting knife and brandished it at the officers. In the ensuing struggle to arrest the intruder, one officer was slashed in the arm; the other, on the nose.[50]

In another incident occurring in Carter's first year as president, another intruder climbed the iron fence and entered the White House grounds. The man was Chester M. Plummer, Jr., a Washington, D.C. taxi driver. He walked 60 feet toward the mansion while carrying a heavy, three-foot-long iron pipe. When a Secret Service uniformed officer ordered him to halt and to drop the iron pipe, the intruder groaned, raised the pipe over his head, and rushed the officer.[51] When Plummer refused to heed a second warning, the officer drew and fired once. Police gave emergency medical assistance but Plummer died two hours after being taken to a hospital. A grand jury looking into the incident decided to file no charges against uniformed officer Charles A. Garland.[52]

Many intrusions are handled without recourse to weapons. One man scaled the White House fence four times during a two-year period while Ford was president. One of these incidents ended in a scuffle with uniformed officers, but the only injury sustained was when the intruder hurt himself climbing over the fence.[53]

Nor do all the risks result from guarding protectees or guarding the White House. In 1980 two Secret Service agents were killed in separate incidents that did not involve directly guarding a protectee and which occurred in cities other than Washington, D.C. On January 15, 1980 a man carrying a gun entered the Service's Denver field office. Hugh Ryan had been committed to a mental hospital the previous year as a result of his attempt to break into the White House grounds. Following this incident, he had also been questioned by the Service in connection with an alleged threat against the president. Ryan complained to Denver agents that he was being harassed by the Secret Service. Recognizing the man's apparent instability, two agents tried to get close to him as he talked; but Ryan drew a 45-caliber pistol and shot agent Stewart Wilkins in the stomach and chest. The second agent then shot and killed Ryan. Agent Wilkins died in surgery.[54]

In June of 1980, a 26-year-old woman agent, Julie Cross, was shot to death in Los Angeles by two armed robbers while she was conducting a stakeout of a suspected counterfeiting operation. The robbery and shooting were not directly connected to the stakeout. Ms. Cross was the first female federal agent to be killed in the line of duty.[55]

Secret Service personnel share something more with the politicians they protect than the fact that much of their work is performed under the public eye and in the political arena. Both occupations harbor an element of danger which may be ignored but is very real nevertheless.

NOTES

1. James F. Kirkham *et al.*, *Assassination and Political Violence: A Report to the Commission on the Causes and Prevention of Violence* (New York: Bantam, 1970), pp. 69-71.

2. *Ibid.*, pp. 71-73.

3. *Ibid.*, pp. 73-76; "U.S. Secret Service, Excerpts from the History of the United States Secret Service—1865-1975," (Washington, D.C.: Treasury Dept.), pp. 29-31.

4. "Appointment in Laurel," *Newsweek*, May 29, 1972, p. 18; "George Wallace's Appointment in Laurel," *Time*, May 29, 1972, p. 18.

5. *Ibid.*

6. "Wallace's Appointment," *Time*, p. 19.

7. James W. Clarke, *American Assassins* (Princeton, N.J.: Princeton Univ. Press, 1982), p. 175.

8. The account of this incident is taken from: *Ibid.*, pp. 175-79; "Appointment in Laurel," *Newsweek*; "Wallace's Appointment," *Time*.

9. "Appointment in Laurel," *Newsweek*, p. 22.

10. *U.S. News & World Report*, May 29, 1972, p. 16.

11. Clarke, *American Assassins*, p. 174.

12. *Ibid.*, p. 183.

13. *Ibid.*, p. 184.

14. Terence Smith, "Reports Hint Bremer Stalked Others," New York *Times*, May 26, 1972, p. 12.

15. "Stalking the Candidate," *Newsweek*, May 29, 1972, p. 18.

16. *Ibid.*

17. "Appointment in Laurel," *Newsweek*, p. 22.

18. Laurens Pierce, "He Carried a Camera and a .38," *TV Guide*, May 1, 1982, p. 22-23.

19. *Ibid.*

20. "Stalking the Candidate," *Newsweek.*

21. *Clarke, American Assassins*, p. 191.

22. The description of this incident is taken from: Bill Kreifel, "Secret Service Always Practicing," *The Lincoln Journal*, Lincoln, Nebraska, Oct. 6, 1981; Robert D. McFadden "Suspect Was Defender of Manson Family," New York *Times*, Sept. 6, 1975, p. 1; Clarke, *American Assassins*, pp. 152–53.

23. McFadden, "Suspect Was Defender of Manson," p. 1.

24. Clarke, *American Assassins*, p. 153.

25. *Ibid.*, p. 153.

26. McFadden, "Suspect Was Defender of Manson," p. 1.

27. This account is based upon: "Can The Risk Be Cut?" *Newsweek*, Oct. 6, 1975, pp. 18–22; Lacey Forsburg, "Cheers, Then a Shot, and Crowd Screams," New York *Times*, Sept. 22, 1975, pp. 1 and 26; Philip Shabecoff, "Suspect Had Been Queried But Freed by Secret Service," New York *Times*, Sept. 23, 1975, p. 1.

28. Gerald R. Ford, *A Time to Heal* (New York: Harper & Row, 1979), p. 311–12.

29. "Can the Risk Be Cut?," *Newsweek*, p. 20.

30. Shabecoff, "Suspect Had Been Queried But Freed."

31. Clarke, *American Assassins*, pp. 159–60; Henry Weinstein, "Suspect Asserted She Helped FBI," New York *Times*, Sept. 22, 1975, pp. 1 and 27.

32. Clarke, *American Assassins*, p. 160.

33. "Interview With Sara Jane Moore," Los Angeles *Times*, Sept. 25, 1975, pp. 1–3.

34. "Can the Risk Be Cut?" *Newsweek*, p. 21.

35. *Ibid.*, pp. 21–22.

36. Moore interview, Los Angeles *Times*.

37. "Ford's Second Close Call," *Time*, Oct. 6, 1975, p. 13.

38. "Can the Risk Be Cut?," *Newsweek*, p. 21.

39. Shabecoff, "Suspect Had Been Queried But Freed."

40. "The New Orleans Plots," *Time*, Sept. 23, 1973, pp. 11–12.

41. New York *Times*, August 21, 1973, p. 20.

42. "The New Orleans Plots," *Time*, Sept. 23, 1973, pp. 11–12.

43. *Ibid.*

44. *Ibid.*

45. New York *Times*, August 21, 1973, p. 20.

46. "The New Orleans Plots," *Time.*

47. Roy Reed, "Charge of Threat to Nixon Dropped For Ex-Policeman," New York *Times*, Aug. 25, 1973, p. 10.

48. *U.S. News & World Report*, Dec. 10, 1979, p. 63.

49. Harry Neal, *The Secret Service in Action* (New York: Elsevier-Nelson, 1980), pp. 104–5.

50. *Ibid.*, pp. 123-4.

51. *Ibid.*, p. 125.

52. "Guard at White House Is Cleared in Shooting," New York *Times*, July 24, 1976, p. 12.

53. "Intruder Captured at White House," New York *Times*, August 15, 1976, p. 22.

54. "Federal Agent Slain in Denver," New York *Times*, Jan. 15, 1980, p. 1.

55. "Female Secret Service Agent Slain on Los Angeles Post," New York *Times*, June 6, 1980, pp. A-14.

5

AN INCREASINGLY
THREATENING WORLD

*Basically, the production of nitroglycerin involves the gradual
adding of glycerol to a mixture of nitric and sulfuric acids
followed by separation of the nitroglycerin from the waste pro-
ducts. The following directions will serve for the laboratory
preparation of nitroglycerin in small amounts.*

Improvised Weapons of the American Underground

In addition to the effectiveness of protective methods, the variables
that most effect security are the scope and nature of threats to protectees.
While the design and implementation of the Secret Service's protective
methods have advanced significantly over the past two decades, threats to
protectees have dramatically escalated in sophistication. Like the
military, which must allocate its resources among various kinds of forces
and hardware, the Secret Service develops its protective tools and procedures in accord with its perception of the nature and magnitude of
potential threats. The Service does not have the resources to defend
against all possible threats (from a UFO attack to a deranged sniper) with
equal vigor: it must, in a real sense, place its bets according to the most
likely sources of an attack.

Since the Service believes that only one attack on a protectee was a
result of a conspiracy (the two Puerto Rican nationalists who assaulted
President Truman in 1950), the organization has traditionally geared its
methods toward combating what it perceived as the primary threat—the
lone, deranged assassin. Within the past several years, however, the Service has begun to give much higher priority to the possibility of assassination conspiracies—not domestic ones, but ones involving foreign

terrorists. Although the Service still regards the lone assassin as the primary domestic threat, changing international conditions have caused it to focus on assassination conspiracies as never before in its history.

The volume of threat cases (of all kinds) has reached the level of 20 new ones per day. The vast majority are domestic in origin and involve threats made by individuals. In a typical year, the Service's Protective Intelligence Section launches 150,000 "inquiries" about actual or possible threats, and this results in the arrest of about 300 persons annually.

The number of potentially dangerous individuals in our society shows no evidence of decline, despite the increased availability of clinical help of various kinds. In 1981 the National Academy of Sciences' workshop on the prevention of assassination noted that the Secret Service's job had become more difficult because of otherwise progressive changes in the treatment of mental illness that have led to the discharge of "large numbers of formerly institutionalized patients."[1] Thus the Service has more cases that require monitoring. On another front, the number of terrorist groups has significantly increased within the past two decades. Most disturbingly, the sophistication and availability of weapons have escalated in recent years, and this is true for both kinds of threats (lone, deranged assassins and terrorist groups).

Within the United States, handguns continue to proliferate and can still be purchased with relative ease. In spite of federal laws attempting to stop the influx of cheap, foreign-made handguns, police records show that these weapons are among the fastest-selling consumer items in the country.[2] Private citizens now own an estimated 50 million handguns. The Treasury Department's Bureau of Alcohol Tobacco and Firearms estimates that one of every three persons over sixteen years of age owns one. Cheap weapons known as "Saturday night specials" (increasingly, foreign-made) can be purchased in some places with little more than proof of age and residence (a driver's license) plus a seldomly verified pledge that the purchaser is not a felon, mental patient, or drug addict.[3]

As if the proliferation of handguns were not problem enough, there is the specter that assailants might load them with the recently invented Teflon bullet, developed by Dr. Paul Kotch, a coroner. This "KTW" bullet is a brass slug covered with a Teflon coating. The coating lubricates the bullet so that upon impact, it slides through matter while retaining its shape instead of mushrooming as would a conventional bullet. The result is awesome: the Teflon bullet has six times the penetrating power of a conventional lead bullet and can go through five and a half telephone books and pierce "bulletproof" vests as if they were made of cardboard. In one demonstration, a Teflon bullet penetrated the equivalent of four bulletproof vests of the kind usually worn by police.[4]

Although more than a dozen states have legislation pending that would outlaw Teflon bullets, the politically powerful National Rifle Association (NRA) opposes such laws on the grounds that they infringe upon the right to bear arms. The package in which the bullets are sold is labeled "for police use only," but it is possible in some areas to order this ammunition COD from a gunshop without police credentials.[5]

For would-be assailants who are more sophisticated about weapons, whether they be loners or part of a terrorist group, there exists an extensive proliferation of weapons and weapons technology, stimulated by a flourishing black market in firearms. For the right price, certain vendors can provide everything from bazookas to heat-seeking antiaircraft missiles. Although silencers are outlawed in the United States, imports from the several European nations that allow their sale can be purchased for $500 to $700 in the United States.[6] The black market price for automatic weapons is $1,000 for an older one, such as a Thompson submachine gun, to $3,000 for a modern M-16.

California Deputy Attorney General Charles O'Brien, testifying before a Senate subcommittee on internal security, claimed that terrorist groups operating in the United States (many of them domestic in origin) have been stockpiling weapons: "We have reported a large number of M-16 rifles and M-3 submachine guns that have disappeared into the radical underground. They have light machine guns and thousands of rounds of stolen ammunition too."[7] One pamphlet entitled "Improved Weapons of the American Underground," while warning the reader that the actual construction of weapons as described in the pamphlet may be dangerous and/or illegal, proceeds to offer detailed instructions concerning the materials and steps needed to craft: nitroglycerin explosives, plastic explosives, detonators, fuses, silencers, and submachine guns.[8]

The increase in the number of potentially dangerous persons whom the Service must keep track of coupled with the increased number of sophisticated weapons available has compounded the Service's basic problem regarding what it perceives as the primary threat to protectees—the lone, deranged assassin. The problem is that the Service has yet to develop a predictive, operational "profile" that would allow it to effectively identify lone assassins before they strike. The existence of a so-called "profile" of the lone assassin has been the subject of much confusion and debate. The myth persists that a fairly precise profile exists and can be used to predict behavior, but such a profile is largely illusory and is composed of traits that are far too nebulous to afford predictive, operational usage by the Secret Service.

In 1970 the Kerner Commission, which studied the causes of violence in America, devoted an entire section of its final report to "the psychology of Presidential assassins." The commission weaved the apparent similarities among American assassins into an historical profile:

> All of those who have assassinated or attempted to assassinate Presidents of the United States (with the possible exception of the Puerto Rican nationalist attempt on President Truman) have been mentally disturbed persons who did not advance any rational political plan.[9]

More specifically, the Kerner panel concluded that:

> Almost all the assassins were loners who had difficulty making friends of either sex, especially in establishing lasting relationships with women.

From one to three years before the crime, each assassin "became unable to hold a job although there is no evidence of physical disability in any case." There is an hypothesis, said the commission, that "the absence of a strong father figure may contribute to the assassin's frame of mind."[10]

Dr. Lawrence Z. Freedman, who has studied assassins extensively and who, after the JFK assassination, worked for the Secret Service in its attempts to develop a profile, wrote (in 1981) a description of American assassins which implied that a fairly precise profile had been developed. Freedman asserted that "presidential assassins" are a "peculiarly American phenomenon," and that they carry out "a profoundly political attack" for confused "personal" reasons.[11] According to Freedman, the profile of these assassins is that they are "emotionally disturbed isolates acting on their own without any rationale except that they, or the party and cause with which they identified, could benefit from the slaying . . . .These lonely assassins performing their murderous acts in solitude were acting against a symbol, not a man."

Professor James W. Clarke, who is not a psychologist but a political scientist, studied American assassins and found a common psychological trait—frustration—which may have contributed to the acts of aggression in all cases except that of James Earl Ray, the convicted assassin of Martin Luther King, Jr. Clarke posited a four-part typology for assassins:[12]

(1) those who view their act as a sacrifice on behalf of a political ideal; (2) those with an overwhelming need for acceptance, recognition, or status; (3) psychopaths who are driven to destroy themselves or to strike out at society; (4) those who have little sense of reality and suffer from cognitive distortions. Although Clark is not an expert in psychiatry or psychology and although his profiles may not endure as the definitive typology for classifying all assassins, his well-documented work serves to remind us that the profile, discussed by the Kerner Commission and Freedman and many others, is simply too limited to provide a meaningful understanding of the range of relevant variables that help to produce assassins.

Apparent similarities among assailants are often used to gloss over some very important differences. It may be true that Lee Harvey Oswald, Lynette "Squeaky" Fromme, and John W. Hinckley shared certain traits, but there are also important characteristics of background and behavior not shared by all three. Oswald was conspicuously calm, unemotional, and apparently rational during his interrogation. He was relatively poor; he had a wife and two children. He had been enmeshed in international political intrigue, having defected to the Soviet Union and offered U.S. radar secrets to the Russians, after serving in the Marine Corps. Fromme was a cult member (the Manson family), had a long criminal record, and was overtly eccentric (dressing in a red cape and turban and seeking media attention in order to dramatize the Manson cause). Hinckley came from well-to-do parents, had undergone psychiatric treatment prior to his assassination attempt and was deeply enmeshed in fantasies centering around actress Jodie Foster. Any complete profile of these and other assassins would continue to turn up dissimilarities of background and behavior which may well have as much of a causal influence as the apparent similarities (difficulty in holding a job, difficulty in sustaining interpersonal relationships, etc.).

Moreover, many of the traits generally employed in fleshing out the profile of the lone assassin are very nebulous and have little or no clinical or protective-research value. Because of their imprecision, they are best described as pop-psychology concepts or folk concepts. There is no better example than the term *loner*. All assassins are *loners*, according to the widely accepted profile.

Just what is a *loner*? If used to describe persons who are not gregarious, lack an extensive social calendar and an impressive circle of friends, and do not interact well by upper-middle-class standards, then, indeed, it seems accurate to label most assassins as loners. But the problem arises when, as is typically the case, researchers or commentators appropriate the term as part of a causal explanation for the assassin's violent behavior or as precluding the assassin's participation in a conspiracy. For, according to Freedman and others, American assassins are always loners—operate alone—whereas European assassins, such as papal assailant Mehmet Ali Agca, tend to be conspiratorially involved.

Regarding the first use of the *loner* concept (as defining a social maladjustment that contributes to violent behavior), the question arises as to how many interpersonal relationships—and of what magnitude and quality—an individual is required to have in order to avoid being labeled a loner? Is a loner someone who has no friends at all? Only superficial relationships? Only unsuccessful relationships? If so, most assassins have not been loners.

Lee Harvey Oswald is almost always classified as a loner.[13] Although he did not appear to have a charming personality and although his marriage was replete with discord, he did have a family (a wife and two children) and a friend and patron in Dallas, George de Mohrenschildt, who invited him to parties and introduced him socially to members of the Russian exile community, during the year prior to the assassination. Two months before the assassination Oswald is known to have traveled in rural Louisiana in the company of David Ferrie, his former Civil Air Patrol instructor, and another man. Shortly before the assassination, Oswald took a bus trip to Mexico during which he went out of his way to greet and chat with fellow passengers who were strangers to him.

There is no clinical, quantitative baseline for the concept of *loner*. Many writers and artists seem to qualify as well as do assassins. Nor is there an established qualitative baseline, although the folk concept holds that any relationship forged by the loner will be unfulfilling, of poor quality. Many persons besides assassins have unsuccessful marriages or love affairs, shift work settings very frequently, are unemployed for long stretches, and often hole up in a house or apartment, sometimes refusing to talk to people who try to see them. This is as much the profile of the Hollywood actor as the lone assassin.

There is a second use of the folk concept of *loner*—to argue against the possibility of conspiracy. Does an assassin have to be a joiner, a socialite, or good at lunch in order to be part of a conspiracy? If an assassin has only one friend, does this preclude participation in a conspiracy even if the friend is a KGB agent, a CIA agent, or a mafioso? Persons who are fairly isolated from others, are alienated, and are devoted to some political cause may not be the best candidates to hatch a conspiracy, to plot it and to recruit others into it; but they might easily be used as pawns or be encouraged by others who appear to them to share their ideals.

Moreover, the profiles of individual assassins, the composite of which forms the general profile, are usually the product of speculative hindsight rather than clinical analysis. Because the individual is known to have shot at the president, his or her life is interpreted on the basis of this event. Shortly after John W. Hinckley's arrest following the Reagan shooting, a network television reporter interviewed one of Hinckley's college professors in Colorado. The professor described his now infamous former student as sitting in class as if he were in a world of his own, dreaming, and not focusing on what was going on. The author suddenly came to the frightening realization that in many of his university classes over the years, there were hundreds of students who exhibited the same behavior—were they all would-be assassins?

Thus, yet another problem with the lone-assassin profile is that it is by no means unique to assassins. If one were to study the psychological traits and backgrounds of low-level intelligence operatives or those in organized crime, or recidivist prisoners, the "profile" would probably overlap extensively with that of the lone assassin in terms of jobs, interpersonal relationships, and family background. If the lone-assassin profile has any use as a distinguishing label, it is in providing a broad clue as to what the person is not rather than what the person is: the person is not the type who would be idealized by churches, the Eagle Scouts, civic groups, or employers as "person of the year"; or, conversely, the person is maladjusted in some broad sense of the term.

Despite claims to the contrary by many historians, psychologists, and journalists, the lone-assassin profile is more a caricature than an operational, clinically defined concept. As then Secret Service Director H. Stuart Knight flatly admitted in 1980 (and it is still true today): "There is no profile of an assassin. We keep searching for it, but there is no sure-fire profile."[14]

Part of the confusion has to do with the definition of a "profile." There is a lone-assassin profile in the sense of a dictionary definition—"a representation of something in outline." A profile exists in the journalistic sense, as in a "profile" of the unemployed, or the inner-city poor. In contrast, the profile sought by the Secret Service is a set of indices which will enable the Protective Intelligence Section to understand and predict behavior well enough to identify assassins before they strike. Part of the proof that such a profile does not yet exist is the disturbing fact that not one person who has tried to assassinate a Secret Service protectee has been on the Service's watch list of 400 dangerous persons or anywhere in its files.

Although 90 percent of the persons in the Service's 40,000 to 50,000 files have a history of psychiatric problems, the challenge to the Service is to figure out which of these persons would actually attempt to kill a protectee, since not all persons with psychiatric problems turn out to be assassins.[15] The Service's files tend to contain a large contingent of potentially dangerous persons who are self-announcing—like the man who called the Service's Chicago office and talked for 33 minutes while threatening President Carter's life, or the man who wrote to Secret Service headquarters announcing that he was coming to Washington, D.C. to kill the president (agents arrested him in Washington and found that he was carrying a knife and a diagram of the White House).[16] Many self-announcing persons are too unstable or inept to carry out a successful attack, although they still constitute a real danger. But it is the other category, those who are psychologically disturbed and who would attack but who do not self-announce, who present an even greater danger. Both types (those who self-announce and those who do not) may be lone assassins, and both may fit the popular profile of the lone assassin; but the two are very different in terms of the difficulty that the Service has in identifying them and in terms of the kind of threat that they pose.

With the possible exception of Sara Jane Moore, none of the modern assailants have been self-announcers. Moore's case serves to illustrate that self-announcing versus non-self-announcing may be a continuum of behavior rather than a bifurcation. While Moore did not directly announce her intention to assassinate President Ford, she strongly hinted as much to police and she attempted to bring herself to police and Secret Service attention in several ways during the 48 hours preceding her attempt.*

The search for a behaviorally predictive profile continues within the Secret Service, aided by outside consultants. In the meantime, the historial caricature of the American assassin that is referred to as "the profile" is much too vague and speculative to meet the Service's needs.

The other major threat, which is perceived by the Service as increasingly dangerous, is the one posed by terrorist organizations. The actual scope of the threat to U.S. leaders posed by international terrorism is very

---

* Moore's case is discussed at length in Chapter 4.

difficult to measure accurately, and it is a topic that seems to galvanize ideological passions, which often color analyses of the terrorist threat. Some observers assert that there exists a large network of interacting, mutually supportive terrorist groups nurtured by regimes such as Cuba, the Soviet Union, Libya, as described by Claire Sterling in her book *The Terror Network*.[17] Other observers claim that the American military and American intelligence have exaggerated the scope of the terrorist threat for purposes of propaganda or of legitimizing certain military and diplomatic actions and politics. Another problem is that one person's "freedom fighter" is another person's "terrorist," depending upon whether the goals of the insurgent group are endorsed or rejected. Allowing for the difficulty of quantifying what is primarily a clandestine activity, and even with the ideological conflicts involved, there can be no doubt that, as far as the Secret Service's protective mission is concerned, the scope and sophistication of potential threats involving terrorists has grown significantly during the past two decades.

The wounding of Pope John Paul II, the assassinations of Anwar Sadat and of Britain's Lord Louis Mountbatten, the kidnapping and execution of former Italian Prime Minister Aldo Moro, the kidnapping of U.S. General James Dozier by Italian terrorists, and the bombings of several American embassies and of the U.S. Capitol building in 1983 all serve as grim reminders of the specter of violence which increasingly haunts world leaders and public officials.

A recently published directory of international guerrilla and terrorist organizations lists 547 different groups.[18] Not all of them engage in violent activities, and they vary greatly in ideology, goals, and methods. Yet the sheer number of these groups (all of which are at odds with one or more established governments) is, by itself, evidence of the complex and volatile nature of international politics. According to one estimate put forth in 1982 in a journal entitled *International Security Review*—its very name indicating the growing concern with the problem—there were 55 foreign terrorist groups operating within the United States.[19]

It is clear that the lone, deranged, domestic assassin is not the only type of assassin with whom the Service must be prepared to deal. One of the most notorious international hit men is 35-year-old Illich Ramirez Sanchez, better known as Carlos "The Jackal," who is believed to have been behind a series of kidnappings and assassinations throughout the world. Carlos is alleged to have masterminded the kidnapping of 11 oil ministers attending an OPEC meeting in Vienna in 1975, as well as the 1972 Munich Olympics massacre and the hijacking of a French airliner to

Uganda (which resulted in the raid on Entebbe airport to rescue the plane).[20] Reports on Carlos' whereabouts are taken seriously by security forces throughout the world. In March of 1982 Mexican authorities believed that he was in Mexico City—close enough to the United States to concern the Secret Service.

As is the case with most facets of the protective mission, the Service's job in dealing with international hit men and terrorist groups is rendered more complex by the nature of the United States political system. Security experts claim that the United States is a favorite location for terrorists seeking rest and relaxation or hiding out, because of its relatively porous borders and comparatively relaxed passport controls.[21] Also, the United States is a very mobile society where, unlike some others, interstate travel is extensive and thus does not raise any suspicions. The United States' polyglot population assures that terrorists of almost any nationality can find an immigrant community or a subculture in which to submerge themselves. As opposed to some political systems in which a pervasive secret police maintains tight control, security experts assert that it is easy for terrorists to take advantage of freedom of movement and pluralism existing in the United States and thereby blend in without detection.[22]

In 1976, U.S. authorities were hunting for Fusaka Shigenobu of the Japanese Red Army. He was reportedly planning to assassinate Japanese Emperor Hirohito, who was visiting the United States for the bicentennial celebration. In 1978 a terrorist from West Germany's Baader-Meinhof gang, Kristina Bersten, was arrested in Vermont after crossing over from Canada. The purpose of her entry into the United States was never discovered.

Although attacks on U.S. leaders have not increased precipitously even with the advent of the terrorist age, the CIA asserts that the same cannot be said for terrorist activity worldwide. In 1979* there were, according to CIA data, 293 major incidents of terrorism worldwide—including 46 assassination attempts, 20 kidnappings, and 13 hostage situations.[23] CIA data, gathered worldwide, claim that between 1968 and 1979, deaths and injuries caused by terrorist attacks increased from 200 to 900; assassinations, from seven to 47; attacks on U.S. citizens or property: from 51 in 1968, to 122 in 1978, to 77 in 1979.

It is not simply the increased number of terrorist groups or the apparent increase in incidents of violence that poses a formidable potential

---

* This is the latest year for which the CIA's annual report on international terrorist activity is declassified.

threat which the Secret Service must protect against: it is also the increased sophistication of assassination technology, which has now reached James Bondian levels. N.C. Livingstone, a private security consultant whose clients have included several heads of state, and James P. Kelly, former Assistant Director of the Secret Service, wrote a controversial 1981 article entitled, "Could the President Survive a Real-Life James Bond Movie?" Their conclusion was *no*—that the Secret Service's existing methods were too archaic to deal with threats posed by terrorists using the most sophisticated assassination techniques.[24]

In the assassination scenarios put forth by Livingstone and Kelly, terrorists: inject deadly nerve gas into the ventillation system of the Kennedy Center for the Performing Arts, killing the president along with the rest of the audience; fire a heat-seeking missile (such as the Soviet SAM-7), destroying *Air Force One*; use a device powered by compressed gas to shoot a tiny poison pellet into the president's hand as he greets a crowd: the dart feels like a slight pin prick, but the president dies moments later. Farfetched? Futuristic? The authors point out that the technology needed for these scenarios has already been developed and is, unfortunately, all-too-available.

While the White House is equipped with sophisticated air and water filtration systems that would foil a nerve-gas attack, most public locations visited by presidents lack such defenses. Livingstone and Kelly assert that several terrorist groups possess the capability to produce GB or VX type nerve gas, .02 of a drop of which killed a dog in less than a minute during an experiment at Fort Detrick, Maryland. Heat-seeking missiles can weigh as little as 25 pounds, cost under $1,000 to produce, and have a range of two miles. Assassins could launch such a missile at Air Force One as it took off or landed. According to Livingstone and Kelly, the gas-powered poison pellet has been used in assassination plots against Charles de Gaulle and the Shah of Iran. As early as the mid-1970s, the CIA developed a poison dart that was shot from a silent device which was accurate up to 250 feet. The dart penetrated the victim's clothing and skin without being felt and injected a lethal dose of a poison that left no trace; then the dart itself dissolved, leaving no trace.[25]

Livingstone and Kelly concluded that the Service is geared too exclusively toward combating the threat posed by the lone, domestic assassin, to the neglect of the more sophisticated threats which they describe. Still, there is no doubt that the Service perceives the terrorist threat as one of its top priorities, as the 1983 installation of concrete barriers and ground-to-air missiles around the White House clearly indicates. The Service has also formed a counterterrorist assault team (CAT), an elite corps of agents with specialized background and training useful in repelling terrorist attacks.

Whether the 1981 case of the Libyan hit squad (five terrorists allegedly dispatched by Libya's Kaddafi to assassinate President Reagan) was real or not, it was a watershed event for the Secret Service, which took extraordinary protective measures for a period of several weeks.* For the first time in history, the president lit the Christmas tree from inside the White House. It was the first publicly acknowledged terrorist threat. Also for the first time, officials in Washington worried openly about missile attacks on the presidential plane and about rocket-propelled grenade launchers being used against the presidential limousine.[26] Although the threat never materialized, the extended, publicly acknowledged, fairly massive increase in security—which included such measures as increasing security on the White House roof, providing Secret Service protection to key members of the White House staff, increasing presidential and vice-presidential protective details, and altering the president's agenda to reduce exposure—clearly indicated that, as far as the Reagan White House and the Secret Service were concerned, the terrorist age had indeed arrived.

Regardless of whether the actual number of threats from either terrorists or lone, domestic assassins has increased, the availability of more lethal weapons has, by itself, created a more threatening environment for protectees—lone assassins with Teflon bullets, terrorists with missiles.

In 1974 law enforcement officials, with help from the CIA, foiled a plot to assassinate President Ford. Authorities arrested Muharem Kerbegovic, a Yugoslavian native known as the "Alphabet Bomber," so named because he would telephone or mail bomb threats to authorities and would designate the bomb's location by using a single letter of the alphabet. At his trial (not for a presidential assassination attempt but for allegedly killing three persons with a bomb planted at the Los Angeles airport), Kerbegovic claimed to be the messiah.[27] Historically, this would seem to give him much in common with other disturbed persons who were would-be assassins—Richard Lawrence, who tried to shoot President Andrew Jackson in 1835, imagined himself to be King Richard III of England; John Schrank, who wounded Theodore Roosevelt in 1912, claimed to have been directed by the ghost of President McKinley; the

---

* The case is discussed in Chapter 6, in the section on protective intelligence.

man who claimed to be John Wilkes Booth reincarnated and who was arrested in Washington, D.C. where he had come to assassinate President Carter.[28] But there is a significant difference. Lawrence and Shrank wielded pistols; the man who thought he was Booth was armed with a knife. When the Alphabet Bomber was arrested, police found in his home all but one of the ingredients needed to construct a nerve-gas bomb composed of a "highly lethal" agent. The missing ingredient had been ordered and only awaited pick-up by Kerbegovic. "He was that close," said a police official.[29]

Throughout most of the modern era, the United States Secret Service has believed that the primary threat to its protectees came not from conspirators hatching plots but from lone, deranged assassins. Within the last five years, however, there has been a perceptible change in emphasis. Protective intelligence-gathering and protective methods are much more concerned with well-planned conspiracies, originating not domestically but internationally. The kind of attack which seemed to the Service to be the least likely, based upon its view of historical precedent, was the politically motivated conspiracy, which the Service believes to have occurred only once (the 1950 assault on President Truman by Puerto Rican nationalists). Now, this kind of threat has become a dominant factor in the Secret Service's performance of its protective mission and will likely remain so, indefinitely.

NOTES

1. E. M. Leeper, "Could the Secret Service Predict Violent Behavior?," National Academy of Sciences News Report, Jan. 1982, pp. 14–19 at p. 19.
2. "Saturday-Night Specials—Plentiful and Easy to Get," U.S. News & World Report, April 13, 1981, p. 29.
3. Ibid.
4. NBC Magazine, July 30, 1982. Report by Jack Perkins.
5. Ibid.
6. John Minnery, How to Kill, Vol. IV (Boulder, Colorado: The Paladin Press, 1979).
7. Ibid., p. 23.
8. "Improvised Weapons⁄ of the American Underground," (Phoenix: Desert Publications, 1981).
9. James P. Kirkham et al. (eds.), Assassinations and Political Violence (New York: Bantam, 1970), p. 78.
10. Ibid., pp. 77–81.

11. Lawrence Z. Freedman, "The Assassination Syndrome," *Saturday Evening Post*, July/August 1981, pp. 66–68.

12. James W. Clarke, *American Assassins: The Darker Side of Politics* (Princeton, N.J.: Princeton University Press, 1982), pp. 13–14.

13. Sources for description of Oswald: *Report of the Warren Commission on the Assassination of President Kennedy* (New York: Bantam, 1964), pp. 596–656; *Report of the Select Committee on Assassinations, U.S. House of Representatives* (Washington: U.S. Gov't. Printing Office, 1979), pp. 56, 123–25, 180, 217–18, 248–55.

14. Francis X. Clines, "Culling the Secret Service's 400 List," New York *Times*, May 8, 1980, p. 51.

15. Leeper, "Could the Service Predict Violent Behavior?," p. 16.

16. "Man Held in Carter Threat," New York *Times*, Oct. 30, 1977, p. 41; Harry Neal, *The Secret Service in Action* (New York: Elsevier-Nelson, 1980), pp. 81–83.

17. Claire Sterling, *The Terror Network* (New York: Berkeley, 1982).

18. Peter Janke, *Guerrilla and Terrorist Organizations: A World Directory and Bibliography* (New York: Macmillan, 1983).

19. N.C. Livingstone, "Taming Terrorism: In Search of a New U.S. Policy," *International Security Review*, Spring, 1982, pp. 17–34, at p. 18.

20. "Mexican Police May Have 'The Jackal'," Boston *Globe*, March 12, 1982, p. 4.

21. Livingstone, "Taming Terrorism," p. 18.

22. *Ibid.*

23. The following data are taken from: "International Terrorism in 1979," Central Intelligence Agency, published by the National Technical Information Service, U.S. Gov't, Springfield, Va., pp. iv, 8, 14–17.

24. "N. C. Livingstone and James P. Kelly, "Could the President Survive a Real-Life James Bond Movie?," *The Washingtonian*, Sept., 1981, pp. 168–76.

25. David Wise, *The American Police State*, (New York: Vintage Books, 1976), p. 205.

26. "Searching for Hit Teams," *Time*, Dec. 21, 1981, p. 17.

27. "Ford Assassination Attempt in 1974 by Nerve Gas Foiled," Boston *Globe*, Dec. 5, 1983, p. 4.

28. Neal, *"The Secret Service in Action,"* pp. 81–83.

29. "Ford Assassination Attempt by Nerve Gas."

6

PROTECTIVE METHODS
AND
PROCEDURES

A reporter asked Secret Service Director of Public Affairs John Warner whether agents were trained to use their bodies as shields in the event of an attack on the President. A pained expression crossed Warner's face. He waved his hand, thereby dismissing the question.

Robert Blain Kaiser
New York Times, Feb. 10, 1980, p. 1

The design of protective methods is a key element in determining the quality of security, as are the nature of the threats faced and the personality and priorities of the protectee. The Service does not like to discuss its methods. The portrait presented here was developed from the public record—Congressional hearings, government documents and reports, print and electronic media. No Secret Service personnel discussed methods and procedures with the author, nor were they requested to do so. The following description is not exhaustive. It serves only to convey the flavor of the Service's methods as a way of rounding out our analysis of various facets of the organization's composition, problems and performance.

In the aftermath of the JFK assassination, the Secret Service undertook the most complete overhaul of its protective methods in the history of the organization. It sought the help of outside experts who authored a series of reports, known as the STAR reports, for the Service to review.[1]

As part of this effort, the Department of Defense made its vast research and development resources available to the Service to find ways of reducing the vulnerability of political leaders to assassination. A series of studies was conducted by such organizations as the Office of Science and Technology, the Office of the Director of Defense Research and

Engineering, the Advance Research Projects Agency. Think tanks also participated—the Rand Corporation, the Research Analysis Corporation, the Institute for Defense Analysis. Thus the awesome expertise of the defense establishment—both public and private research groups—was applied to the task of improving protective methods.

The studies generated by this extensive effort dealt with a full range of protective problems and variables—coordinating security among Secret Service, White House, federal agencies and local police; advance planning and publicity for public appearances; the use of body armor; attacks on the protectee from the air; methods for screening and credentialing; the use of shields, evasive action, surveillance techniques; collecting and processing data about potential threats; threat detection.

Another study done by the Research Analysis Corporation dealt with protective methods relevant to travel and public appearances. It proposed the use of highly sophisticated weaponry, such as "cold liquid" weapons and "liquid stream projectors." The study analyzed how attackers might penetrate protective barriers and confuse or distract Secret Service agents. It examined the possible use of non-lethal protective weapons (gas-propelled impact projectiles) and explored methods for detecting small arms fire via an acoustical early warning device. It researched how to armor nearly everything—cars, chairs, helicopters, podia.

Meanwhile, the Institute for Defense Analysis studied threats: What motivates assassins? What methods and weapons are they likely to use? Computerized simulations and war-game techniques were employed to test the effectiveness of various protective methods. Reaction times of agents were tested. Even the use of doubles or false identities by assassins were studied. To repel threats, the Institute proposed some highly futuristic devices—special lighting systems that would blind an attacker, an energy field that would deflect ballistic projectiles away from the protectee.

The results of these expert analyses were presented to the Service in the STAR reports between 1963 and 1966. But the revolutionary improvements in protective methods that the think tanks and defense strategists envisioned never came about. The Secret Service was not transformed into something like a corps of Jedi warriors wielding light sabers and other fantastic devices.

The experts who dreamed up the *avant-garde* techniques were not constrained by the political context in which the Secret Service must operate: They did not have to worry about a White House staff or anti-democratic images or media reaction. To the ivory tower consultants, it was perfectly logical to protect the president by any means possible. So they suggested such things as a huge truck-mounted optical scanner that would roll along in motorcades and provide complete electronic surveillance of crowds and buildings, a smoke-screen device on the president's limousine designed to go off when anything went wrong, a complete suit of body armor for the president, a device that created high-pitched noises that would disorient attackers, a protective shield that would automatically pop up and surround the president whenever there was a threatening noise.

None of this hardware, nor anything even approximating it, was adopted by the Service. It was not for lack of money or technology: it was because the Service knew full well that no president could accept the political image created by the presence of smoke screens, pop-up shields, leviathan monitoring devices and weird noises. Even the far less obtrusive, standard methods adopted by the Service are applied only when the president and the White House staff will permit it.

Since the STAR reports, the Service has continued to draw upon outside experts from both public and private organizations, in order to continue the modernization of its methods. This continuing process of soliciting expert advice, although useful in many ways, is always constrained at the operational level by political culture and by the priorities and the personality of the protectee. Technical improvements that are not obtrusive and do not cramp the political style or invade the privacy of protectees are more likely to be implemented. For example, most politicians use a podium of some kind, so that bulletproofing it is not a conspicuous addition to protection. In the last two decades there has been tremendous improvement in the armor and maneuverability of limousines, with no sacrifice of style or comfort.

HOME SWEET HOME

The protective detail should occupy at least one complete protective ring, immediately surrounding and completely blocking all avenues of access to the rooms or general area being occupied by the president.

Secret Service training manual

In some ways, it is the safest place a president can be. The protective detail loves it when presidents are in the White House: the environment is controlled, every inch of it is familiar turf, all the protective procedures are standard and well-rehearsed. In contrast, the president's private home is comparatively unfamiliar to agents and usually requires extensive physical adaptation before effective security can be achieved.

For all its advantages, the White House also presents its own unique challenges. It is the symbol of the American Presidency. As such, it acts as a lightning rod for political passions. Theodore Roosevelt once described the mansion as "the loneliest place in the world," but not for lack of visitors. Many persons who wish to conduct some kind of political protest or who want to catch a glimpse of their president—their hero or their villain—are likely to head for the White House if time and resources permit. The mansion also serves as a place of business as well as a home. Congressmen, White House staff, bureaucrats, press, consultants, diplomats, gardeners, and delivery persons come and go by the dozens. Screening and checking the credentials of this heavy traffic is a full-time job for the Service. The White House is the people's house too. Each year nearly two million visitors brave long lines to tour through it.

As predictable and secure as it is in some senses, the White House is still a hectic, quite public environment that demands a tremendous protective effort from the Service. The basic problem is to allow authorized traffic to flow smoothly while maintaining tight security for the president and other protectees. This is not easy to accomplish.

On the evening of May 13, 1930 a well-dressed man strode purposefully to the front door of the White House and walked inside without hesitation or haste. A Washington, D.C. policeman stood guard outside the door; two more were stationed inside. None of the three questioned the visitor. After the man had passed through, a policeman asked one of his colleagues who the man was. "I don't know," came the reply, "but I think he's a Secret Service agent."

The policeman was wrong. Within moments the mystery visitor had entered the dining room where President Hoover sat eating. The startled president looked up at the intruder. A real Secret Service agent quickly took charge of the man and escorted him outside. He turned out to be an average American who had come to the White House to see his president —"just sightseeing."

Hoover was understandably concerned about how a stranger walked into his dining room. He was informed that the D.C. police guards were not under Secret Service supervision and control. That very evening, the President ordered that the Service be placed in charge of the police guards. Two months later Congress passed the necessary legislation.

Times have changed. The Hoover White House lacked the sophisticated security of the modern era—elaborate credentialing, electronic warning systems. Still, the problems are very similar. In 1977 President Carter was in the Oval Office working with appointments secretary Tim Craft when a stranger appeared on the veranda outside the Office's glass doors. The man casually opened one of the French doors and asked for directions to get to the office of one of Carter's staff assistants.[2] Carter gave directions.

Evidently the man was encouraged by Jimmy's accessibility and cheeriness. "Well," said the visitor, "while I'm here can I have a minute with you?" The answer was a flat *no*, and the visitor was sent on his way. He was a freelance writer who had entered the White House as a guest of presidential aide Mark Siegal. The writer had been issued a temporary visitor's pass at the gate. According to security procedures, the visitor had no more right to be in the Oval Office than a delivery person or a grounds keeper, or than the stranger in Hoover's dining room.

It was not that Carter had thrown open the gates of the White House as a symbol of his nonimperial presidency. In fact, security procedures at the Carter White House were stricter than in any previous administrations and had generated great frustration among official visitors who had suffered through long delays caused by the extensive screening. The system simply failed. Needless to say, the Service conducted a thorough review to discover the flaw in their system.

On October 3, 1981, only six months after the assassination attempt on President Reagan, a man drove up to the northwest gate of the White House, sounded his horn, and flashed what appeared to the uniformed guard to be a White House pass. The man entered (accompanied by three members of his family who were in the car) and drove up to the mansion. He then parked and the group proceeded toward the Oval Office. The intruders were on the White House grounds for ten minutes before they were finally stopped by a Secret Service agent, but not before they had reached the Oval Office. The man not only had a history of mental disorder but was on the Service's list of dangerous persons. As a result of the security lapses, the uniformed guard was fired and two agents were suspended for five days.

Even the most advanced security technology and procedures are not foolproof, but they are still formidable and, for the most part, very effective. Three eight-hour shifts of agents provide round-the-clock protection at the mansion, supplemented by Uniformed Division guards who man the guardhouses. At each of the white guardhouses there are usually two uniformed guards. One sits behind the tinted glass at a panel of communications equipment and electronic monitors that looks like the cockpit of a small plane; the other stands outside. There are guardhouses not only at the perimeters (at each gate) but inside the grounds as well. One ajoins the mansion itself.

There are additional guardhouses at the entrances to the Old Executive Office Building (EOB) located next to the White House. Both the White House and the office building are surrounded by a six-and-one-half-foot, black iron fence. West Executive Avenue, a narrow strip of pavement that runs between the mansion and the EOB, is closed off at both ends by gates with guardhouses. The White House fence walls off the EOB so that even high–level government employees who are cleared through the outside gates and enter West Executive Avenue cannot walk onto the White House grounds without a separate security check.

The points atop the iron fence are not sharp and it can be scaled fairly easily. Neither the fence nor the high mounds of lawn that screen the White House from view along East Executive Avenue (between the White House and the Treasury Building) contribute much to security. That is provided by the elaborate systems of electronic sensors and video surveillance that cover the White House grounds. The seismatic sensors hidden in the ground are so sensitive that even the lightest tiptoeing can be picked up. At night, cross–aimed spotlights bathe nearly every inch of the vast lawns in soft white light. TV cameras—some buried in the ground, some hidden under bushes, others disguised as lanterns—provide complete video surveillance of the 18.7 acres surrounding the mansion.

Armed, uniformed Secret Service guards visit the White House roof periodically to check the various antennas and national security devices and to survey the grounds. Their colleagues patrol the roof of the huge Treasury Building across from the White House and look down on the mansion.

Inside the White House, security is strict. Even top presidential advisors are required to wear a security badge with their picture on it, at all times. Agents strive to maintain a constant protective ring around the president, designed to prevent or at least blunt any attack. To that end, agents will don white ties and tails so that they can preserve the ring at formal receptions without being conspicuous. During the annual Easter egg roll in 1982, an agent was right at Reagan's side—dressed as an Easter bunny. A canine squad with dogs trained to sniff out explosives periodically roams the mansion, especially during the hours when public tours are in progress.

Electronic sensing devices hidden in the walls, floors, and ceilings provide early warning of unauthorized movement. The monitoring system extends to protectees as well as intruders. Each protectee (president, first family member, vice-president, etc.) is assigned a number. The president is always number one. A computerized system tracks and reports the location of each protectee and flashes the data to Secret Service agents— *#1-East Room*. When the protectee changes location, the data is inputted and the change is reported electronically.

When the president is in the Oval Office, a Secret Service agent is stationed outside the glass doors, probably in response to the Carter incident. Another agent guards the Office's inside entrance by standing in the corridor. There is a panic button behind the president's desk. It is located knee high and is extremely sensitive. A president can thus summon help while appearing to shift his posture. Within seconds after the button is nudged, a bevy of agents will descend upon the Oval Office. The panic button sometimes gets pushed by accident as the lanky Mr. Reagan moves around behind his desk. Visitors to the Reagan Oval Office have, on occasion, been startled when the Secret Service suddenly burst into the office for no apparent reason.[3] As part of the increased security during the Reagan presidency, agents began to escort Mr. Reagan as he moved from place to place within the mansion (from the family quarters to the Oval Office and vice versa).

The Service constantly monitors anything and everything in the White House environment. Agents run periodic tests on the air, checking for bacteria and noxious gases. All incoming packages are opened and inspected. Food receives special scrutiny. Don't bother to mail jelly beans to President Reagan: The Service may munch on them if they look particularly wholesome; otherwise, they will be discarded. But in no case will they be given to the president to consume. The laboratory analysis necessary to certify food as safe for the president is too expensive and time consuming to conduct, except in rare instances.

Even with all the technical devices and monitoring systems, human vigilance is the key factor in the protective system. Agents constantly watch for any sign of trouble—quick movements in the White House tour line, a man entering the West Wing wearing a raincoat on a sunny day, a face that does not match the picture on an ID badge.

There is much more to guard against than assaults from deranged individuals or intrusions from over zealous admirers. To this end, there is a bomb shelter under the East Wing and an underground tunnel leading to it. The zigzag tunnel was built early in World War II. The Service has an arsenal of weapons with which to repel terrorist attacks, whether they are launched from the ground or the air. Portable but powerful Redeye, shoulder-fired antiaircraft guns stand ready to knock out planes that assault the mansion.

There is no more vivid illustration of the trade-offs between politics and protection in our democratic culture than the White House tour. The tour reflects a very egalitarian notion—that the White House is not the private, royal domicile of a ruler but a national monument that belongs as much to the citizens of this democracy as to the leader whom they elect. But egalitarian notions usually create protective nightmares.

The White House—"home" to every president except George Washington, a major symbol of our political culture. Two million visitors a year are guided through the five rooms that constitute the tour route. They gaze at the State Dining room, the East Room, and the Red, Blue, and Green rooms, then exit through the North Portico and walk down the oval driveway to the exit gate.

The tour is highly restricted. No pictures can be taken inside though they can be snapped outside. There are 132 rooms that are off-limits to the public. The tour takes place on the east side of the Mansion; the Oval Office is in the opposite wing, far removed from the crowds. Still, the protective challenges presented by mass public access are formidable. Tuesday through Saturday from ten in the morning to one in the afternoon, an endless stream of visitors flows continuously through the Mansion. For the public, it is free; for the Service, the costs are high in terms of resources and manpower.

Secret Service uniformed guards, augmented by uniformed rangers from the National Parks Service, keep the thousands of waiting visitors in as orderly a queue as possible. The line often extends around the entire perimeter of the mansion. As they enter, visitors must walk through metal detectors operated by uniformed Service personnel. Hand-held detectors are used to check anyone who looks suspicious or who sets off a walk-through detector. All packages, handbags, and so forth are opened and carefully inspected.

It is now standard procedure to confiscate, as politely as possible, all newspapers from entering tourists. Newspapers too easily serve as a shield for a weapon or for some surreptitious activity. Closed circuit television cameras watch visitors at every step of the tour. There are uniformed Secret Service officers and plainclothes agents in every corridor and in each room on the tour. Among other duties, these guards make sure that visitors stay within the red ropes that define the proper route. A Secret Service command post in one of the corridors is staffed by several uniformed officers and at least one agent and is packed with communications and monitoring equipment.

Plainclothes agents mingle with the crowds and are ever alert. Despite all the gadgetry, an agent's eyes and ears provide the best means for thorough and swift threat detection. The Service is all-too-painfully aware that in any group of two million persons there are bound to be some problem cases. If a visitor becomes a pest or manifests strange behavior while in the tour line, he or she may get a tour they did not anticipate—of the special section of the psychiatric ward at St. Elizabeths Hospital in Washington where the Service packs off problem cases for observation.

In 1980 a man broke out of the tour line and unfurled a banner protesting nuclear weapons and nuclear power. The incident presented no threat to the President but it is indicative of another fact of life concerning the White House. As the primary symbol of the presidency and, along with the Capitol Building, as a major symbol of American government, it is an enticing setting for the expression of political beliefs and frustrations. Even late at night one usually finds some protest group, however small or motley looking, camped along the north fence of the White House on the sidewalk of Pennsylvania Avenue.

The causes vary from Serbo-Croatian independence to the banning of microwave ovens to the lack of Christianity in government policies. Sometimes there are only a few people in a group; sometimes, twenty or thrity. Many groups distribute leaflets to passersby or carry placards by day, then sleep on the sidewalk at night. Part of the allure is that all of this transpires in the shadow of the White House, where the chief executive resides. Many demonstrators must hope that the president will catch a glimpse of them and inquire: "Who are those people?" What do they want?" Most demonstrations are orderly. Washington, D.C. police see to it that pedestrian traffic is not impeded—Pennsylvania Avenue has very wide sidewalks—and that demonstrators do not reach through the White House fence or dump leaflets on the lawn.

The mansion's political magnetism draws more than lawful demonstrations. It also attracts unstable and threatening persons. Even though many such persons are so mentally unstable that they are more of a threat to themselves than to the president, the Secret Service must deal with every potential threat as if it were skillfully planned and represented a real danger to the president, until evidence to the contrary appears. From the Service's perspective, there is no such thing as a "harmless" prank. A good protective system must assume the worst.

The airspace above the White House is off limits to all but officially cleared aircraft. Yet, a twenty-year-old soldier flew a stolen helicopter over the grounds and buzzed the mansion itself. Agents and uniformed officers forced the chopper down with gunfire. The pilot was arrested immediately. Had he intended to harm the president? Was it a kamikaze attack? "No," claimed the pilot, "I was just kissing off. I wanted to buzz everything that was popular."[4]

Every little lapse in security has its price in terms of reduced protection, at least potentially. In 1973 a young man drove his Mercedes-Benz through a White House gate that had been accidentally left ajar by the uniformed officer manning the guardhouse. The gate was slightly damaged as the man sped through on his way up the driveway toward the north portico. He was quickly stopped and arrested. The Service determined that the incident "was not of a threatening nature" but sent the driver off to St. Elizabeths for observation.[5]

Two years later another driver crashed his car through a supposedly impregnable White House gate that was not left ajar. He too was quickly apprehended, with no immediate danger to the president. The gates were heavily reinforced to withstand assaults from vehicles.

In 1983, in response to such developments as a bombing of the Capitol building in Washington and bombings of the U.S. embassy in Kuwait and of Marine headquarters in Lebanon, and also in response to intelligence data suggesting the possibility of a terrorist attack upon the White House, the mansion's defenses were strengthened dramatically. For a two week period around Thanksgiving, a string of dump trucks (light-green ones from the National Parks Service) filled with sand were positioned outside the White House gates. They were first placed there in response to bomb threat. Their purpose was to prevent a fast-moving vehicle laden with explosives from crashing through a gate. In Beirut, Lebanon over 249 Marines were killed by a suicide truck-bombing. The White House trucks were moved to allow slow-moving vehicles to pass and then be checked at the gate.

In early December the trucks were replaced by three-foot-high, fifteen-foot-long concrete barriers.[6] The barriers were spaced so that a slow-moving vehicle could squeeze through, and they were set up in such a way that vehicles were required to make a sharp turn to get to the gate after passing through the barrier, thus insuring that a vehicle could not build up speed as it approached the mansion.

Then, on December 10, 1983, a *Time* magazine report (picked up by all of the wire services) indicated that, for the first time in history, fixed-based ground-to-air missiles had been installed to protect the White House.[6] The locations of the missiles remains secret, and it is not clear whether they are controlled by the Secret Service, the military or a joint command. But it was revealed that the missiles are controlled from the Executive Office Building next to the White House.

ON THE ROAD

Roll back and examine all rugs insofar as practical. Then go over the entire surface of rugs, pressing down firmly with fingertips to locate any small objects that might be concealed therein....Carefully examine all pictures — tap for hollow frames....All lights in the area should be monitored with a photo cell to detect the presence of sound-modulated light waves.

Secret Service training manual

Presidential travel presents more of a challenge to the Service than providing protection at the White House. The environments traveled to range from familiar to completely unknown, from friendly to hostile. The difficulty of advance work varies accordingly. The amount and quality of advance security preparations also varies with the number of agents available to the Service for a particular advance mission and with the amount of cooperation and information provided by the White House staff. Although there are certain procedures that are always followed when the president (or any other protectee) travels, there exist no pre-designed (canned) protective packages for advance work. As the Treasury Department admits:

Thus, the [advanced] procedures do not include such matters as how far from the president crowds should be kept, under what circumstances doors should or should not be locked or guarded, or even how many Special Agents should be assigned to a particular visit. The standards which Special Agents apply in individual cases seem to be the product of their experience in similar circumstances, modified by two other factors: the level of manpower available to the Service; and the need to reach a practical accommodation — there being no written agreements — with the occasionally conflicting demands of

the White House advance staff for greater exposure of the
president.[7]

Good advance work requires good coordination among the White
House staff, Service field offices and the White House detail, and local
police. If coordination or communication among these participants
breaks down, lapses in protection are likely. For a Presidential trip, one
or more agents are assigned to do the advance work, depending, in part,
on the complexity of the itinerary. Usually, at least one agent from the
White House detail will meet with the agent in charge of the field office
closest to the destination and they will work with local police.

Depending on the agenda and the amount of preparation that is
possible, any or all of the following procedures are executed. At airports a
special area for *Air Force One* is set aside and secure routes of entrance
and exit for protectees are established. Military airfields are used
whenever possible because they present fewer travelers and traffic and
are more easily controlled. Motorcade routes are planned and traveled
over; alternate routes are selected in case of blockage or emergency.
Emergency sites—hospitals to which the president can be taken if there is
a medical emergency—are selected, and routes to them are planned.
Buildings, subways, and streets are surveyed all along the route to
discover potential hiding places for snipers and to decide where to position counter-sniper teams. These teams carry binoculars and rifles and
are usually stationed on rooftops. The site of any planned stop is surveyed
to determine where the rope barriers and other crowd-control mechanisms should be positioned. The Secret Service does not have anything
approaching the personnel needed to perform these tasks: it depends
upon the efforts of local police, without whom the job would not get
done.[8]

If the press is involved, the Service must set up credentialing procedures to make sure that only *bona fide* reporters are allowed the close
proximity to the president which the media are accustomed to. In times of
strict security, such as following the wounding of President Reagan,
reporters are searched after their ID's are checked. To avoid chaos and
minimize discontent, these procedures must be well-planned in advance.

The White House staff and the president's media advisor play a
crucial role in advance work involving the press, for they know reporters
much better than the Service does. One of the major problems in checking credentials on the road is that there are local reporters in addition to
the national press pool. If the President goes to Rapid City, South Dakota

to dedicate a dam, the familiar faces from the Washington press corps might tag along, but there will also be local press who must be screened for this particular event. The Service may know the New York *Times* reporter by sight, but is there really a Rapid City *Bugle*, and is Joe Woodstein really a *Bugle* reporter? The Secret Service field office working with White House media people must find out.

Even thousand-dollar-a-plate dinners attended only by the party faithful must have screening procedures. Recently, such elite guests have been subjected to metal detectors as they file in for a black-tie dinner with the president.

Every room the president will enter must be thoroughly inspected for electronic surveillance devices, bombs, toxins, and fire hazards. In Washington the Service has its own bomb carrier in which it can transport any bomb it finds. Bombs are driven to isolated areas for examination and detonation. The bomb carrier looks like a cement mixer on a trailer, and it is pulled by a small van. Outside the Washington area, the Service must rely on police bomb-disposal vehicles.

A secure escape route is planned for every room, garage, and corridor that the President will enter. Hotel elevator cables must be freshly inspected and escape routes from stalled elevators planned out. At every location where the president will sleep, eat, or visit, lists of employees are obtained—for hotels, catering services, airports. Lists are cross-checked with Secret Service files to identify any dangerous persons.

In recent years, bulletproof attire and devices have been used increasingly for presidential appearances, especially by President Reagan following the attempt on his life. Reagan began wearing his bulletproof vest at most public appearances and at all events where the Service had any hint of danger. On his European diplomatic tour of June 1982, he wore it constantly.

In contrast, Gerald Ford wore a vest for only one day after the second attempt on his life within a month. Ford found the vest too bulky and quite uncomfortable. Reporters could see the protective attire bulging under the President's shirt and distorting the shoulder line of his suit coat. Ford's vest appeared to those who saw it close up to be about one-half-inch thick.

Reagan's consistent use of the vest, in contrast to Ford, may not be due entirely to the fact that Reagan was seriously wounded and Ford was fortunate enough to escape unharmed. The Service's constant research efforts to produce lighter, less bulky bulletproofing has most likely made Reagan's model considerably more comfortable and less obtrusive than the one Ford rejected seven years earlier.

Bulletproof podium shields are now universal—at presidential speeches, national political conventions, and dinners. The glass reviewing stand used by President Reagan for his inauguration was entirely bullet-proof. When he visited the Knoxville World's Fair in May 1982, he ad-dressed the crowd from behind a glass shield that, unlike the smaller podium shields commonly used, protected him from head to toe.

At every moment in the president's itinerary, whether he is in a ban-quet room, exiting an airplane, or riding in a motorcade, the primary pro-tective goal is to maintain a *safe zone*. It has been called, at various times, "the outer perimeter," a "zone of security," the "sanitized zone." It means that whatever the context or location, the Service will gear its ef-forts toward establishing and maintaining a safe area around the pro-tectee. The size and shape of the safe zone vary according to such factors as the number of agents on duty, the situation, and what the protectee will allow. Ideally, from the Service's viewpoint, the zone ought to be the size of a football field; in reality, it is usually measured in feet rather than dozens of yards. It is supposed to surround the protectee completely (360 degrees), whether the protectee is stationary or moving. Whatever threats arise, the zone will give agents a better chance to prevent an attack or, failing that, to blunt an attack. As a Secret Service manual describes it: "to absorb the shock to such an extent that the results will not be tragic."

Unfortunately for the Service, the zone is often more imaginary than real. Presidents will frequently sprint out of it in order to reach out-stretched hands. Enlarging the zone so that the protectee has more leeway is usually prohibited by lack of personnel and by democratic culture (it is not politic to clear out several city blocks just because a president is about to enter a hotel). The zone is usually small and fairly fragile, but it is better than no zone at all.

As with protective procedures, the ultimate effectiveness of the zone is dependent upon the eyes, ears, and reflexes of agents. No matter how big or small the zone is, it is up to agents to detect and stop threats; the zone only provides more time. Agents attempt to divide the 360 degree perimeter into visual surveillance zones, so that every inch of the zone's imaginary boundary is being watched. As we know from football, zone defenses are difficult to execute without lapses, especially when the Secret Service's protectee is moving rapidly or, worse, erratically.

Advance work requires attention to hundreds of small details, neglect of any one of which could prove fatal to the protectee under a given set of circumstances. For example, emergency blood of the correct type must be stocked for the president at the designated emergency hospitals.

Advance work also means homework for agents—a great deal of it. Lists of key telephone numbers must be committed to memory (police, hospitals). Photos and dossiers of dangerous persons known to be in the area to be visited are studied carefully.

In recent years secrecy concerning presidential travel has become a more prominent protective method. This is largely because presidents and their staffs have come to perceive it as necessary and have allowed more of it. The Service has always wanted the White House to keep travel plans secret; now, more and more, the Service is getting the secrecy it wants. Details of itinerary are no longer announced in advance, to the extent that it is politically feasible. Precise arrival and departure times, travel route to and from hotels and airports, even the location of certain appearances are often kept secret so that would-be assassins will be prevented from stalking the president and will not have the luxury of planning ahead. For the first time in the history of the modern presidency, Mr. Reagan's daily schedule is no longer published with geographic details as to cities, hotels, times, and so forth.

When President Reagan decided to visit a black family in Maryland who had been subjected to a cross burning, the Service instructed the family not to tell anyone about their impending meeting with the president. The family was told to make other excuses for absences from school and work. So secretive was the visit that the family thought that they were going to the White House; instead, without advance warning, the president showed up at their house.

Sometimes the element of surprise works against protection rather than for it. This occurs when a president, or any protectee, suddenly has a whim to do this or that, with little or no advance warning to the Service. In such instances, the kind of careful advance work required for effective security is impossible. A Service training manual politely refers to these events as "off-the-record trips." In agent jargon they are called "pop-ups." The president spontaneously decides that he must visit the home of a friend or confidant, within the hour; or he decides that he has to play golf—in fifteen minutes. In the latter case, there is nothing agents can do but sprint for their golf bags, stuff a high-powered rifle in with their clubs, and rush to tee off (either with the president or right behind him). For the Service, pop-ups reduce protective methods to catch-as-catch-can.

Agents must go where the protectee goes. Skiing with Ford or horseback riding with Reagan were not considered difficult duty; but, sometimes, the protectee's idea of a fun trip creates logistical and life-style nightmares for agents. Consider Vice-President Walter

Mondale's vacation to lakes Elsie, Manitou and Brennan—in the Canadian outlands. The wilderness trek was surely a culture shock for the Washington-based protective detail whose main exposure to nature consists of walking across perfectly manicured lawns under the stately shade trees that dot the nation's capital.

For ten days at Lake Brennan a small tent city was erected.[9] Supplies and equipment were brought in by helicopter including 1400 pounds of food, electric generators, and seven motorboats. Agents had so many duties in their combined role of Boy Scout-Indian guide that it is a wonder they had any energy left to devote to preserving the *safety zone.* They had to pitch tents, tote and assemble communications gear, police the site for trash and garbage so as not to offend their Canadian hosts, and paddle Mondale on his long fishing expeditions. The menacing "no-see-um" flies inflicted bites that swelled and itched distractingly. Because the Canadians would not allow helicopters to disturb the most pristine areas of their wilderness, agents were forced to execute long portages to satisfy the vice-president's passion for trout. In one instance agents carried boats and equipment for six miles between lakes. At least Mondale brought his own cook, so agents were spared that duty. One can imagine the trepidation felt by the White House detail when a president or vice-president is overheard to say that he has always wanted to hunt moose.

Perhaps somewhat surprisingly, foreign travel is not always more difficult for the Service than domestic travel. It depends upon how cooperative the foreign hosts are, what the political climate is, and what the protectee's mission is. The Service gets plenty of help from American military personnel and from the security forces of the host country. Coordination and manpower tend to be the two biggest problems in advance work. Foreign advance work generally has fewer manpower problems—plenty of personnel are made available to the Service—but greater problems of coordination. A visit to a country where domestic unrest and/or international terrorist attacks are commonplace can be very dangerous for the protectee. In 1982 President Reagan visited West Germany and Italy. Both countries have had a continuing problem of assaults on political leaders by hard-core terrorists. Imagine the frenzied advance work necessitated when former Presidents Nixon, Ford and Carter all flew to Cairo for the funeral of assassinated President Anwar Sadat.

On occasion, a foreign trip can be easier to handle than a trip to New York or Chicago. Most of the agents who accompanied President Nixon on his 1972 trip to China fondly remember the sojourn as a logistical dream, superior in coordination and cooperation to most domestic trips. The Chinese regime, firmly in control of its country, provided a multitude of unobtrusive security men and plenty of English-speaking liaison personnel to see that everything ran smoothly. The hosts made sure that every Chinese citizen who came in contact with the American visitors— waiters, chauffeurs, guards—could speak fluent English. This was important to security for it gave the Service the ability to exercise more control over people and settings (with no language barrier to confuse things).

Chinese planning for the trip was described by one American as "absolutely meticulous in every respect."[10] The Chinese politely looked the other way at American agents carrying weapons. Foreigners are forbidden to carry weapons in China, by long-standing tradition. The hosts provided an enormous security force of both plainclothes agents and army and militia personnel. Yet the Service was allowed such latitude in implementing its own security that American agents, not Chinese, were allowed to check credentials and screen guests at the doors of the Great Hall of the People where Nixon and Mao were to watch a ballet. The Chinese allowed the Black Box (the locked briefcase, carried by a military officer, that contains the codes to activate America's nuclear arsenal) to be brought into the Great Hall.

IN CASE OF ATTACK

Usually weapons should not be used to subdue an attacker if any other defense will effectively suppress a threat.

Secret Service training manual

As the service is well aware, its role in a crisis is "reactive." Protection depends upon instant and appropriate reaction to an assault. As one agent put it," . . . we have to give away the first shot."[11] Even then, the first priority of reaction is *defense*. "Our job," said Secret Service Public Affairs Director Jack Warner, "is to protect the person from being hit by an object any way we can."[12]

Agents closest to the president do not really need guns for their crisis response. Their job is to immediately surround the President, shield him, move with him to a safe place, and, once there, cover him with their bodies (as was done to LBJ when shots were fired in Dallas and to Ford after he was pushed into his limousine following a shot that narrowly missed him). This is defensive protection, not offensive. After the president is protected from the immediate threat, the next priority is to get him to a safer environment as quickly as possible—to a safe home base (the White House) or to a hospital if there is any possibility that he has sustained an injury.

The agents who are not surrounding the president have different crisis-response priorities. Their first job is to screen the president from the assailant(s). Early in 1976 candidate Ronald Reagan had an opportunity to watch agents taking target practice. As a former cowboy actor, Reagan noticed that the agents fired from a standing position instead of a crouch. "Doesn't that make you too big a target?" Reagan inquired. "That's just the point," an agent answered. "The reason we shoot standing is to better protect your body with ours."[13] Agents are trained to remain upright at all times and to make themselves as large a target as possible, while interposing themselves between the President and the attacker.

This procedure was valiantly executed by Agent Timothy McCarthy during the attempted assassination of President Reagan. McCarthy can be seen on the videotape walking directly toward Hinckley as Hinckley fired at the President. McCarthy, who was seriously wounded, neither crouched nor dodged but created as big a screen as possible.

The president's protection has priority over capturing assailants or helping those injured in the attack. Despite their training in lifesaving and first aid, agents are instructed not to assist the injured until the President has been safely evacuated. However, agents not directly involved in the first-priority response (evacuating the President) can help the injured or subdue or capture assailants, and then work at sealing off the scene of the attack (to preserve evidence).

The protection of captured assailants from an outraged public or from trigger-happy law enforcement personnel is important. Only by a full and thorough investigation can the nature, scope, and origin of the attack be discovered. Was it a lone assassin, a domestic conspiracy, a foreign terrorist plot, an isolated incident or a coordinated attack on all political leaders? Dead suspects cannot be interrogated.

In April 1979 the Service developed written procedures to be followed by operative personnel in crisis situations.

The crisis procedures have no provision for an automatic reinforcement of presidential protection in case of attack. If the second-in-command of the protective detail, whose decision it is as to whether reinforcements are needed, is too distracted or too injured to give the order, then reinforcements could be delayed or might not arrive at all. Without quick reinforcements, it is conceivable that the Presidential detail could be pinned down by snipers, unable to evacuate the president.

Moreover, the agents at the scene may not be in the best position to accurately determine the nature of the threat. Suppose, for example, that the second-in-command perceives that there is only one attacker, that the attacker is in custody, and that the president, though wounded, has left for the hospital—no need for reinforcements. At the scene, things may appear to be under control, but this may be illusory. Other attackers may await the president at the hospital or might assault his limousine. Lacking reinforcements, the protective detail (diminished by casualties or simply by having left some personnel at the scene) may not be strong enough to repel a second attack.

The Service fears that an automatic increase in presidential protection following an attack might overcommit personnel, putting too many agents in the wrong place at the wrong time—"overmanning," the Service calls it. If, for example, there were a massive increase in the number of agents assigned to the president but the attack on the president was only one of a series of attacks, on the vice-president and several other protectees, the Service might not be able to respond effectively to the additional attacks. This is a valid concern. Still, if requiring an automatic increase in protective personnel after an attack on the president is too inflexible, it is too nebulous to have the decision rest exclusively with a single agent who might be enmeshed in the crisis. Some middle ground needs to be found.

THE SIXTH SENSE

Be alert for signs of danger . . . . Look for persons who are acting unnaturally . . . . Look for unnatural appearance of places, objects, and situations.

Secret Service training manual

"The sixth sense," as agents term it, involves being able to anticipate danger and know when to take quick preventive action. The alertness and swift reactions of agents are the key for effective protective methods, no matter how sound or technically advanced those methods are. Safety zones, bulletproof vests, and good intelligence data can help, but it is the reflexes and skills of agents surrounding the protectee that make the biggest difference in the outcome of an attack.

As former agent Rufus Youngblood describes: " ... you are constantly on the alert for the individual who somehow does not fit. You scan the crowd, the rooftops, the doorways, the windows, ready to take whatever action may be necessary."[14] Each agent watches some chunk of the 360 degree safety zone—the visual zone defense. If an agent fails to spot a quick or suspicious movement within his zone, or if the zone breaks down, agents may find themselves screening the president from a hail of bullets instead of clamping down on a potentially threatening person.

Good reaction is not synonymous with a quick draw to return the fire of an assailant. As previously described, agents' first priority is to protect the president, not draw and shoot. There is a very good reason for this, as a Secret Service training manual describes:

> In some instances the time needed to put weapons into action may be sufficient for the attacker to accomplish his mission. Example: on the average it takes an officer at least 2½ seconds to react, draw, and aim his revolver from a hip holster. During this time the attacker could run 75 feet. If the President is in a car which is moving in a direction generally toward an attacker at 20 miles per hour, it would travel 73 feet in 2½ seconds. Therefore, the attacker and the president could cover a distance separating them of 148 feet (approximately 9 car lengths) while the officer is attempting to draw and fire his gun.[15]

Yet, as crucial as quick reaction time is, there are several factors that militate against it. If agents react too quickly and their actions turn out to be unnecessary, the president may be embarrassed—by being pushed to the ground and smothered by agents or shoved into a limousine—and the agents could be in deep trouble. If bystanders are pushed around or trampled over as a result of some precipitous action by agents, the Service faces a bad press or even litigation. Agents simply cannot afford to operate like frontier marshalls or Chilean security forces—use force first, ask questions later.

By far, the most inhibiting influences on quick reactions are stress and fatigue. In 1978 the Service hired Dr. Frank Ochberg, a psychiatrist and associate director of the National Institute of Mental Health, to conduct a year-long study of the job-related stress suffered by agents. The results of the study remain confidential, but Ochberg indicated that the travel routine and the intense nature of the work combine to produce considerable stress and fatigue.

The eight-hour shifts are tiring. Presidents and candidates travel so extensively that jet lag becomes chronic. Then there is *shift* lag—the protective detail works in three eight-hour shifts and agents are rotated among shifts. With shift lag, jet lag, and tension, it is a wonder that agents don't bumble around like zombies. There is an instant method for reducing stress and fatigue—shorter shifts and more stable assignments. But this would require drastic increases in Service personnel levels (and a conspicuous rise in budget).

There is a different kind of stress that plagues the nine hundred men and women who serve in the Secret Service's Uniformed Division. They must stand guard for hours at a variety of locations, from the White House gates to the doors of foreign embassies along Embassy Row in Washington. The major source of stress and fatigue, the major inhibitor of quick reaction, is boredom. As one uniformed officer describes: "If you're standing guard on the midnight shift and no one comes by to say hello for hours—well, that can get very boring." Another officer says of fixed-post guard duty: "Sometimes you wish something would happen so you could see some action."[16]

Several years ago, the Uniformed Division tried rotating duty assignments every two hours. Uniformed guards would be on duty for two hours; off, for two. The schedule drew heavy criticism for being too cushy. Also, the protective duties of the Uniformed Division were expanded. This combination caused a return to standard eight-hour shifts. Guard-post assignments are changed frequently to ease boredom; but no matter how novel the surroundings, eight hours of standing and watching is boring.

PROTECTIVE INTELLIGENCE

Obtain pertinent protective information—names, photos, descriptive information on known subjects in area to be visited. Determine as to current status of subjects—hospitalized, in custody, at liberty and where.

Secret Service training manual

Protective intelligence gathering seeks to obtain strategic warnings about potential threats and tactical warnings about specific plots in progress. Because its staff and data base are limited, the Service must concentrate on known potentials for attack: it does not have the resources or expertise to monitor a broad universe of conceivable threats, on speculation that a threat *might* develop. Its data system is small compared with that of the CIA and the FBI. The Service cannot hope to gather data on every person or group, so it must determine, even if by guessing, what kinds of individuals and groups are most likely to present a threat to protectees.

The Service's Office of Protective Research gets its data from three basic sources: the White House, Secret Service field offices, and other federal agencies. White House personnel turn in reports on any calls or letters that seem threatening to any protectee. Anyone who comes into or near the mansion and exhibits threatening or strange behavior is automatically reported to the Service, which then interviews the person or, in extreme cases, sends them for psychiatric observation. Thus, all self-announcing oddballs or threateners who come to White House attention end up in the Service's data bank, along with those who come directly to the Service's attention.

In the field, the Service's own field offices, those of other federal agencies (especially FBI), and state and local agencies provide data on potential threats. The Service claims that in recent years there has been a drastic decline in the amount of intelligence it receives from these sources—a result of the Privacy Act, which restricts governmental circulation of information on individuals, and the Freedom of Information Act, which the Service claims has curtailed information provided by the public and by undercover informants because such sources fear that their anonymity cannot be protected. It is alleged that there has been a forty percent reduction in data and that the biggest dip is in the raw data needed to predict threats.

In addition to information laws, the Service contends that restrictive guidelines for the investigation of individuals, issued by Attorney General Edward Levi in 1976, have severely hampered its ability to follow up on its data by checking out potentially threatening persons. Also, the Service claims that the FBI, which is its major supplier of raw data, has changed its data-gathering priorities in recent years—away from the general domestic intelligence needed by the Service and toward the more specialized criminal intelligence demanded by prosecutors. With all of the declines in data cited by the Service, it still obtains between five and six thousand new pieces of information every month.

The Service has *memoranda of understanding* with other federal agencies regarding the kind of information that they should pass on to the Office of Protective Research. The memoranda are very general, even vague. There are no mechansisms in place for monitoring whether the agreements are being adhered to, whether other federal agencies are cooperating fully.

The typical memorandum of understanding specifies seven categories of data that should be provided:[17]

1. Information concerning attempts, threats, or conspiracies to injure, kill, or kidnap persons protected by the USSS or other U.S. or foreign officials in the U.S. or abroad.
2. Information concerning attempts or threats to redress a grievance against any public official by other than legal means, or attempts personally to contact such officials for that purpose.
3. Information concerning threatenting, irrational, or abusive written or oral statements about U.S. Government or foreign officials.
4. Information concerning civil disturbances, anti-U.S. demonstrations or incidents or demonstrations against foreign diplomatic establishment.
5. Information concerning illegal bombings or bombmaking; concealment of caches of firearms, explosives, or other implements of war; or other terrorist activity.
6. Information concerning persons who defect or indicate a desire to defect from the United States and who demonstrate one or more of the following characteristics:
    a. irrational or suicidal behavior or other emotional instability
    b. strong or violent anti-U.S. sentiment
    c. a propensity toward violence.
7. Information concerning persons who may be considered potentially dangerous to individuals protected by the USSS because of their background or activities, including evidence of emotional instability or participation in groups engaging in activities inimical to the United States.

The Secret Service maintains a Watch Office in Washington, complete with a switchboard that operates twenty-four hours a day, seven days a week. The Watch Office screens incoming data (State Department cables, intelligence reports from the CIA, FBI, Defense Department,

National Security Agency). It alerts Secret Service and Treasury officials (via the switchboard) when there is an unusual event or emergency.

There are no written guidelines for defining an *emergency* or an *unusual event*. It is up to the on-duty officer at the Watch Office to determine what is important enough to warrant sending out an alert. When in doubt, the watch officer can consult with the White House or with intelligence agency personnel regarding their interpretation of an event or condition, but the officer must make the final judgment about emergency notification.

The Protective Research data bank has files on groups and organizations, people, and past events and incidents. All of these are indexed and cross-indexed. There are 20,000 persons on file who, for one reason or another, have been previously investigated as potential threats. Each year the file grows, as approximately 1500 new problem individuals come to the Service's attention. Among these, there may be as many as five hundred arrests and two to there hundred convictions for threatening public officials.

The data system is, as the Service describes it, "primarily directed toward identifying dangerous individuals." There are over 40,000 Americans in the Protective Research files. They are there because of some actual or potential threat or some problem or characteristic that makes them potentially dangerous. It is this group who is cross-checked against lists of employees at the hotels and airports frequented by protectees.

When the President is on the road, the basic file of over 40,000 persons is checked to identify potentially dangerous persons in the geographic area that the president will visit. This is called the "trip file." It may contain as many as one hundred names. With the help of state and local law enforcement officers and federal field officers, the Service will attempt to check out and account for every person in the trip file. Agents will seek to discover whether these individuals are still in the area; whether they are in jail, hospitalized, or at liberty; and what their current condition is, which usually necessitates an interview. A few such persons will, as a result of the interview or other data, be detained during the president's visit.

A second list of names is prepared for each trip. These are the individuals in the area who are considered to be definitely dangerous (as opposed to potentially dangerous) or who remain unaccounted for after the efforts to check out each person in the trip file. The second list becomes the "album." A photo and profile of each individual is put together in an album to be studied by every agent in the protective detail. Particularly dangerous cases are red-flagged with a "look out," as are previously-accounted-for individuals in the trip file who suddenly become unaccounted for (escape from prison or from a mental institution).

Agents will often pose as newsmen or photographers and mingle in friendly crowds or among demonstrators, both at the White House and on the road. This is done for two reasons. First, it is a good way to spot problem types whose pictures are in the album or who have a *look out* posted for them. Second, it is a source of new protective intelligence: a person previously unknown to Service files may show up at several events in different places, raising the possibility that he or she is "stalking" the president.

Aside from any particular trip or event, Protective Intelligence maintains a constant list of persons considered dangerous, a nationwide list of four hundred people. Individuals on this "Watch List" receive special attention even when no protectee is visiting their area. Each person is checked out every three or four months (to update their status, location, and condition). Violent or dangerous persons who are incarcerated are not on the list, but as soon as they are released from hospitals or prisons they are put on the Watch List.

There are strict legal limitations on the Service's ability to deal with dangerous persons on the Watch List or in the album. Constitutionally, agents cannot scoop people up and lock them away on speculation simply because the president is coming to town. There must be a demonstrable reason for incarcerating a person. Often, it is difficult for agents to make a good case that a person is "dangerous" because (as we shall see later in this chapter) the Service's data is not very refined and it is not possible under existing privacy laws to obtain data from psychiatrists without the patient's permission. In some cases, however, the family of a person on the Watch List will voluntarily cooperate with the Service and will commit a troubled individual to a hospital for the duration of a presidential visit. In order to lock up a person without family cooperation, agents must have specific, concrete data which, in many cases, they do not possess.

In addition to domestic data, the Service gets foreign intelligence from all agencies within the American intelligence community (CIA, NSA, military intelligence, Department of Defense). In recent years, such data has focused increasingly on international terrorists and their activities.

At a glance, the Protective Intelligence system appears to be impressive and effective—computerized, specialized, logically organized, possessing files on more than 40,000 potentially dangerous Americans, adding a thousand pieces of data every week. Yet there is a striking fact, the implications of which cannot be ignored. As valuable and modern as the system is, no person who has actually shot at a protectee has been on the Watch List or in the Service's basic files—not Lee Harvey Oswald or Sirhan Sirhan or James Earl Ray or Arthur Bremer or Lynette Fromme or Sara Jane Moore or John W. Hinckley.

This does not mean that the system is useless. We do not know how many would-be assassins have been foiled; how many potential assassins have been identified, investigated, and incarcerated. There are sixty arrests each year of "very dangerous" persons, thanks to the protective intelligence system and to the effective work of agents. Perhaps each group of sixty contains two or eight or twenty people who would have shot at the president if they had not been arrested. But it is still a problem of the first magnitude that those who actually show up and shoot at our political leaders are, without exception, unknown to the United States Secret Service.

As this by itself indicates, there are significant deficiencies in the protective intelligence system. One of these involves the system's technical capacity. While the Service's main complaint is that raw domestic-intelligence data has decreased drastically in recent years, the Service's data system seems to have trouble effectively processing whatever quantity of data it gets. By the Treasury Department's own admission, the quality of data analysis has suffered because of the Service's inabiltiy to develop the statistical tools needed to mine the data effectually.

Although the Service has received considerable help from outside consultants who, since 1969, have urged various improvements in the data-analysis system, the Service has generally not followed these recommendations.[18] Secret Service administrators have consistently felt that the consultants failed to grasp the complexities of protective work and of the Service's data needs, especially regarding the role of field offices vis-à-vis the Washington headquarters.

The Service takes the position that *more is better*—that if it could only obtain sufficient raw data, its intelligence system would better meet the demands of the protective mission. But the system needs considerable upgrading before it can efficiently deal with the data already on hand. Increased volumes of data are only useful if the Service knows what to look for and if its data system knows how to find it.

The Hinckley case is a primary example of existing problems. John W. Hinckley was arrested at the Nashville Airport on October 9, 1980 as he attempted to board a plane while carrying three pistols. The incident, which occurred less than six months before Hinckley shot Reagan, coincided with presidential campaign activities in Nashville: candidate Reagan had just cancelled a planned trip there, scheduled for October 8; President Carter was conducting one of his town meetings at the Grand Old Opry. To most Americans, the fact that this incident did not earn Hinckley a place on the Watch List or at least inclusion among the 40,000 or so potentially dangerous persons, seems like a classic bureaucratic foul-up: either the Nashville police or the FBI should have reported him, and agents should have been looking for him as they protected President Reagan.

As logical as this criticism seems, consider the case from an intelligence-gathering perspective. As a Secret Service agent in charge of a field office said of the Hinckley case:

> Take the same situation of someone in New York City being arrested for carrying a gun before a president is supposed to visit. Is the Secret Service supposed to look into every incident? We'd need ten thousand agents.[19]

The en masse addition of this category of persons to the protective files—all persons arrested for carrying firearms in proximity to the president or to candidates—would, within a couple of years, swell the data system by several thousand dossiers. But the basic problem would only be exacerbated. The Service has limited personnel. It can only interview or check out a tiny sample of the more than 40,000 files. The real problem is how to choose *which* cases should be selected for the Watch List of 400 persons and then given special attention. The problem remains unsolved, and this is the critical weakness of the protective intelligence system. There are, at present, no precise profiles or indices for picking out the next Bremer or the next Hinckley, and this would be true if the Service had 120,000 dossiers.

With nothing more on his record than a previous firearms arrest which occurred in proximity to a President, John W. Hinckley would have remained a faceless person undeserving of special attention—even if he *had* been reported and had been in the files. Without more to go on, without more refined clues, there would have been no way to distinguish Hinckley from the several thousand other persons in his category, and there is no way that the Service could treat them all as if they belonged on the Watch List. We must remember that the Watch List contains three to four hundred persons not because that is the actual number of dangerous people in America but because, in addition to representing the Service's best guess as to who the most dangerous persons are, it represents the approximate number of cases that the organization can deal with and keep track of given its existing personnel and methods.

Had Hinckley been arrested for two such incidents or had he been spotted at several presidential functions, and thus been reported, the data system might have picked him out as a man whose association with guns and/or presidential events made him a "stalker" or a problem case. But this would not have happened if the FBI had reported only the Nashville incident. Without another report, without profiles or indices capable of sorting Hinckley out of the pack, he would still have been *unknown* to the Service in any sense that would have better protected President Reagan outside the Hilton Hotel in March of 1981.

The Hinckley case is but one example of a more fundamental problem. Despite the impressive progress in the fields of computer technology and psychiatry, the Service has few clues as to how to look for potential assassins. Without a reliable set of profiles or indices that can be used to identify those who are actually dangerous, as opposed to *potentially* dangerous, neither the agents nor their computers can derive much benefit from increased quantities of intelligence data. The goal of the protective intelligence system is, according to the Service, to identify dangerous persons. But this goal can only be realized when the computers can be instructed as to what to look for, when the Secret Service and its consulting psychiatrists come to know enough about what makes a *dangerous* person tick to select one out of a group of one thousand seemingly dangerous persons. To date, no such knowledge exists.[20]

How *does* the Service come up with its Watch List of four hundred persons? It does so not by using hard scientific concepts from psychology and psychiatry applied to the files through the analytical genius of modern computers. It is, instead, wholly a matter of judgment. The Watch List is the product of educated guesswork. It is reviewed periodically. Some individuals are dropped from the list because they no longer appear to be acutely dangerous; others are added. The list is checked to see that there is some degree of overall consistency, some commonality to the four hundred individuals (so that the list will not become a hodgepodge of cases). This is done by Secret Service personnel, not by computers. It is a process of judgment based on experience and insight, and there is nothing automatic or scientific about it.

This is true of dangerous groups as well as individuals. The computers do have a series of specialized profiles on the *modi operandi* of groups and organizations known to be dangerous. These can be cross-checked with files on individuals and on potentially dangerous groups. How does the computer decide which groups present a real danger to the president and which groups are merely flamboyant or a political nuisance? It doesn't. Again, this is a judgment call for the Service, not a scientific calculation by its computers.

What about the relative *dangerousness* of various environments visited by protectees? How does the computer rate Cairo, Egypt or Charleston, West Virginia? It doesn't: there are no criteria or indices by which it can perform such a task. It does help agents do their advance-work homework. The computer assembles all of the relevant data on a particular environment. Agents study it and reach conclusions about how dangerous the trip will be and what advance work is needed.

It is not as if the Service hasn't tried to discover scientific indices for *dangerousness*. Throughout the 1960s and 1970s it employed outside experts to develop a "profile" of the potential assassin. It seemed promising: experts on human behavior and mental pathology would find the common elements that shaped and motivated assassins and would develop a profile that could serve as a baseline for the protective intelligence system. After all, similar efforts had given corporations a profile of what makes a good executive and NASA a list of the traits needed to be a successful astronaut; psychologists had profiles of the true-believer, the high achiever. Why not the assassin?

Disappointingly, the consultants did not produce any profiles which the Service considered useful. In the 1980s the Service changed the goal. Instead of trying to develop profiles of assassins, consultants were asked to pursue "broader indices" for identifying dangerous persons. In March of 1981, the Service held a symposium, under the auspices of the National Academy of Sciences, to try to further the development of such indices.

The results of the symposium, though useful in a heuristic sense, were hardly comforting for the Service and may have worsened its fears that scientists spend too much time in the ivory tower to be of much help in protective work. The symposium reached the conclusion that a great deal of empirical research is needed before it could be determined *which* items of information about a subject are more important than others. Lacking the "requisite knowledge base" to rank order the import of various pieces of data gathered on subjects, it is not possible to develop indices to identify dangerous persons.

The Service had asked the symposium:

> What are the objective indicators of dangerousness, and what items of information should be collected to make this determination?

The answer was:

> Propensity toward violent behavior or dangerous behavior should be viewed as fluctuating over time and elicited by particular settings or mental states of the individual. No one can make reliable long term predictions as to whether and when a person might try to harm himself and others.[21]

The Service was already acutely aware that dangerous behavior fluctuates over time, as indicated by its changing Watch List. It seems that it will be a long time before the scientists have the kind of precise, predictive knowledge that the Service requested from them.

The symposium was fairly grim in its assessment of prospects for further research. One problem is that the Service cannot open its files to consulting scientists because of privacy laws; and without access to the more than 40,000 dossiers, it is difficult for consultants to find specific ways to improve the protective-intelligence system. Another problem cited by the symposium is that a key scientific component of behavioral research, the use of a *control group*, is not feasible. The idea of having one group of dangerous persons who are dealt with by the Service via its usual methods and a similar group that is purposely left alone (the control group) is, as the scientists put it, a "possibly tragic method for evaluating Secret Service methods."

The symposium seems to have put the Service in a position analogous to that of a patient who recognizes that he has an emotional problem and consults a psychiatrist who, after lengthy analysis, tells the patient: "Boy, do you have a problem!"

The scientists' bleak assessment of the present and future prospects for developing indices with which to find dangerous persons may have been disappointing to the Service, but the recommendations about protective methods must have been even more unsettling. It was the general feeling of the experts that the least coercive methods possible should be adopted in dealing with dangerous persons. In an era of tight federal budgets and reduced personnel, the Secret Service was surely nonplussed when it was recommended that new methods for dealing with dangerous persons during a presidential visit might include "sending the individual on a vacation to a distant place" and "assigning an agent-escort" to the person for the duration of the visit. The idea of becoming travel agent and babysitter for hundreds of dangerous persons is not one which the Service is likely to embrace.

In addition to all of the problems of data analysis, the protective intelligence system has other difficulties created by its dependence on external sources. The system's internal limitations and weaknesses are magnified by the fact that so much of its vital data is gathered and reported by other agencies. Since the Secret Service is unlikely to be allowed to triple its present size and become a major intelligence-gathering agency on a par with the FBI or the CIA, it will always be a net importer of data within the American intelligence community.

This dependence extends to state and local levels as well as federal. When a protectee visits an American city, there may be a greater number of identifiably dangerous persons in that city who are unknown to Service files than are known. The intelligence-gathering efforts of local police are therefore a crucial element in determining the effectiveness of protective research.

The quality of local intelligence-gathering varies greatly, and the Service must, in a very real sense, take what it can get and hope for the best. Almost every big city police department has an intelligence squad or unit that gathers data—by both overt and covert methods—on local individuals and groups. Like the police departments in which they exist, these units vary in their competence, priorities, and cooperation with the Service. The Service's strained relationship with the New York City Police Department may permeate to the intelligence unit, affecting the coordination of cooperative efforts at intelligence gathering. Some departments (Chicago, for example) have a tradition of concentrating on political intelligence (the surveillance and infiltration of radical and dissident groups). Other departments direct their intelligence efforts primarily toward organized crime.

When the Secret Service field office and advance team ask a local department for data on *dangerous* individuals in their city, the list from one city may be full of underworld types; from another, full of political radicals. Since there are no set definitions of what constitutes a *dangerous* person, different police departments have divergent ideas about who should qualify for the list that they pass on to the Service. Also, some departments may be unwilling to share certain criminal intelligence with federal agencies because of fears that the Feds will make a premature arrest that would botch a complex case, or fear that the FBI will move in and take all the credit.

The Service depends on federal agencies for much of its protective intelligence data. These agencies vary in terms of the quality of data provided and their willingness to provide it. The CIA is fairly stingy, allegedly because so much of its intelligence relates to sensitive espionage matters. If the Service develops a rivalry with a particular agency, or if—as the Service alleges of the FBI—an agency redirects its intelligence-gathering away from areas needed by the Service, or if a particular agency passes on unreliable data, then the protective intelligence system is in trouble.

It now appears that the Secret Service expended vast amounts of time and energy protecting against a perceived threat that was based on inaccurate intelligence. To the extent that the Service misdirects its protective efforts and misappropriates its scarce personnel because of poor data from other agencies, its effectiveness in dealing with real threats is diminished.

Throughout November and December of 1981, the Service's biggest concern was protecting against a Libyan hit team allegedly dispatched to the United States by Libyan President Muammar Kaddafi to assassinate President Reagan. Reagan himself announced that there was "hard evidence" of the plot, presumably provided by the CIA. News coverage gave the impression that intelligence data on the Libyan plot was detailed and reliable: the hit team was reported to be composed of three Libyans, three Iranians, and an East German; the hit team was in Mexico; it entered the United States; one assassin wore cowboy boots and smoked English cigarettes; sketches of the assassins appeared in the newspapers. The sources for all this data were "security officials," "Capitol Hill sources," or simply "It's been learned."[22]

It turns out that the intelligence data that put the Secret Service on perpetual alert for two months was less-than-solid to say the least. As ABC newsman Sam Donaldson put it: "We've never confirmed any hard evidence about a hit team inside the United States." Two members of the Senate Intelligence Committee who were primary media sources for the Libyan story subsequently felt that they were misled—"entrapped" by the CIA briefers who told them about the plot and about the alleged evidence. Was the whole affair the result of faulty intelligence gathering or analysis? Was it all a CIA concoction designed to provide leverage against Kaddafi or to discredit him? Like the rest of us, the Secret Service will probably never know.

The Service may adopt a more hard-nosed, skeptical attitude about the validity of CIA bombshells, at least in the short run. But it cannot afford to ignore CIA data on protective threats. Because the Service has neither the personnel nor the sources to develop its own intelligence networks in a league with the CIA or the FBI (or even to verify the work of other agencies), it must—to a certain grudging degree—take intelligence reports at face value, perhaps with a little discount for past performance. In the final analysis, however, no matter how weak or dubious the data base appears, the Secret Service is not in any position to dismiss a report that a foreign assassination team is out to get the president. The Service would rather risk the distraction and embarrassment of a wild goose chase than the parade of the riderless horse.

CONCLUSION

The Service steadfastly insists that its protective methods and procedures are applied equally to all protectees—presidents, candidates, children of former presidents. When asked whether precautions were the same for an outing by President Reagan as for a Houston shopping trip by Lady Bird Johnson, Secret Service spokesman Jack Warner replied: "The process is the same for everyone. Only the number of personnel varies depending on the notoriety of the person. We certainly would screen all the people in Houston who might be a threat. We wouldn't be doing our job otherwise."[23]

This may be a laudable goal, but it is far from a reality. Protectees vary greatly regarding the number and kind of protective procedures that they will allow or abide by. Moreover, the effectiveness of most protective methods depends greatly on the number of agents available. Protective intelligence is not a mechanized, scientific process but one dependent on agent judgment. If the agents are overworked or have too few colleagues to consult with, the quality of intelligence suffers. Whether establishing a safety zone or checking every inch of the rugs and walls of a strange room, the implementation of the procedure is affected by the number of agents involved. The "process" may be somewhat the same for all protectees but the results of the protective process, the effectiveness of implementation, vary according to a range of variables. Foremost among these are the number of agents assigned and the cooperativeness of the protectee.

Secret Service methods are a complex mix of modern technology and judgment calls, of precision and guesswork, of professional insight and shibboleth. When protection is implemented effectively and unobtrusively, as it usually is, the United States Secret Service gives the impression of being a precision-honed protective machine. Behind the facade of routinized, computerized, robot-like security procedures lies the key element in successful protection — the experience, insight, good judgment and quick reactions of the agents on the line.

NOTES

1. STAR Reports are discussed in James B. Kirkman *et al.* (eds.), *Assassination and Political Violence* (New York: Bantam, 1970), pp. 118–21.

2. Charles Mohr, "Oval Office Intruder Asks Carter for Directions," New York *Times*, August 2, 1977, p. 12.

3. *Newsweek*, April 13, 1981, p. 16.

4. Harry Neal, *The Service Service in Action* (New York: Elsevier-Nelson, 1980), p. 123.

5. New York *Times*, Feb. 10, 1973, p. 17.

6. Boston *Globe*, "Barriers Beef up White House Security," Dec. 5, 1983, p. 5.

7. "Management Review on the Performance of the U.S. Dept. of the Treasury in Connection with the March 30, 1981 Assassination Attempt on President Ronald Reagan" (Washington, D.C.: Treasury Dept., 1981), p. 41.

8. Joseph F. Sullivan, "Security Forces Prepare for Ford Visit to Newark," New York *Times*, Oct. 2, 1975, p. 83.

9. Neal, *Secret Service in Action,* pp. 110–11.

10. John Burns, "Security Men Still Keep Nixon under Close Guard," New York *Times*, Feb. 25, 1972, p. 14.

11. *Newsweek*, April 13, 1981, p. 50

12. Robert Blair Kaiser, "Presidential Candidates Disagree on Value of Secret Service Watch," New York *Times*, Feb. 10, 1980, p. 1.

13. *Newsweek*, April 13, 1981, p. 51.

14. Rufus Youngblood, quoted in *Newsweek, Ibid.,* from his book *Twenty Years in the Secret Service.*

15. U.S. Secret Service, *Secret Service Training Manual, 1954.* National Archives record group 22, Warren Commission documents, p. 98.

16. Howie Kurtz, "The Executive Protection Racket," *Washington Monthly,* October, 1978, pp. 47–49.

17. Treasury Dept., *Management Review,* p. 28.

18. *Ibid.,* p. 36.

19. Kevin A. O'Reilly, "Presidential Protection" (Paper presented at Seminar in Political Assassinations and Violence, Southeastern Mass. Univ., Professor Philip H. Melanson, Dec. 1981). O'Reilly interview with Special Agent Charles Collins, head of the Secret Service's Boston field office.

20. Treasury Dept., *Management Review,* p. 35.

21. E. M. Leeper, "Could the Secret Service Predict Violent Behavior?" National Academy of Sciences *News Report,* January, 1982, pp. 17–18.

22. John Weisman, "Why American TV Is So Vulnerable to Foreign Propaganda," *TV Guide,* June 12, 1982, p. 12.

23. Stephen Chapman, "The Secret Service's Biggest Secret," *New Republic,* Jan. 24, 1981, pp. 18–21.

7

PRESIDENTIAL PSYCHOLOGY

To understand what actual presidents do and what potential Presidents might do, the first need is to see the man whole—not as some abstract embodiment of civic virtue, some scorecard of issue stands, or some reflection of a faction, but as a human being like the rest of us, a person trying to cope with a difficult environment.

James David Barber, The Presidential Character

The Secret Service develops strict rules concerning what presidents should and should not do. But presidents make their own rules as to what advice, restrictions, and security procedures they will accept. The extent to which a particular president conforms to the Service's rules depends upon a complex mix of factors, including the president's personality and political situation. There is a law that requires that presidents must be afforded Secret Service protection: there is no law requiring presidents to accept protecton or to comply with the procedures demanded by effective security. Thus the personality, the psychological orientation, of a particular president is a—if not the—key variable in determining how well or poorly protected our commander-in-chief is at any given time.

There are two basic categories of psychological variables that shape the interaction between a president and his protectors. First, there are the potential conflicts that are more or less inherent in the role of president, and which therefore exist for any president. Second, there is the personality of the incumbent, a variable that drastically alters the nature of the Service's protective work with each new chief executive.

It is a facet of what has been called the imperial presidency that presidents seem larger than life, to the point where our political culture often regards them as quintessential national symbols rather than flesh-and-blood human beings who labor at an overwhelming job. Yet, in reality, the presidency is a job—one generating its own occupational stresses. Unlike some well-publicized high-stress occupations (air traffic controller, for example) presidential job stress is often masked by the aura of the imperial presidency, or, in its physical manifestations, by the skilled hands of the White House makeup technician.

Some of the job-related stress of the presidency has a direct impact upon the Secret Service's interaction with the president. First of all, as every president is well aware, the ever-present possibility of assassination means that there is an inherent element of danger. Like men and women in other occupations in which there is personal risk—policemen, test pilots, prison guards—most presidents (and politicians) seem to cope with occupational dangers by adopting a fatalistic attitude. Were presidents or politicians to allow themselves to fret constantly about the spector of assassination, both their job effectiveness and their psyches would suffer greatly. To varying degrees, most presidents adopt the view that the risks to their person come with the territory—an occupational fact of life.

John F. Kennedy's fatalism is now legend. According to White House advisor Kenneth O'Donnell, JFK viewed the risk of assassination as part of the price for an open democratic process and was not at all perturbed by it; he even asserted that assassination was the Secret Service's worry, not his.[1] Still, this did not banish the problem from Kennedy's mind. The night before his assassination he remarked to O'Donnell: "Last night would have been a hell of a night to assassinate a president. . . . Anyone perched above the crowd with a rifle could do it."

JFK's fatalism was not atypical among modern presidents. As Franklin D. Roosevelt put it, "Since you can't control these things [the threat of assassination], you don't worry about them."[2] President Johnson opined: "If anyone wants to do it, no amount of protection is enough. All a man needs is a willingness to trade his life for mine."[3] Dwight D. Eisenhower remarked to his friend and confidant Sherman Adams, "If anybody really wanted to climb up there and shoot me [he pointed to a fire escape outside his Denver hotel room], it would be an easy thing to do. So why worry about it."[4]

Herein lies one of the potential conflicts: the Secret Service must worry about. A fatalistic attitude helps to enable a president to go from crowd to crowd, handshake to handshake, without dwelling on the possibility that an outstretched hand may point a gun, and without flinching, jumping, or ducking at every odd noise or sudden movement. In contrast, Secret Service agents around the president must constantly focus on potential danger and must regard everything with suspicion. In short, they must worry about everything that the president would like to forget. The more the president puts the dangers out of mind, the more the Service's warnings and restrictions are an intrusive reminder of vulnerability and mortality.

After a threat against President Carter turned out to be a hoax, one Secret Service agent remarked: "They [presidents] never think it can happen to them, and when something like this happens it reminds them of the hazards."[5] But most presidents seem acutely aware that it can happen to them, which is precisely why they tend to become fatalistic. Under normal conditions and on a day-to-day basis, it is Secret Service personnel and procedures that provide the most graphic reminders of "the hazards."

In the final analysis, it is the president's personality more than the depth of his occupational fatalism that will determine his willingness to comply with protective requirements. Both Eisenhower and Kennedy were very fatalistic about assassination, but Kennedy rebuffed Secret Service advice to a degree that at times must have appeared to the Service as bordering on reckless disregard for personal safety. Although Eisenhower felt that the Service's sometimes-intricate protective procedures were largely a waste of time and energy, he complied graciously and cooperatively.[6]

Another built-in tension between protectors and protectee is that most presidents get tired of having their lives managed, while the Secret Service aspires to manage extensively its protectees. Presidents normally attain the office via a long punishing campaign trial that is now measured in years rather than months. Elizabeth Drew, who interviewed several presidential candidates, concluded that the process was "both strange and brutal" and that "few human beings could emerge whole."[7]

One aspect of this intense experience is that virtually every facet of a candidate's life—from speech, to clothing, to makeup and hair style—is managed by professional experts, until the distinction between public and private life, between the candidate and the campaign, blurs or disappears altogether, as the candidate is programmed for electoral success. According to Drew, it is a truism in presidential politics that "candidates wives hate schedulers and advance men." And why not, for these men control their husband's lives to a degree that must sometimes seem like institutionalization.

Candidates themselves can become testy or even downright rebellious toward their political keepers. One story emerging from Reagan's unsuccessful 1976 campaign for the Republican nomination is that he insisted on getting eight hours sleep per night, arguing that he could not function well on less sleep. His inventive managers, frantic to overcome Gerald Ford's slim delegate lead, took to resetting clocks and watches and manipulating time-zone changes to give the candidate the impression that he had had a full eight hours, while actually working him longer. Reagan caught on and was reportedly furious.

When the candidate wins and enters the White House, the intensity of the control exercised by political managers is likely to subside, at least somewhat, in comparison to the often robot-like programming of the candidate that occurs during a heated election. The intrusions on privacy and mobility created by Secret Service protection, which during the campaign were mild compared with those inflicted by the political managers, are likely to become more conspicuous in the White House, as the political pace subsides and the Secret Service's efforts intensify.

The successful candidate has now ascended to one of the most powerful offices in the world. He may be, as Lyndon Johnson was fond of describing the office, "the leader of the free world." Yet, according to the requirements of his protectors: he cannot shake hands with everyone he wants to; he must sometimes stay inside when he wants to be outside; he cannot go to his favorite restaurant unless Secret Service agents dine at the next table and unless the kitchen and food are checked, causing long delays in food service.

Once in office, it is the Secret Service that most conspicuously impinges upon the privacy of the president and his family; on the campaign trail, it was the political managers. Some presidents, like some presidential candidates, enjoy having Secret Service agents around, at least for a while. Their presence is, after all, a trapping of the imperial presidency. To be watched over, escorted, and chauffeured by dozens of respectful, well-dressed functionaries is a visible reminder of the power and prestige of the office. But presidential protection is not a nine-to-five operation conducted only at the president's office or place of work. It is constant and, as far as the Service is concerned, applies to the president's private life as well as public life. Because of this, the Secret Service's welcome can quickly wear thin, despite the fact that its presence may contribute to an aura of political power.

When a president wants to avoid the burdens of office for a few hours (by visiting a friend, perhaps), the Secret Service is there to turn the outing into a complex logistical problem that can easily spoil the illusion of leisure or normalcy that the president may be trying to create. John F. Kennedy was very irritated to discover that stepping out of the White House to a party in nearby Georgetown for a few hours of fun and relaxation was turned into a mass production of protective procedures.[8]

Eventually, most presidents come to feel that the Service intrudes upon much more than their social life. When the Secret Service requested additional office space, Lyndon Johnson refused. "No, hell no," said LBJ. "Secret Service would have absolutely no hesitancy in occupying my bedroom!"[9]

Johnson would have included the kitchen as well. The Secret Service's policy of inspecting all foodstuffs brought into the White House has been a particular problem for the more epicurean chief executives. Franklin D. Roosevelt's well-known fondness for exotic fish and game resulted in a continuous stream of gifts to the White House kitchen—everything from Peking duck to Maine lobster. FDR objected strenuously when Secret Service agents insisted on sidetracking all of the incoming treats to a laboratory where they could be analyzed. Even worse for Roosevelt's palate, agents took to consuming some of the allegedly more questionable gifts; others, they simply tossed into the garbage.[10]

The Service's intrusion into the private lives of presidents and their families (to the extent that they have a private life) is a very real source of friction. It must surely feel strange when even a trip to the bathroom is an event worthy of security precautions. LBJ once admonished an agent who was on his first tour of duty at the Texas ranch: "If you hear rustling in the bushes near the old man's bedroom door during the night, don't shoot. It's probably him taking a leak."[11]

Even when, unlike LBJ, protectees are inclined to use indoor plumbing exclusively, agents are not far away. Aboard *Air Force One* when a president or member of the first family goes to the lavatory, protective procedures call for an agent to stand outside the door. Betty Ford recalled that on one flight during which there was some unexpected turbulence while she was in the lavatory, the Secret Service agent standing guard outside the door yelled, "Sit down, Mrs. Ford! Please sit down." The First Lady responded, "I *am* sitting down."[12]

Eventually there often develops a kind of game or contest between presidents and their protectors—one in which both sides attempt to define to their advantage the boundaries of the president's privacy. Sometimes the game is good natured, sometimes not. Harry Truman's desire to stay close to his roots as *everyman* caused him to seek out ordinary activities as if he were still a private citizen. He decided, for example, that he would leave Blair House (where he was living while the White House was being refurbished) and stroll to the bank a few blocks away. The problem was that Truman was not an ordinary citizen depositing his paycheck. The pied-piper effect of the president strolling the busy streets of downtown Washington soon caused vehicular and pedestrian traffic to snarl, creating a potentially dangerous situation for presidential security.

The Service responded imaginatively: henceforth it had the traffic lights along the president's walking route fixed in advance so that they would turn red in all directions, thus stopping all traffic and clearing the way for a swift and safe presidential walk. But Truman soon noticed the strange phenomenon of the four-way red lights. He ordered the practice stopped. "I'll wait for the light like any other pedestrian," he huffed.[13]

One of the more interesting give-and-take interactions between the Service and a first family member involved First Lady Eleanor Roosevelt. Both she and the president became annoyed by the Service's ubiquitous presence and by its restrictions. The first lady allegedly made life quite unpleasant for agents whose unlucky assignment was to hover around her. Finally, the frustrated Secret Service took the unusual step of letting the first lady protect herself. She was given a revolver and taught how to use it for self defense. In trade for her promise to carry the weapon with her at all times, the Service promised to allow Mrs. Roosevelt to gallivant on her own. As is often the case in a game without enforceable rules, both sides cheated. The first lady kept the gun in her dresser drawer and never carried it at all; the Service planted undercover agents at all of her public appearances.[14]

In 1981, then Secret Service Director H. Stuart Knight described the ego-dimension of the conflicts between presidents and the Service. "To tell a president he can't do something because he might get hurt assaults his ego. He has to feel like a man, not a puppet, and you've got to figure out a way he can save face."[15]

The problem is that there is not always—or even usually—a way for the Service to implement effective protection in a face-saving manner, without assaulting the president's ego, or privacy, or psychological defense mechanisms for coping with the threat of assassination. One result is that, in one way or another, most presidents eventually rebel against their protectors. The degree and kinds of rebellion depends upon the personality of the incumbent. Sometimes it is good-natured; sometimes, vindictive. The common denominator is that the president finds a way to assert himself against those who intrude upon his style, his privacy or his psyche—by lashing out at them or besting them, even humiliating them.

John F. Kennedy would sometimes snarl at agents who cramped his political style. "Get those ivy league types off my back!" he ordered the head of the White House detail. The two agents who were riding on the back bumper of the President's limousine were promptly removed.

Franklin D. Roosevelt took pleasure in playing inventive pranks on his protectors. FDR liked to relax in the swimming pools at his Warm Springs, Georgia retreat. There were three pools, connected by underwater passageways. The president would splash about until the agents guarding him would look in another direction, then dive deep underwater and swim through a passageway, surfacing in another pool and staying out of the agents' view. Aware that FDR was partially paralyzed from having contracted polio, and assuming that he was still underwater, the agents would plunge in, suits and all—to FDR's great delight.[16]

Another of FDR's pranks involved persuading an agent to fetch a ladder and climb onto the roof of the president's home in Hyde Park, New York, under the pretext of having the agent retrieve something or check something. Roosevelt would then order his handyman to remove the ladder, leaving the agent stranded and temporarily out of FDR's way.[17]

Franklin Roosevelt also pioneered an activity which Lyndon Johnson would later elevate to an art form—vehicular hide-and-seek with agents. While driving near his rural Hyde Park home, FDR made a quick U-turn on a narrow country road. This was no problem for his small car, but the larger Secret Service vehicles following him had difficulty in executing the same maneuver, allowing Roosevelt to speed away and escape for a short time.[18]

At the White House Lyndon Johnson would demonstrate his independence from Secret Service agents by walking outside without informing them, jumping into the limousine, and ordering the driver to "just drive," forcing the White House detail to scramble to catch up.[19] But it was on LBJ's home turf, the Texas ranch, where the chase really became frenzied. There, Johnson would drive himself, speeding his big Lincoln over the endless maze of dusty roads that criss-crossed his vast acreage.

The Secret Service had to struggle to catch up, but they usually did. Lyndon's Lincoln always carried a copious supply of beer. Johnson would cradle a can between his legs and quaff it as he zoomed around the ranch. Eventually, this resulted in his having to make increasingly frequent pits stops, which gave agents an opportunity to overtake him.

At one such stop the earthy Johnson accomplished literally what some presidents may well have thought about doing figuratively. When he pulled his Lincoln to the side of the road and got out to relieve himself, agents quickly caught up and closely surrounded him. As a stiff breeze swept across the plains, a surprised agent sputtered, "Sir, you're pissing on my leg." Johnson continued. "I know," he drawled. "That's my prerogative."[20]

The more generic sources of conflict between the president and the Secret Service (those that stem from the inherent tensions between the role of president and the role of protector) profoundly influence the nature of the Service's work. But the variable that has an even greater impact upon interaction and upon the quality of protection is the personality of the president. (The influence of political demands and pressures is discussed in the next chapter.) Because there are no laws or enforceable rules pertaining to how much of what kind of protection a president must accept, personality becomes a crucial determinant. Thus, many of the behavioral dimensions of the Secret Service's protective task will change precipitously with the arrival of a new president.

How much will a president resent protective intrusions upon what remains of his private life? To what degree will he rebel against them? How fatalistic will he be concerning danger? Will his attitude toward the Service be one of cooperation, indifference, or stubborn resistance? Personality is the key.

Political scientist Dwight L. Tays has offered a typology for classifying presidents according to the way in which they react to security precautions.[21] He posits three basic types, developed by analyzing each president's comments about security, his experiences in "critical incidents" involving protection, and the observations of those around him. The first is the "less-restrictive" president who largely discounts the need for protective procedures and attempts to conduct his activities with "as little regard for security as possible." The second type, the "passive-cooperative," does not see the need for protective measures but goes along with them anyway and usually does not make things difficult for the Service. The third is the "supportive-preference" type, who is generally receptive to protective procedures and tends to enjoy the seclusion (the isolation from the public) which such procedures provide. Regardless of whether distinctions among presidential orientations toward protection are clear enough to sustain a tripartite model, Tays' analysis is useful in highlighting the significant differences in presidential personality.

According to Tays, John F. Kennedy was a prime example of a *less-restrictive* president. He was one of the most difficult (and recalcitrant) of modern presidents, as far as Secret Service protection was concerned. A strong-willed man who was accustomed to doing what he wanted to do, Kennedy complained to friends shortly after taking office that he felt like a virtual prisoner in the White House because of protective restrictions.[22]

His interaction with the Secret Service was tense, often abrasive. He groused about procedures, snapped at agents, and constantly ordered them not to do what they perceived as essential for his protection. To the chagrin of agents, he would spontaneously command his limousine to stop and would then exit and plunge into a crowd to shake hands, with no deference to security precautions. He refused to allow agents to ride on the running boards of his limousine, as Secret Service procedure dictated.

Franklin D. Roosevelt was much like Kennedy. He too was irritated by protective measures and tended to actively resist them. Colonel Edmund Starling of the Secret Service described FDR as "utterly fearless, contemptuous of danger, and full of desire to go places and do things, preferably unorthodox places and unorthodox things—for a president."[23]

Although less resistant than JFK or FDR, Lyndon Johnson surely belongs in the tough-to-protect group. To Johnson, spontaneous contact with the public was as much a compulsion of his personality as a political necessity, and he liked to do it as often and as extensively as possible. On one occasion when LBJ unexpectedly waded into a crowd—pumping hands, kissing women, posing for the cameras—an agent blurted: "We've got to have some restraints." Johnson replied, "I've got to press the flesh."

At the opposite end of the continuum is a group of presidents who were very cooperative with the Service and much easier to protect, whom Tays would label the *supportive-preference* type—Eisenhower, Nixon, and Reagan.[24] Eisenhower did not believe that security was necessary, but (like a good soldier) he cooperated. Nor did he share LBJ's nearly compulsive need for public contact or Kennedy's strong-willed independence, or FDR's penchant for "unorthodox" activity. Eisenhower got along well with the Service, which he described as "one of the finest, most efficient organizations of men I have ever known."[25] He seemed to be impressed with little things about the Service that reminded him of the military, like the fact that agents had to be on duty at Christmas and away from their families.[26] In contrast, Kennedy and Roosevelt would probably have been pleased if all of the agents went home for Christmas and stayed there until the next Christmas.

When the Secret Service suggested that Eisenhower should not sit out on the White House lawn to do his oil painting—one of his favorite pastimes—because he presented too good a target, he moved his easel indoors, with no rancor.[27] Ike once reflected ruefully that he "apparently worried these protectors by my unthinking disregard for their advice."[28] A Secret Service dream come true—a president who felt guilty about not following procedures.

Richard Nixon was perhaps the easiest of all presidents to protect. "Protecting Richard Nixon," said one veteran agent, "was like "protecting a robot."[29] Mr. Nixon was disinclined toward public contact and spontaneous outings, tending to prefer the confines of the White House or of his San Clemente home. He was generally cooperative (although, as we shall see in the next chapter, the same cannot be said of his political aides). At times, he would even request additional protection—a request that the Service is not used to receiving.

On a given day, however, even an easy-to-protect, cooperative President like Nixon can present problems, can rebel against procedure. During the 1973 inaugural parade, the Service requested that Mr. Nixon keep the windows of his limousine closed because trouble was expected from demonstrators. This aggravated Nixon, who proceeded to open his window even though protesters were hurling a barrage of objects. The missiles, mostly eggs, turned out to be harmless; but, at the time, neither Nixon nor the agents knew this for sure. Even "robots" malfunction now and then.

Ronald Reagan has been quite cooperative with his protectors. Then Secret Service Director H. Stuart Knight told the press that Reagan "will wear protective attire anytime we ask him to,"[30] which has not been true of most presidents. After the assassination attempt in March of 1981, the Service significantly increased security. Reagan, who was cooperative before the attempt, seemed even more so afterward, even with stricter procedures. In part this was probably due to the fact that Mr. Reagan was extremely impressed with how agents performed during the assassination attempt, especially agent Timothy J. McCarthy, who was wounded while walking directly into the gunfire in order to shield the President. After the shooting, Reagan seemed to feel a kind of combat-born camaraderie with agents.

One might think that Reagan's attitude was predictable, that he would gladly accept increased security without complaint since he had nearly lost his life. But two assassination attempts on President Ford seemed to have the opposite result: Ford became almost more disregarding of precautions in his attempt to prove that he would not be intimidated by the threat of assassination.

Between the two extremes is the type of president Tays calls the *passive-cooperative*—the middle-range group who do not regard protection as very necessary but, for the most part, go along with it anyway. Truman, Ford, and Carter fall into this category. Carter was basically cooperative, but, like all presidents, he was occasionally resistant or unpredictable. At his inaugural parade he suddenly decided to walk the length of Pennsylvania Avenue, from the Capitol to the White House, creating a logistical and security nightmare for the unprepared Secret Service.

Although he did not resist protection, Carter's aloofness bothered the men who guarded him. He never developed the friendly relationship with agents that Ford and Reagan had and was regarded as a "cold fish."[31]

Truman had come to terms with the Secret Service presence while he was vice-president. He did not view protection as necessary and it inhibited his desire to do things in an ordinary manner, but he generally accepted it. Shortly after becoming vice-president he saw a man hanging around outside his Senate office. Truman asked an aide who the man was and what he wanted. The aide responded that the man was a Secret Service agent. "Well what the hell is this? When did this happen?" Truman asked. He approached the agent and shook his hand. "I don't see much sense in this," he said, "but if you fellows are detailed to do it I'll give you all the cooperation I can."[32]

A president's orientation toward protection can undergo a marked transformation during his tenure in office because of changes in attitude and in political circumstance. Lyndon Johnson, who was a cantankerous and capricious protectee for most of his presidency, was very different during his last two years in office. As opposition to his conduct of the Vietnam War increased, he became a political recluse. The man who once thrived on "pressing the flesh" now holed up in the White House or visited those few places guaranteed to have a friendly audience (mostly military bases). With his loss of enthusiasm for public contact, he became a much more docile protectee.

Moreover, as his sense of isolation increased, he seemed to worry more about the possibility of assassination, especially in the wake of the assassinations of Robert F. Kennedy and Martin Luther King, Jr. (both in 1968). After King's death LBJ was scheduled to attend a memorial service. The President telephoned agent Clint Hill, head of the White House detail, three times the night before the King memorial service, once at 4:00 A.M. According to Hill, Johnson "had a premonition that something was going to happen to him." The president requested that Hill stay as close to him as possible.[33]

Gerald Ford underwent a similarly striking transformation in the opposite direction. Although he was a basically cooperative protectee, two assassination attempts within seventeen days in September 1975 seem to have been perceived by Ford as a direct challenge to America's democratic system. The day after the second attempt he asserted: "The American people are a good people and under no circumstances will I—and I hope no others—capitulate to those who want to undercut what's good in America."

Ford declared that if a president could not walk among the people, "something has gone wrong in our society."[34] He vowed to continue personal contact with the public. Ford kept his promise but, in the process, became a less cautious, almost Kennedy-style, protectee. In his efforts to prove that American democracy would not be paralyzed by the fear of assassination, he campaigned for a second term from open limousines; he plunged into crowd after crowd. In Dallas he rode in an open limousine along a preannounced parade route, constantly waving at the crowds that lined the streets. He eschewed a bulletproof vest (he wore it only once then shed it because it was too confining and uncomfortable).

The United States presidency is in many respects a very personalist institution. The political and public-policy success of an administration is inexorably linked to the strengths, weaknesses, and idiosyncrasies of the president's personality and character. It is not surprising, then, that the quality and style of protection is so much influenced by the psychological orientations of the incumbent. To an important degree, each president sets his own *rules* for protection, based upon his personality and political style.

NOTES

1. Arthur Schlesinger, Jr., *A Thousand Days: John F. Kennedy in the White House* (Boston: Houghton Mifflin, 1965), p. 1024.

2. James Roosevelt and Bill Libby, *My Parents: A Differing View* (Chicago: Playboy Press, 1976), pp. 200–1.

3. *U.S. News & World Report*, April 13, 1981, p. 28.

4. Sherman Adams, *Firsthand Report* (New York: Harper, 1961), p. 84.

5. "Guarding the President: The Job Gets Tougher." *U.S. News & World Report*, Oct. 2, 1978, p. 74.

6. Adams, pp. 83–86.

7. Elizabeth Drew, "Running," in *Behind the Scenes in American Government*, 4th ed., ed. Peter Woll (Boston: Little Brown, 1983), pp. 20–41, at p. 21.

8. N. C. Livingstone, "From JFK to Reagan: What the Secret Service Thinks of the Presidents They Protect." *The Washingtonian*, Sept. 1981, p. 170–71.

9. Jack Valenti, *A Very Human President* (New York: W. W. Norton 1975), pp. 175–76.

10. Dwight L. Tays, "Presidential Reaction to Security: A Longitudinal Study," *Presidential Studies Quarterly*, Fall 1980, pp. 600–9, citing Michael F. Reilly, *Reilly of the White House* (New York: Simon and Schuster, 1947), p. 17.

11. Frank Cormier, *LBJ: The Way He Was* (Garden City: Doubleday, 1977), p. 136.

12. Betty Ford with Chris Chase, *Time of My Life* (New York: Harper & Row, 1978) p. 177.

13. Tays, "Presidential Reaction to Security," p. 603.

14. *Ibid.*, p. 602.

15. "Can the Risk Be Cut?" *Newsweek*, April 13, 1981, pp. 18–21, at p. 18.

16. Roosevelt and Libby, *My Parents*, pp. 89–90.

17. *Ibid.*, p. 201.

18. Tays, "Presidential Reaction to Security," p. 602 citing Edmund W. Starling, *Starling of the White House* (New York: Simon and Schuster, 1946), p. 312.

19. Livingstone, "JFK to Reagan," p. 170.

20. *Ibid.*, p. 171.

21. Tays, "Presidential Reaction to Security," pp. 600–9.

22. Livingstone, "JFK to Reagan," p. 170.

23. Tays, "Presidential Reaction to Security," p. 601, citing Starling, xviii.

24. Tays does not deal with or categorize Reagan; the author has categorized Reagan as a "supportive preference" type, based on the author's own research.

25. Dwight D. Eisenhower, *Mandate for Change 1953–1956* (Garden City: Doubleday, 1963), p. 75.

26. Tays, "Presidential Reaction to Security," p. 604.

27. Adams, *Firsthand Report*, p. 84.

28. Eisenhower, *Mandate for Change*, pp. 269–70.

29. "Can the Risk Be Cut?" *Newsweek*, April 13, 1981, p. 18.

30. *Ibid.*

31. Livingstone, "JFK to Reagan," p. 170.

32. Margaret Truman, *Harry S. Truman* (New York: William Morrow, 1973), pp. 200–2.

33. Mike Wallace interview with Clint Hill, Vital History Casettes, *Encyclopedia Americana*, CBS News Audio Resource Library, Dec. 1975, tape 2, side A.

34. "Ford Won't Capitulate to Would-Be Killers." New York *Times*, Sept. 23, 1975, p. 26.

8
THE PRIMACY
OF
POLITICS

*We are not a political agency. Our guys are bipartisan public
servants.*

**Secret Service Public Affairs
Director Jack Warner, 1980**

There is no Democratic or Republican way to pave a street. So goes
the hoary urban-reformist shibboleth. Nor, ideally, should there be any
partisan or political dimension to presidential protection. Like public
health or transportation safety, protecting the lives of political leaders is
a governmental function that *should* be divorced from politics.

The Secret Service has an apolitical image, something akin to that of
the British civil service (which prides itself on serving Conservative or
Labor governments with equal effectiveness). The Service will protect
any occupant of the White House with maximum efficiency, whether
Democrat or Republican. It has a merit personnel system complete with
entrance exams and civil service job protections. This appears to insulate
the organization from patronage politics.

The Director of Secret Service is, by tradition, a career Service person. Although the Director serves at the pleasure of the Secretary of the
Treasury, who is a presidential political appointee, there is no tradition of
sacking the old Secret Service head when a new President takes office.
Even the agents who head up the White House protective detail
sometimes continue in their post after a change of presidents—testimony
to the neutral, nonpolitical nature of the job. Agent Jerry Parr headed
the White House detail under Carter and continued for the first year of

the Reagan Presidency, though the two Presidents were as different in personality as in party label.

Thus the Service's protective mission would appear to help insulate it from the strong currents of politics that swirl about the American Presidency. The protective mission is, after all, a consensual one: neither the Congress, nor the press, nor political interest groups will argue against trying to keep presidents alive or against the necessity for a protective organization. This too is an apolitical influence. Bureaucratic entities whose very existence is constantly questioned (the Department of Education) or whose mission is constantly being redefined by the push and pull of competing political interests (The Environmental Protection Agency) often get so enmeshed in politics that it is difficult for them to perform effectively.

Still, in spite of all of its apolitical advantages, the operation of the United States Secret Service is highly political: political priorities, dynamics and realities shape the style and effectiveness of protection. The Service's internal processes and external relationships are, in a very real sense, dominated not by merit and consensus but by the vagaries of politics. There is *politics* in the best sense—the Presidency as the highest political office in the land, an elective office beholden to the governed for its powers; there is *politics* in the worst sense—patronage, corruption of organizational mission, partisan/political subversion of methods and procedures. We will now explore the myriad ways in which political influences shape the Service's performance.

To begin with, the Service may be a neutral, apolitical merit bureaucracy; but its most important protective work is done vis-à-vis our most fundamentally political institution—the presidency. There are no laws or accepted rules governing the interaction of the Secret Service and the president. Therefore, there is no buffer that might insulate the Service from the overwhelming sense of politics that dominates the institution. The American presidency—the only branch of our government headed by one person, the only nationally elected office (except for the vice-presidency), the linchpin of our public policy process, the quintessential symbol of our democracy. When an apolitical organization works with a highly political institution without benefit of formal rules of the game, chances are that the organization will become extensively politicized.

The Treasury Department report on the attempted assassination of President Reagan concluded: "The means exist to fully protect the president; unfortunately, he must decide whether in availing himself of these means he will reduce his ability to lead and his effectiveness in office."

Presidents are politicians—by definition, very successful ones. They did not get to the White House by isolating themselves but by effectively relating to the public; they cannot effectively exercise the presidential power by being reclusive. There is a public expectation in American democracy that politicians will get out and campaign to be president, and to remain president. As former McGovern campaign manager Frank Mankiewicz put it: "There's no way you can run for President on TV or riding around in a bubble-top limousine."[1]

The public seems to agree. When they come out to greet a presidential candidate and they are thwarted by Secret Service protection, they don't like it one bit. One reporter describes an incident in the 1980 presidential campaign, an incident that recurs frequently on the primary trial and in the general election:

> In Iowa, George Tanes, a *New York Times* photographer, said that many of those who went to see Governor Reagan told him the protection 'was overdone and they resented it.' Said one disaffected Republican, 'I shook George Bush's hand but when Reagan was here I couldn't get near him.' "[2]

Politics is a marketplace. If one candidate appears too distant or reclusive, one or more of his challengers will—by virtue of his personality or of advice from his campaign managers—present a contrasting image of accessibility and gregariousness. Whatever style of campaigning will get the most votes is the one that candidates will adopt. In American politics, especially presidential primaries, pressing the flesh works well.

If, once elected, a President tries to hole up in the Rose Garden, his opponents and the press will criticize his unwillingness to "stay in touch with the people," his "increasing isolation." Even if the public accepts presidential isolation because of some protracted crisis or because the president has an immense reserve of popularity, the political marketplace will make it advantageous for some challenger or successor to present a contrasting image of political extroversion. One reclusive president, even if popular and successful, would not be enough to permanently change expectations about accessibility, because such a phenomenon would require unique conditions which would be unlikely to recur.

Modern presidents have become reclusive usually when their power was already in decline (Richard Nixon) or when they became lame ducks (Lyndon Johnson). Presidents like Jimmy Carter who seem at the time to have a valid excuse for prolonged isolation (the Iranian crisis) may find, as Carter did, that the political costs of such isolation are only deferred, not avoided.

Sometimes American political culture rebels against its own expectations. Gallup Polls occasionally show that as much as forty-five percent of the public will agree that the "old-style" politics—shaking hands, kissing babies—is just too risky for our leaders. But the majority will not subscribe to that view even in the abstract. One suspects that many among the forty-five percent who do subscribe will feel quite differently at primary or caucus time, that they would be miffed if tight security denied *them* their handshake with, or their close-up look at, their favorite candidate.

After an assassination attempt, everyone talks differently. "This macho stuff has to stop," snapped a Ford aide, referring to direct public contact in the aftermath of Ford's second brush with death. Senate majority leader Mike Mansfield said, in the same context: "I do not think a president has a right to place his life in danger. It is not the man concerned, it is the office, in effect, which is of paramount importance."[3] But after the trauma of an assassination attempt subsides, American politics-as-usual gradually takes over.

Even after the election is won, the expectations of public contact continue. And Gerald Ford is not unique among presidents in having taken these exceptions as his own: "The American people ought to have an opportunity to see first hand or to listen more directly with their President . . . " As long as contact between candidates and voters, and between elected leaders and citizens, is veiwed as an important element in our civic culture, the editorials, gripes, and abstract rhetoric that it is archaic and dangerous will remain just that—rhetoric.

Nor is contact with masses of voters the only public accessibility demanded by our system of selecting a president. Candidates must campaign for money as well as for votes. Fund raising is essential, even if it is only as a prerequisite for federal matching funds. Once a candidate becomes president, there is still fund raising to be done—for other candidates, or to reduce the president's own campaign debts or those of his political party. Whether as candidate or president, such fund raising requires dinners, cocktail parties, handshakes, and contact with thousands of people who are courted primarily for their dollars instead of their votes.

Moreover, it is not that candidates and presidents find public contact distasteful or frightening but feel compelled to engage in it because they are helpless to alter the primal rituals of political culture. Some, like

Walter Mondale, have made it clear that they find handshaking, backslapping, and kissing babies to be a punishing chore from which they would welcome dispensation. But most politicians seem to thrive on it, if not love it. With Lyndon Johnson, "pressing the flesh" was nearly an obsession. As Hubert Humphrey explained, there are two reasons that politicians do it: first, it is good politics; "second, and most important, it makes you feel good. It makes you feel very good."[4]

Public contact is more than a norm of political culture. In the last two decades, American voters have helped to create a presidential nominating system whose formal rules of the game render physical, face-to-face contact a necessity. It was once possible to become the party nominee by meeting with only a few dozen people—the political bosses who tightly controlled large blocks of convention delegates via their state or city political machines. As late as 1968, when Humphrey and Nixon were nominated, there were only seventeen primaries, and the vast majority of convention delegates were selected without the direct input of the voters. In state after state over the last fifteen years, the voters were given a chance to express their preference for a nominee, to have *their* chance to see the candidates. There are now thirty-seven primaries, which select eighty percent of the delegates.

The timing and sequence of primaries is another factor that demands public contact. There is no single national primary or primary day. Instaed, there is a long, winding trail of primaries starting in New Hampshire. So candidates must court small chunks of the American electorate, piecemeal. This lends itself more to physical contact and less to campaigning via giant media blitzes than would a one-shot, nationwide primary.

Some small states take on disproportionate importance because their primaries or caucuses are scheduled early. New Hampshire is, of course, the quintessential example. Its tiny, pampered electorate would not warm up to any candidate whose approach was purely electronic. Granite State voters expect *real* candidates to trudge through the snow from factory to coffee klatch. Even a front-running nominee with tens of millions of supporters or an incumbent president seriously challenged for the nomination will comply, meeting people in person by the hundreds instead of projecting to them through a TV screen by the millions.

Personal contact is so crucial in our political system that politicians refuse to eschew it for protection. In fact, they will often avoid protection to render contact more politically effective. In the 1980 presidential campaign seven candidates who qualified for Secret Service protection refused it at various points during the process. John Connally — himself no stranger to political violence, having been wounded during the assassination of President Kennedy — was one who refused. George Bush refused protection in Iowa, preferring not "to look like a big shot," and wanting to "roll up his sleeves and talk with people."[5]

Five Republican candidates refused protection at one time or another, as did independent candidate John Anderson and Democratic candidate Jerry Brown. The California Governor asserted that "Agents get between me and the people." Said a Brown aide: "In Iowa we saw Senator Kennedy's protection blocking highways, getting in the way of the kind of one-to-one contact we prefer — we don't need that."[6]

The dominance of the political nature of the Presidency over protective concerns is by no means limited to campaigning. The president's foreign-policy role has its own political demands that often play havoc with procedures. President Johnson's 1964 trip to Mexico is a classic example. Mexican political culture has an even more rigid norm about the democratic symbolism of public contact than does America. It is an unwritten law in Mexican politics that presidents can never appear in public with any barrier between themselves and their people — no bulletproof shields, no bubble-top cars, nothing.

It was assumed in the wake of President Kennedy's assassination that his successor would never ride in an open car. But LBJ had two choices regarding his motorcade into Mexico City: he could ride in an open car with the president of Mexico, or he could ride in a closed car without his host. It was *not* an agonizing decision for Johnson, though it generated great anxiety among his staff and near apoplexy within the White House protective detail. In the interests of diplomatic harmony and political courtesy, Johnson rode in an open care alongside the Mexican president.[7]

Political considerations and political culture influence the protectors as well as the protectees. One Secret Service Director, H. Stuart Knight, described presidential protection as "a living nightmare in a democracy."[8] Because the Service operates in a constitutionally defined system, there are political-legal limits on the methods and tactics that can legitimately be employed in safeguarding a protectee. An American president who cares about his public image cannot afford to have a protective detail that creates the impression of a police state. If the protectors are perceived as bullies or if they manifest any hint of insensitivity to consititutional rights, they become a political liability to the president. The mere appearance of toughness or of a chip-on-the-shoulder attitude by

Secret Service agents can create political flak aimed at the White House as well as the Service.

When the Service overreacts or appears overzealous in handling a crowd or screening a press corps, it is roundly criticized by the public and the press, and, sometimes, by the White House itself. It is not as if the Service is unaware of its place in a democratic system. John Warner, the Service's Public Affairs Director, described the problem of establishing protective barriers: "We would like to move people back farther, but those we protect and the media would not allow it and it's not realistic in a democracy."[9]

After an assassination attempt, the press and the politicians usually beat the drums for tighter security, for tougher controls. However, if the Service implements stricter security when there has been no recent assassination attempt or when the trauma of the attempt has passed, the media, politicians, and the public will usually decry such procedures and will bring political pressure to bear upon the Service until they ease up once again.

This is especially true with regard to the Washington press corps. Whenever the Secret Service tightens its procedures for checking credentials and screening the White House press pool, reporters feel abused. Tremendous friction develops betweeen the press and the Service. Since, as former Nixon aide John Erlichman once described it, the proper "care and feeding" of the White House press corps is a key element in the success of any administration, the President cannot risk having a cranky press with which to deal. Before long, it might be the president who is having trouble with the press, especially when the press knows that the president has the political clout to pressure the Service into loosening up.

In one classic case in 1972, the Service tried to strengthen security for the president and for presidential candidates by implementing tighter security checks on the press, to prevent a would-be assassin from infiltrating the press corps and gaining close access to the protectee. The Service informed all reporters who wished to cover the Democratic national convention in Miami that they must submit their names and considerable personal data to the Service for a security check. Tougher procedures for the White House Press Corps were also instituted.

Reaction was swift and intense. A committee of reporters accused the Secret Service of usurping from the Democratic National Committee the press-accreditation process for the Democratic Convention. Several reporters who were denied convention press passes on security grounds took the Service to court. One reporters' organization called the stricter procedures "an unprecedented veto over who might cover the convention," and a "threat" to freedom of the press.[10]

The Service responded that it had no interest in any reporter's ideology or associations: It simply wanted to make sure that no individual who had previously made threats against any protectee would be afforded tha special access provided by a press pass. The constitutional issues involved in conflicts between freedom of the press and effective security were hotly debated. In the end, the reporters generated enough political pressure to force the Service to back down, to abandon its stricter standards. But the conflicts between freedom and protection remained unresolved.

The constitutional-democratic context affects the implementation of protective methods as well as their design. The Secret Service is supposed to implement effective security without trampling on constitutional rights. This is often difficult to adhere to, especially under conditions of stress. The Service pays a heavy political/legal price when it appears to go too far in its pursuit of protection.

After the back-to-back assassination attempts on President Ford, agents were especially keyed up when dealing with crowds. In Skokie, Illinois a young man stood in a crowd of spectators as President Ford approached. The man's hands were thrust deep into his pockets. An alert Secret Service agent ordered the young bystander to take his hands out of his pockets, as a security precaution. The man refused. A struggle ensued and the spectator was overpowered by police and agents. Afterward, it was determined that the man presented no threat to the president, and that was the end of it.

Other such incidents do not end so painlessly for the Service. In 1980 the organization made a public apology to Jane Margolis, a militant San Francisco union leader, and gave her $3,500 in an out-of-court settlement for her suit against the Service. Ms. Margolis had charged false arrest in a 1979 incident in which she was dragged from a union convention and held by agents for forty minutes. She had planned to berate President Carter for his alleged "anti-labor practices" when he arrived to address the convention. Instead, she was ejected from the hall, handcuffed, and detained.

The Service said that it was all a misunderstanding. The agent involved was merely assisting a Detroit police officer; the police officer "believed that the arrest was being made for violation of federal law." Ms. Margolis termed the Secret Service apology "a victory for free speech."[11]

When agents become fatigued or unusually tense, they are sometimes overzealous in their implementation of security precautions. The resulting political consequences depend a great deal upon the status of persons who are the targets of the alleged overzealousness. Immediately after the wounding of presidential candidate George Wallace, an incident of this type occurred at the hospital where the Alabama Governor was being treated. A New York *Times* reporter, Nan Robertson, was using a telephone in the hospital's outpatient clinic to phone in her story. A Secret Service agent ordered her to leave, but she ignored him and continued to dictate her story back to New York. According to the *Times*, Special Agent Joseph Herman then picked Ms. Robertson up, put an arm lock on her, and threw her out into the hall. The diminutive reporter was alleged to have "crashed on the floor and skidded down the corridor head first into the opposite wall."[12]

The press was outraged. The Washington Press Club filed a formal protest with the Service, as did the Reporters' Committee For a Free Press and the New York *Times*. Max Frankel, the *Times'* Washington bureau chief, sent a letter to Secret Service Director James Rowley calling the incident "an unprovoked and malicious assault."[13]

Constitutional and political factors also have a limiting influence on the Service's protective intelligence and preventive methods. Some agents complain that they are afraid to place suspects under surveillance for fear of being sued or being accused of using police-state tactics. The Service must operate within the boundaries of *an assumption of innocence until proven guilty* and *rights to privacy*.

According to Professor Charles R. Halpern, Director of the Institute for Public Representation at Georgetown University Law Center, being identified by the Secret Service as a "threat" to the president can have "devastating effects of the life of the person" thus identified. Halpern asserts that the Service can legally intervene to incarcerate a person identified as a potential threat only if the person is "arguably mentally ill."[14] The problem for the Service is that many individuals whom they perceive as a threat do not fall into this category.

The evidence that a person is mentally ill can be difficult to come by, even if the Service regards the person as such. Under existing privacy laws, the Service cannot talk to the psychiatrist of any suspect, no matter how "dangerous" the person is perceived to be, without the person's permission. Without psychiatric data, the Service is, in some cases, hard pressed to demonstrate mental illness, and it could be subject to lawsuits for false arrest if it takes action against an individual without sufficient proof.

Rights to privacy also prevent the Service from employing consulting psychiatrists to analyze its files of potentially dangerous persons in in order to discern patterns or to develop indices. Without such guideposts, the Service has great difficulty in making effective use of its data, but it is forbidden by law from opening its files to consultants without the permission of the forty thousand subjects involved.

While the mental health and psychiatric professions cooperate extensively with the Service in its efforts to identify dangerous persons and to predict violent behavior, the cooperation is informal. These professions seem committed to keeping a safe distance between themselves and the Service, lest they be — or appear to be — co-opted by the government. Some psychiatrists fear that extensive linkages with the government might create the appearance of an emerging totalitarian state in which, as in the Soviet Union, definitions of "insanity" often become political, and "treatment" is often a euphemism for the political incarceration of dissidents.

Part of the Service's problem is that the boundaries of constitutional rights are far from clear-cut — that's why the United States Supreme Court has more work than it can handle. Another part of the problem is that the Service receives conflicting inputs from our political system. The press, politicians, and public who — in the wake of a violent incident — demand tougher action, will then turn on the Service and charge it with running amok. One Secret Service agent observed bitterly: "The Congressmen who are howling now [for tougher security] are the first to complain when one of their constituent's rights have been violated."[15]

Even the Service's arsenal of protective devices is as much a product of American political culture as American technology. The National Commission on the Causes and Prevention of Violence concluded in 1970 that an impressive array of awesome, albeit James-Bondian, protective devices were available, but "they could not be utilized when the dangers inherent in them or the impression they would make upon onlookers were considered."[16]

Like all public agencies, the Secret Service also has its share of bureaucratic-organizational politics. Its relationships with Congress, with the Treasury Department in which it exists, and with federal and local agencies create a rich political tableau. The Service's interactions with other organizations are not well-defined by law or organizational charts or in the *Federal Register*. Organizational relationships are formed on the battleground of interagency politics. Sometimes, informal treaties between agencies produce cooperative, productive relationships; sometimes, there is bureaucratic guerrilla warfare.

As with nations, bureaucratic entities change their relationships over time. The FBI and the Secret Service now seem to have a good rapport — a cordial working relationship, a joint political interest in pressuring Congress for changes in Freedom of Information and privacy laws. But as we saw previously, in the 1930s the Bureau was the Service's fiercest bureaucratic enemy. Hoover's FBI actually muscled onto the Service's turf, performing duties of presidential protection for President Roosevelt.

The Secret Service is very dependent on local police for data concerning potential threats and for help in implementing protective procedures. Yet there are no laws or even accepted rules governing the Service's relationship to police departments with whom it must work intimately, though sporadically, in order to protect presidents, candidates, and visiting dignitaries. The Service's relationships to various police departments ranges on a continuum from friendly to hostile, depending upon a complex mix of interpersonal and bureaucratic dynamics.

The tension between the Service and New York City police seems deep-seated and long-standing. One twenty-year veteran of the NYPD chided the Service for "treating local police as if they were Keystone Cops."[17] When President Carter visited New York City in 1976, coordination of protective efforts between police and Secret Service was less than smooth. The Service told the police that it was Service policy to have agents armed with rifles positioned on selected rooftops. Police Commissioner Michael Codd had an icy response: "If anybody does that he'll be arrested. That's basically a job for us." The Service deferred to New York's Finest. In many other cities where organizational rapport was in better repair, the Service would have been allowed to deploy its counter-sniper teams.

Another political context in which the Service is heavily involved is the politics of information. Every government agency with an intelligence or data-gathering mission (IRS, FBI, CIA, military intelligence, National Security Agency, and Secret Service) engages in such politics — seeking to expand its own data nets, often at the expense of rival agencies, and trading information with friendly agencies. The American intelligence community is noted for its rich history of interagency squabbling and duplicity, and lack of coordination.[18]

The Service has lobbied vigorously, through the press and on Capitol Hill, to be allowed to broaden its data base and to have fewer limitations on the use of its data. It has complained that restrictions issued by the Carter Justice Department in 1979 severely hampered its ability to monitor persons and groups who might pose a threat to protectees. "There's so much we don't know about suspicious individual organizations," lamented then Secret Service Director H. Stuart Knight.

In the late 1970s the Service joined with the CIA and FBI in lobbying for Congressional relief from the Freedom of Information and privacy laws. Director Knight told Congress that in 1976 alone, there had been a fifty percent decrease in the quantity of information that the Service received from local police and federal agencies, and that the quality of data had declined an estimated twenty to twenty-five percent.

The Service, like other data-gathering agencies, argues that the Freedom of Information Act, which provides public access to government documents under certain specified conditions, has destroyed the confidence of informants regarding anonymity; and that the Privacy Act makes authorities too timid about forwarding data on individuals, for fear of being sued. Neither the Secret Service, nor any other federal agency, has been able to offer direct evidence of this alleged cause-and-effect. The Service's file of potentially dangerous persons has allegedly shrunk in recent years. As we saw in Chapter Six, however, the Secret Service's biggest problem is not the amount of data available but an inability to develop indices or handles for analyzing whatever data it has.

One of the problems noted by both the Warren Commission in 1964 and Treasury Department report on the attempted assassination of President Reagan in 1981 was that there are no set policies governing what information other agencies should provide to the Secret Service. In the arena of bureaucratic politics, the trading of information results from a bargaining process and is by no means automatic because of an agency's legally defined mission or needs. The amount and kind of data that the Service exchanges with other agencies is shaped not only by interagency politics but by the larger political climate as well.

The Service's exchanges with the FBI in the late 1960s seemed to relate more to the Bureau's surveillance campaign against antiwar groups than to the Service's protective mission. Some of the exchanges were controversial and were of the type later outlawed by the Privacy Act of 1974. The FBI provided the Service with data from its COINTELPRO project — a massive, if not indiscriminate, surveillance of hundreds of dissident groups and thousands of persons. In return, the Service gave the Bureau its data on potentially threatening persons.[19] The FBI data contained very little protective intelligence: the vast majority of groups and persons targeted in COINTELPRO were in no way violent or threatening. The vast majority of persons in Secret Service files were not subversive.

The exchange seemed to satisfy each organization's lust for data more than it aided the performance of their missions.

In the early 1960s, however, the Secret Service changed its mission in a manner that made the FBI data more useful. The Johnson White House pressured the Service into protecting the president from "embarrassment" as well as from harm. The Secret Service began to use the FBI data on political dissidents in its advance work for presidential travel and appearances. The Service tried to avoid peaceful demonstrations as well as threats to security. This highly political mission represented a major change in the Service's duties and was of dubious legitimacy.[20]

In the early 1970s the paranoias of the Nixon White House concerning political enemies and Communist subversives — two groups who often appeared to the Nixon administration as one — combined with the intelligence agencies' voracious appetite for domestic surveillance to produce an orgy of domestic spying. The Secret Service again joined in and became involved in some highly political, constitutionally questionable exchanges of data.

The Service became one of the users of the National Security Agency's project MINARET, which involved intercepting and opening the mail of thousands of American citizens and hundreds of organizations — in clear violation of statutes forbidding mail opening. Although the FBI and CIA were the main users, the Service got in on the act, requesting the National Security Agency to intercept the mail of groups and individuals who were on the Service's *watch list.*

This was illegal, but it was at least related to the protective mission. The same cannot be said of the Service's other use of MINARET, which seemed more related to protection from embarrassment than threat. As Frank Donner describes in his detailed chronicle of domestic spying, *The Age of Surveillance:*

> The functional responsibilities of the requestors [for MINARET data] were largely ingored, notably in the case of the Secret Service which submitted the names of individuals and organizations active in anti-war and civil rights movements not considered a direct threat to protectees on the theory that they might participate in demonstrations against U.S. policy that would endanger the physical well-being of government officials.[21]

In exchange for the mail-intercept data, the Secret Service traded its *watch list,* providing the National Security Agency (NSA) with all of its data on groups and persons potentially threatening to protectees. The fact that NSA had no protective mission was ignored by the Service; the fact that the Service had no legitimate political-surveillance mission was ignored by NSA.

Under pressure from the Johnson and Nixon administrations, the Service had shifted its mission beyond protection. Its forays into gathering data on political dissidents, running political interference for beleaguered presidents by "protecting" against peaceful demonstrators as well as physical threats, and trading its *threat* files to any agency who had something to give in return were clearly beyond the Service's legitimate protective mission. It was not entirely caused by White House pressures: the lure of trading data with the illustrious agencies of the American intelligence community — CIA, FBI, NSA — was probably irresistable for an organization that had always aspired to be a full-fledged intelligence agency but had not succeeded since World War I.

The extensive use of the Service in the Johnson and Nixon years as an advance political detail as well as a protective detail is only one manifestation of a larger problem — the politicization of the Service's mission and operation by presidents and their staffs. *Secrecy* is a mixed blessing for the effectiveness of any organization whose turf has heavy doses of it. On the one hand, it provides a certain advantage in dealing with Congressional oversight committees, with the public, and with the press: "The Secret Service cannot discuss its protective methods and procedures." To some degree, this helps to insulate the organization from criticism and second-guessing. On the other hand, the *Secret* Service cannot or will not blow the whistle when presidents misuse it for political or personal purposes.

If a president misuses the National Park Service, a ranger or Park Service administrator can leak to the *Washington Post* or complain to a Congressional Committee, with only the usual political/career risks inherent in whistle blowing to worry about. In contrast, the Service — much like the CIA — lives by a code of secrecy under which any disclosure of *who does what, when, and how* is regarded as increasing the risk that protectees will be harmed. When presidents misuse the Service, this too falls behind the cloak of secrecy, partly because the Service cannot tell about what is wrong without disclosing what is right (how things normally operate).

Equally important is the fact that the Service cannot work with a president in a give-and-take situation with no formal rules if it becomes his critic or if he views it as a political enemy. A president could retaliate by freezing the Service out, by not cooperating and/or using other federal employees to provide protection (as FDR did with the FBI). Individual agents who refuse to do a president's bidding or who are critical of his orders may find themselves transferred out of the White House protective detail, even if they are right and the president or his staff are technically wrong. Because the Service is very secretive and very available, a great temptation exists for the White House to misuse it.

One misuse is to have the Secret Service perform political chores unrelated to its protective mission. President Nixon asked the Service to tap his brother Donald's phone. They did. Donald Nixon was no threat to the president in the protective sense, but he was in the political sense.

In the latter days of the Johnson presidency when he was hounded by anti-Vietnam War demonstrators at every public appearance, the Service was pressed into political duty to save LBJ from embarrassment. Prior to a Johnson speech at the University of Rhode Island, Secret Service intelligence learned that a professor planned to walk off of the platform in the middle of the speech in protest against the war. The professor's protest was aborted when, as he strode off the stage, two uniformed nurses rushed up and escorted him, thereby creating the impression that it was illness rather than political opposition that caused the sudden departure.[22]

Richard Nixon used agents to help him stage political dramas. During the 1970 Congressional elections when he was stumping for candidates who backed his Vietnam policy, he instructed the Service to allow a few hecklers to remain in the crowd to provide a foil for his speeches. In addition to suspending judgment about whether the hecklers presented a threat to the president and should have been removed, the Service had the complex and distracting political chore of making sure that there was just enough heckling to provide drama and counterpoint but not enough to disrupt the speech.

Nixon also used the Service to prevent protest. At White House urging, the Service began disbursing protesters or removing them from proximity to Nixon regardless of whether there was any identifiable threat to the President. The tactic resulted in an injunction issued by Federal District Court Judge James B. McMillan against Secret Service agents, preventing them from depriving protesters of their political rights. The 1973 injunction required that a threat to the president's personal safety be identified before demonstrations could be disbanded.[23]

The press complains periodically that presidents use agents to keep reporters at a distance and to avoid probing questions. The Washington press corps alleged that at times during the Nixon presidency, agents would physically intervene to squelch a reporter's question during Nixon's press encounters. Sometimes the Service is tougher with the press than with the general public, fueling press suspicions that the Service is running political interference for the president. This happens with candidates too. In New Hampshire in 1980, one reporter was turned away by an agent guarding Reagan. Though the reporter had no fewer than six security badges, one required badge was missing. The reporter simply stashed all of his badges and walked into the event as an ordinary citizen.

In addition to politicizing the Secret Service in ways that detract from its protective mission, the president and his family tend to *personalize* the Service—to require agents to do personal chores unrelated to security. This may seem like a minor corruption of the Service's mission compared with using it to perform political chores, some of which are of dubious legality. But the negative impact upon the effectiveness of protection is equally serious, perhaps more so. No agent can adequately guard the First Lady when his arms are full of hat boxes; no agent can guard the president while toting a beer cooler.

But the agents are always there, standing around. The temptation to use them as errand-boys is usually irresistable. And agents are not in a position to complain. As one put it: "You do what the man wants." Some presidents want more than others. As Governor of Georgia, Jimmy Carter had been accustomed to being surrounded by a bevy of state troopers to whom he would delegate menial chores. At first, he viewed the Service in much the same way—as bag carriers.[24] The "favors" requested of agents by presidents and first families run the gamut from baby sitting to carrying packages, to providing a fourth for bridge. All such activities detract from an agent's ability to provide protection.

One of the most personal uses of the Service by presidents, and one of the most awkward from agents, is covering presidential trysts. If a president should entertain or visit a female friend, it is impossible for him to do so without Secret Service complicity—not often, anyway. In the alleged liaisons of various presidents from Harding to Kennedy, the Service's stealth and secrecy may well have been necessary for "protection" of a different kind—protection of the president's political career, of his image with friends and family, of the safety and anonymity of his female companions.

Presidential residences present another temptation for misuse of the Secret Service—a financial temptation. The Service has the legal authority to request improvements on a president's private home if it believes that such improvements will reduce threats to safety or enhance security. Before 1973, the Service had to request the necessary funds from the General Accounting Office; in 1973 the Service was given its own fund for security improvements, though it still has to answer to Congressional oversight committees about how it spends the money.

Congress may be increasingly cost conscious, but presidential-protection expenses are as difficult for it to deal with as those related to national defense, and for similar reasons. Congress wants the best possible protection for presidents, and it usually defers to the Service's expert judgment in such matters about whether a new communications center at Reagan's ranch is an absolute necessity.

If Congress becomes miserly without fully understanding the security consequences of its refusal to appropriate funds, a president could be placed in increased jeopardy. That is a risk Congress would rather not take. Unless the expenditure seems blatantly unrelated to security, Congress is likely to comply—especially if both the Service and the White House agree on what needs to be done (as they usually do). As Tex Gunnels, a staff member for the House Appropriations Subcommittee which oversees Service expenditures, remarked: "We can't afford to have a president killed. My God, the whole country goes into shock.[25]

The apex of controversy regarding security improvements on presidential homes came during the Nixon administration. A total of about ten million dollars in "security" improvements was spent on three Nixon residences—San Clemente, California; Key Biscayne, Florida; Grand Cay, the Bahamas; and also at the residence of Nixon's daughter. The range of improvements included: communications facilities, guards, offices, Coast Guard patrols, boats, fences, heaters, bulletproof windows, and landscaping. Private security consultant N.C. Livingstone also asserted in an article written with James P. Kelly that Vice-President Spiro Agnew "disguised hundreds of thousands of dollars in non-security improvements to his home under the cachet of security."[26]

The press and Congress questioned whether Nixon's improvements were legitimately related to security—especially the landscaping. It was also alleged that the improvements benefited Nixon friends Aplanalp and Rebozo. The White House responded that the Rebozo house in question was rented by Julie Nixon Eisenhower and her husband David, thus justifying the expenditure; and that the President's frequent visits to Aplanalp's island home at Grand Cay necessitated improvements there. The White House also pointed out that it was the Secret Service that ordered all of the work to be done. This was technically true, but the

Service remained secretive about whether the impetus for the renovations came from the Service or from the White House. And, of course, the Service would not publicly criticize the White House.

Criticism mounted when it was discovered that the Service was paying a California firm $12,000 a year for special care of the grounds on Nixon's San Clemente home, in order to "keep the landscape from interfering with security."[27] In all, the government spent $500,000 more on improvements for the San Clemente and Key Biscayne properties than Nixon had originally paid for them, prompting Senator Howard Baker to quip that, "Someone might decide to run for president so the Secret Service could make improvements on his home."[28]

The Secret Service's view of the security-improvements fund is that the Service is required by law to immediately correct any situation that threatens presidential security, and that there is no choice but to pay for "justifiable security improvements." Thus, in the Service's view, it has little discretion. The key word is *justifiable*. When seventy thousand dollars is spent for a communications command post at the Ford residence in Alexandria, Virginia, there is no problem. But what happens if, like Nixon, a president decides that less than perfect landscaping constitutes a threat to his security? The Service can acquiesce and authorize the expenditure or it can buck the president and risk a public, and private, feud with the White House.

The inhibiting factor that has apparently prevented a repetition of the spectacular abuses of the Nixon administration is not the Service's tougher stand, for there is no evidence of that, but the potential political costs for a president who is discovered to be refurbishing his home at taxpayers' expense. Still, the potential for abuse exists as long as the Service feels compelled by law to spend money for anything related to security and compelled by its political situation to accept White House definitions of what is *justifiable* and to refrain from whistle-blowing at all costs.

In 1981 President Reagan's Pacific Palisades home was put up for sale at 1.9 million dollars. Although the first family had not been seen there in eight months, the Secret Service provided round-the-clock guards for the expensive piece of real estate.[29] Protecting presidential investments by baby-sitting with property until it is sold is not within the Service's job description. The Secret Service did not complain—not publicly, anyway.

The dynamics of presidential politics pervade every facet of the Service's existence down to the nuts and bolts of protective methods and procedures. In classically understated bureaucrateze, the 1981 Treasury report on the attempted assassination of President Reagan asserts:

The political mission of the White House staff conflicts at times with the security mission of the Secret Service; security measures taken to protect the president are often determined by give-and-take between the two groups.[30]

What the report didn't say is that, typically, the White House staff takes much more than it gives and usually gets its way. Former agent Charles M. Vance told a Senate committee:

I have personally seen many, many incidents during which the Secret Service strongly objected to a movement or situation involving a president or vice-president and stated that agents could in no way provide adequate security under the circumstances and yet were overruled ... by White House staff members who wanted more "press exposure" or "public impact" or "a good camera angle."[31]

Whenever we get a close-up look at the operation of the White House protective detail, the primacy of politics can be seen clearly. In most administrations the tail wags the dog, from a security point of view: the White House staff very often tells the Service what to do. Sometimes, the conflicts between the political mission of the White House staff and the protective mission of the Secret Service generate an intense animosity. One agent assigned to the White House detail confided to an associate his frustration with Nixon's top aides: "You know what we say to each other now, don't you?" asked the agent. "We say that 'come the revolution be sure and save two bullets—one for Haldeman and one for Erlichman.' "[32]

One problem for effective protection is that the White House staff's political goals cause Secret Service's judgments to be overruled or its procedures to be set aside. Another problem is that the interference of the White House staff and the infighting between staff and agents can erode the Service's morale and thus impair the effectiveness of what which the Service *is* allowed to do. The danger is that the agents on the White House detail may get retooled—socialized to White House notions of protective procedure to the displacement of Service training and professionalism.

For example, agents are trained to stay in close proximity to the protectee at all times and to do so in tight formation. Nixon White House staffer Bruce Wheliham recalls that in order to give the press a clear view of Mr. Nixon interacting with friendly crowds: "I'll sometimes go in with a hook and yank out agents who were too close."[33] One cannot help but wonder whether after a few months of such treatment agents weren't distracted from the intense concentration demanded by crowd control—second-guessing themselves about whether they were so close to the president that they would suffer the embarrassment of being hooked.

These problems are compounded by the fact that agents serving on the White House detail are in the same position that House Speaker Sam Rayburn described for junior members of Congress: they *have to go along to get along*. Despite their civil service status and protections, agents on the White House detail who feud with the White House staff or who displease the president or the first family will probably find themselves transferred to other duty. Civil service may protect their job with the Secret Service but not their assignment to the presidential detail.

Herein lies a fundamental weakness in the protective system. It is one thing for the protectee to overrule or ignore protective procedures; it is another thing when the protectee has the power to remove protectors who displease him. The White House detail is selected on the basis of merit, and when agents depart that detail they will operate in a merit bureaucracy. But while they serve on the White House detail, they serve—at least to some degree—at the pleasure of the president. Much of the time this is not a problem: agents do the best job they can and their assignments are left to Service administrators. Sometimes, however, personalist influences become a formidable hindrance to effective protection.

When a president or a first lady take a liking to an agent, they sometimes request that the agent go along on this or that trip. Jacqueline Kennedy felt comfortable in the presence of agent Clint Hill; presidents discover that certain agents are fun to chat with. Such rapport, as natural as it is, can create problems if it interferes with the normal rotation of assignments and shifts within the seventy-agent White House detail.

What happens if an agent and a protectee develop a friendly relationship? One possible outcome is that the agent may use his interpersonal leverage to persuade the protectee to accept more security, to follow protective procedures. An equally likely outcome is that the leverage works the other way. That is, that the rapport makes it more difficult for an agent to avoid running errands or to sternly suggest that proper procedures be followed.

At the other end of the interpersonal continuum, problems exist too. Agents who are conspicuously stern and humorless, who give the president the creeps by acting like a robot or a jailer, will have little influence in persuading the president to do anything he doesn't want to do. As professionally competent and efficient as such an agent might be, it will do little good for the quality of protection if the agent is always "getting the hook" because the White House media advisor doesn't like his somber image, or if the agent becomes such an unsettling presence for the president that he is transferred off of the White House detail. It is truly a Catch-22 existence for agents working with the president.

The degree to which the president, First Family, or White House staff meddle in agent assignments varies with administrations and with the situation. The Service steadfastly denies that the problem exists, claiming that assignments are strictly based on merit and transfers from the White House detail to other kinds of work are dictated solely by established policies of personnel rotation.

A classic illustration of White House power over the presidential detail occurred in 1973. The head of Nixon's detail, Robert H. Taylor, and his second-in-command, William L. Duncan, were transferred out of presidential protection after four years of service. Secret Service Director James M. Rowley claimed that the reassignments were in no way political but were simply in keeping with the Service's standard policy for rotating supervisory personnel.[34] The record indicates differently.

Sources close to both the Service and the White House said that Taylor's departure was triggered by a feud with H.R. Haldeman concerning protection versus politics.[35] In one incident in Providence, Rhode Island, Haldeman was said to have ordered that a protective barrier be removed so that Nixon could get closer to the crowd. Taylor refused, on security grounds. At the inaugural parade, Nixon's White House staff was irritated because agents trotted alongside the presidential limousine, interposing themselves between Nixon and the crowds that lined Pennsylvania Avenue. After these incidents, Haldeman allegedly sought to have Taylor transferred out of the White House detail. White House sources told the press that Secret Service Director Rowley had acquiesced to Haldeman's demand.

Imagine the impact that this kind of "transfer" must have on the morale and effectiveness of the White House detail, regardless of the actual cause of the transfer. Agents were said to have been deeply demoralized and worried about the sanctions that might ensue from just doing their job.

The White House detail is a kind of political niche within a larger merit bureaucracy. As such, it is shaped by personalism, politics, and doses of patronage. Presidential protection is most effective when it is allowed to function professionally and autonomously, but it functions this way only to the extent that the president and his staff will adopt a *laissez-faire* attitude. Typically, political pressures and priorities compel the politicoes to intervene into the Secret Service's professional domain, to the detriment of protection. Behind a cloak of secrecy and with no rules of the game to help preserve the integrity of its mission, the Service's White House operation succumbs to the American presidency's most potent dynamic—politics.

It is only in an ideal world that "politics and protection don't mix." Politics and *effective* protection do not mix—at least, not well. In our present system of presidential protection, politics mixes with virtually every aspect of protection. And politics often dominates.

NOTES

1. *Newsweek*, May 29, 1972. p. 19.

2. Robert Blair Kaiser, "Presidential Candidates Disagree On Value of Secret Service Watch," New York *Times*, Feb. 10, 1980, p. 1.

3. *Newsweek*, Oct., 6, 1975, p. 19.

4. *Ibid.*

5. Kaiser, "Presidential Candidates Disagree."

6. *Ibid.*

7. Jack Valenti, *A Very Human President* (New York: W. W. Norton, Co., 1975), pp. 119–20.

8. *Time*, Oct. 6, 1975, p. 12.

9. "Did the Secret Service Drop Its Guard?" *U.S. News & World Report*, April 13, 1981, pp. 27–29.

10. Fred P. Graham, "Tighter Security Rules Stir Friction in Capitol," New York *Times*, June 26, 1972, p. 24.

11. "Secret Service Settles Suit for False Arrest," New York *Times*, June 26, 1980, p. B7.

12. Graham, "Tighter Security Rules."

13. *Ibid.*

14. "Could the Secret Service Predict Violent Behavior?" National Academy of Sciences *News Report*, January, 1982, pp. 14–19, at p. 16.

15. *Newsweek*, Oct. 6, 1975, p. 19.

16. James B. Kirkham *et al.* (eds.) *Assassinations and Political Violence* (New York: Bantam, 1970), p. 120.

17. Kaiser, "Presidential Candidates Disagree."

18. See William R. Corson *The Armies of Ignorance: The Rise of the American Intelligence Empire* (New York: Dial Press, 1977); Frank J. Donner, *The Age of Surveillance* (New York: Vintage Books, 1981).

19. Morton Halperin et al., *The Lawless State: The Crimes of U.S. Intelligence Agencies* (New York: Penguin, 1976), pp. 130, 166.

20. *Ibid.*, p. 130.

21. Donner, *The Age of Surveillance*, p. 227. See also pp. 283–85, 275–77.

22. Frank Cormier, *LBJ: The Way He Was* (Garden City, N.Y.: Doubleday, 1977), pp. 71–73.

23. "Presidential Bar of Dissent Eased," New York *Times*, August 1, 1973, p. 23.

24. N. C. Livingstone, "From JFK to Reagan: What the Secret Service Thinks of the Presidents They Protect," *Washingtonian*, September, 1981, pp. 170–71.

25. Loretta Tofani, "A Totally Up Front White House," Boston *Globe*, April 8, 1982, p. 10.

26. N.C. Livingstone and James Kelly, "Could the President Survive a Real-Life James Bond Movie?" *Washingtonian*, September, 1981, p. 177.

27. New York *Times*, July 26, 1974, p. 29; funding shifts to Secret Service: New York *Times*, Nov. 3, 1974, p. 23.

28. New York *Times*, July 3, 1974, p. 23.

29. Lloyd Shearer, "Intelligence Report," *Parade Magazine*, August 9, 1981.

30. U.S. Treasury Dept., "Management Review on the Performance of the U.S. Department of the Treasury in Connection with the March 30, 1981 Assassination Attempt on President Ronald Reagan," Wash., D.C.: U.S. Govt., pp. 49–50.

31. "Danger For Presidents Seen in Political Moves," New York *Times*, Sept. 23, 1981, p. 17.

32. Dan Rather and Paul Gates, *The Palace Guard* (New York: Harper & Row, 1974), p. 23.

33. "Can the Risk Be Cut?" *Newsweek*, April 13, 1981, p. 51.

34. "Secret Service Aide Explains Transfer," New York *Times*, February 18, 1973, p. 5.

35. The account of the Taylor incident is taken from: *Ibid.*; Philip Shabecoff, "Chief of Nixon's Guard is Removed," New York *Times*, February 14, 1973, p. 1, p. 12; Shabecoff, "The Flap Over Guarding Nixon," same edition, Sect. IV, p. 3.

9

LOSING LANCER*:
THE SECRET SERVICE'S
WORST CRISIS

Jim Rowley [Secret Service Director] is most efficient. He has never lost a president.

John F. Kennedy

The assassination of John F. Kennedy was not only a national trauma but an organizational one as well. The United States Secret Service had failed at its most important assignment—to protect the life of the president. Prior to November 22, 1963, the Secret Service had never lost a president. It did not have legal responsibility for presidential protection when President McKinley was killed in 1901, the last president to be assassinated prior to JFK.

In the aftermath of the Kennedy assassination, the Treasury Department lobbied hard to restrict access to post-assassination analyses of Secret Service methods, fearing that public exposure of protective procedures would increase the risk of future assassinations. Treasury Department lawyers sought to preclude the Warren Commission's report and recommendations from dealing with Secret Service methods, but the Commission responded that it was "unwilling to agree in advance to any limitation upon its prerogative of suggesting any change in arrangements for presidential protection which it may consider desirable."[1] However, Commission lawyers did promise the Treasury Department to respect Secret Service inputs about restricting public access to information

---

* Secret Service code name for President Kennedy.

dealing with protective methods. The Warren Commission's desire to have its records sealed for a generation failed; and with the passage of the Freedom of Information Act in 1966, more and more documents were released.

In 1982 the author initiated a Freedom of Information Act request with the Secret Service for additional documents relating to the JFK assassination, documents that might not be contained in Warren Commission files that are available to researchers at the National Archives in Washington, D.C. (Commission file number 22, "Records Relating to the Protection of the President"). The Secret Service responded that in 1979 it had turned over to the National Archives all remaining documents pertaining to the Kennedy assassination. I then queried Mr. Marion Johnson, the chief archivist in charge of Warren Commission records, about whether the 1979 material was contained in the Commission files which I had already reviewed. It was not. Because of a shortage of staff, the six boxes of "new" material remained unprocessed: the documents had not been catalogued and security cleared. Within two weeks of my query, the additional material had been processed. I went to Washington to review it and found additional data relating to the Service's duties and performance.

The Secret Service documents in Warren Commission files provide a clear picture of the organization's protective efforts for the president's trip to Dallas. While the record indicates that the Service's performance was constrained by the political priorities of the president and the White House staff and by the mistakes made by local law-enforcement units, it also reveals significant failures of performance—failures for which the Secret Service itself was responsible.

President Kennedy's trip to Texas was purely political in purpose. The state's Democratic party was bitterly divided. The President's policies, on a whole range of issues from Cuba to civil rights to the oil depletion allowance, were very unpopular in Texas. Kennedy had narrowly won the state's sizable chunk of electoral votes in 1960, but even with LBJ on the ticket it had been close. Now there was a real chance that Texas might vote Republican in 1964. The two-day trip, designed for political repair, had the president in San Antonio on November 21, in Fort Worth on the morning of the twenty-second, then flying to Dallas for a lunch-hour motorcade and a luncheon at the Trade Mart with Dallas business and civic elites.

There was concern about president's safety. Only the week before Kennedy's visit, United Nations Ambassador Adlai Stevenson had come to Dallas to speak to the local United Nations Association. He was greeted by demonstrators who cursed him, spat upon him, and shoved to get at him. One picket sign struck the ambassador on the head.[2] It is little wonder that Stevenson called Kennedy advisor Arthur Schlesinger, Jr. and urged that the president not go to Dallas. Democratic Senator J. William Fulbright warned the president: "Dallas is a very dangerous place. I wouldn't go there. Don't you go."[3]

Kennedy was too fatalistic to worry about protection. And as far as the Secret Service was concerned, this was just another trip, not one uniquely fraught with danger. With the minor exception of trying to identify the demonstrators who had bothered Stevenson, the Secret Service simply followed its standard protective routine, which it perceived as providing adequate protection. Moreover, the man they were protecting was not amenable to being restricted by tight security, except under the circumstance of a well-defined threat. During a previous motorcade, Kennedy had made an exception and allowed his limousine to be flanked by police motorcycles, because of a specific threat to his safety discovered in advance by the Service. The House Select Committee on Assassinations generally described Kennedy as "almost recklessly disregarding of Secret Service protection," a fact that the Service has not hesitated to invoke, on numerous occasions over the years, as a contributing factor to the tragedy.[4]

Kennedy used the motorcade as a primary political tool, as he had during the 1960 presidential campaign. According to White House aide Kenny O'Donnell, motorcades were used to provide "extended public exposure."[5] Having agents on the running boards or having the president ride under the transparent bubble top reduced that exposure and impinged upon political effectiveness. In Dallas the violent thunderstorms that drenched the city in the early morning hours had given way to a bright, cloudless sky by the time *Air Force One* landed at Love Field. The bubble top, which was not even bulletproof, would not be necessary in Dallas.

Secret Service documents manifest, again and again, the dominance of politics over protection in planning for the trip. The president's protectors were not informed about the trip until political planning and publicity were well underway. The idea of a presidential visit to Texas had been discussed by President Kennedy, Vice-President Johnson, and Texas Governor John Connally on June 5, 1963 in a Texas hotel room. On September 13, the trip was confirmed by the White House and the Dallas papers announced it as forthcoming, although the dates and itinerary were not settled. On October 4 John Connally visited the White House to work out the basic agenda — a motorcade and a luncheon. On November 1, Connally held a press conference in Dallas and announced the visit. It was not until three days later, on November 4, that the Secret Service was first informed by the White House staff that the president would be going to Dallas. This occured after the basics of the trip had been planned and after the event had been publicized in Dallas.[6]

On November 4 the head of the Secret Service's Dallas field office, Agent Forrest Sorrells, was directed by the head of the White House protective detail, Gerald A. Behn, to check out possible luncheon sites. The two possibilities were the Trade Mart and the Womens Building. The Secret Service preferred the Womens Building because it had fewer entrances and seemed better suited to security; some of the White House staff preferred it because it could seat 4,000 people (far more than the Trade Mart).[7] Yet all indications are that the selection of the Trade Mart was a foregone conclusion, only the Secret Service did not know it.

Governor Connally was given primary responsibility for arranging the political agenda. The purpose of the luncheon, which was planned on October 4 when Connally visited the White House, was to repair the president's image within the Dallas business elite. The brand new, richly appointed Trade Mart was the symbol of the city's burgeoning economy. As far as Dallasites were concerned, the Trade Mart was the only location that made sense, given the political purpose of the luncheon.[8]

In contrast, the Womens Building had low ceilings with beams that hung even lower, giving it a claustrophobic ambience. It also had "exposed conduits." Most importantly, it did not have adequate food-handling facilities for a catered luncheon.[9] When John Connally heard that the luncheon might not be held at the Trade Mart, he threatened to boycott the entire trip.[10] As the host politican whose political image was on the line, Connally was not about to be associated with a politically disastrous luncheon held at an inferior facility. Thus the Secret Service had been sent on a fool's errand when told to look for a luncheon site(s). Politically, there could be but one site — the Trade Mart.

Like the rest of the trip, the selection of a motorcade route was, in great measure, politically determined. As White House aide Kenny O'Donnell described it, the Secret Service was so generally attuned to White House political priorities that "it would be automatic" for the Service to arrange a route which, in the time allotted by the president, would take him "through an area which exposes him to the greatest number of people."[11] On November 14, Agents Sorrells (from the Dallas field office) and Winston G. Lawson (from the White House detail) were riding over the proposed routes when they were informed by a member of the Democratic National Committee that the luncheon would definitely be held at the Trade Mart. Given the Love Field Landing and a downtown motorcade, the Trade Mart luncheon site dictated most of the motorcade route, including passing through Dealy Plaza and in front of the Texas School Book Depository.[12] The final route was thus selected November 14.

Two days later, the Dallas *Times Herald* announced the general route, stating that it "apparently will loop through the downtown area probably on Main Street en route from Dallas' Love Field."[13] The precise route was published by Dallas newspapers on November 19, three days before the president's visit.[14]

There was no attempt to exercise any secrecy regarding the President's itinerary or the motorcade route. The closest thing to secrecy seems to have been the way in which the politically determined plans concerning the trip were not made known to the Secret Service until the last minute. Publicity was, if fact, an absolute necessity if the motorcade was to be a political success. If Dallasites did not turn out in large numbers and line the motorcade route, the media might label the president's trip a failure. A well-advertised route was essential if people were to make plans to see the president on their Friday afternoon lunch hour.

As was usual for the Secret Service, it met with local law-enforcement authorities in advance of the trip in order to obtain their help in implementing protection. On November 18 Agents Lawson and Sorrells and two representatives of the Dallas Police Department drove over the motorcade route, taking notes on crowd control, traffic patterns, the location of intersections, overpasses, and railroad crossings.[15] They discussed how to seal off the motorcade route from other traffic so that there would be no tie-ups. Police were to be assigned to each of the overpasses along the route to keep spectators off of them and thereby protect the president's open limousine from being hit by any falling objects. Police would also be stationed at all railroad crossings and would control the switching mechanisms.

Secret Service agents and police checked out the Trade Mart and Love Field, where the president would land. At the Trade Mart, it decided that rope barriers, guarded by police, would be set up to keep the crowd at a safe distance. A police officer would be assigned to guard the only stairway leading to the Trade Mart roof to prevent anyone from having access to the rooftop while the president was entering or leaving; a Trade Mart security guard would be assigned to guard the roof of the building across the street. Trade Mart security guards would guard the facility overnight and would be joined by Secret Service agents the morning of the luncheon. No freight deliveries would be allowed while the President was there. All entrances except the main one would be closed, and only persons with appropriate credentials would be allowed to enter.

Designing security arrangements for the Trade Mart luncheon was the most complex of the advance protective-tasks. Lists of employees who worked for the Trade Mart and for the catering firm that would service lunch were obtained and cross-checked against the Service's protective-research files in Washington. No problem was discovered.

Various identification badges, a different one for each role, were manufactured and issued — a badge denoting local press, one for White House press, others for the airport reception committee, waiters, plainclothes police. Dallas police were shown, and given samples of, the color-coded lapel pins worn by Secret Service, White House staff, and White House communications personnel. At Love Field arrangements were made for landing and taxiing routes for *Air Force One*. Air Force personnel were called upon to secure the routes.

This meticulous advance work did not include checking the tall building along the motorcade route, either in advance (by checking lists of employees against Secret Service files) or at the time of the motorcade (by physically checking them just before the motorcade passedby). As Secretary of the Treasury Douglas Dillon explained to the Warren Commission in a confidential memorandum:[16]

> Except for inauguration and other parades involving foreign dignitaries accompanied by the president in Washington, it has not been the practice of the Secret Service to make surveys or checks of the buildings along the route of a presidential motorcade. . . . With the numbers of men available to the Secret Service and with the time available, surveys of hundreds of buildings and thousands of windows is not practical. . . . Nor is it practical to prevent people from entering such buildings or to limit access in every building to those employed or having business there. Even if it were possible with a vastly larger force of security officers to do so, many observers have felt that such a procedure would not be consistent with the nature and purpose of the motorcade to let the people see their President and welcome him to their city.

The number of personnel who performed tasks directly or indirectly relating to presidential safety and protection was not atypically large, but was impressive nonetheless. A post-assassination "estimate" by the Secret Service concerning on-duty personnel levels is as follows:[17]

Dallas Police uniformed officers

at the Trade Mart	180
along the motorcade route	90
motorcade escorts	20
at Love Field	55
cruising around the city	100

Dallas Police plainclothes personnel	40

Texas Department of Public Safety

uniformed	40
Rangers	5
plainclothes	16

Dallas Sheriff's Office	14

Dallas Fire Department	26

As for Secret Service agents, the combined total from the White House protective detail, vice-presidential detail—Vice-President Johnson had come with the president—and the Dallas field office was 28 agents.[18]

White the advance security preparations for the Texas trip were adequate according to Secret Service standards and procedures, the performance of some Secret Service agents was not adequate by any standards. Following the assassination, Washington columnist Drew Pearson alleged that Secret Service agents stayed out late drinking the night before the president was shot. The first unofficial response from the Service was that the establishment patronized by agents was only a coffee house and served no liquor at all. The problem with this explanation was the fact that at many clubs and restaurants in the Dallas-Fort Worth area, it was customary, given local liquor laws, for patrons to bring their own liquor, with the management providing set-ups. Thus, the fact that this establishment was not licensed to serve liquor did not assure that none was consumed.

In fact, Warren Commission investigators found that a "breach of discipline" had occurred, involving nine Secret Service agents.[19] After President and Mrs. Kennedy had retired for the night in their Fort Worth hotel, nine of the 28 agents went to the Fort Worth Press Club for beer and mixed drinks. Agents stayed there for times varying from a half hour to two hours. Two agents went back to the hotel but a group of seven agents assembled at The Cellar, a coffee house offering live entertainment. Six agents remained at the coffee house until between 1:30 A.M. and 3:00 A.M.; one stayed until 5:00 A.M.

Even if the Warren Commission investigation is correct in its conclusions that the agents drank moderately at the Press Club and consumed no alcohol at The Cellar, every one of the agents involved had been assigned protective duties that began no later than 8:00 A.M. the next morning. The president was scheduled to give a breakfast speech in Fort Worth at 8:30 A.M., then fly to Dallas.

The Dallas protective assignments for the nine socially inclined agents were as follows: one was assigned to provide security at Love Field, four were assigned to the Trade Mart, four were in the follow-up car behind the presidential limousine in the motorcade.

Secret Service regulations strictly forbade the consumption of alcohol at any time during travel that involved protective assignments. Agents traveling with the president were considered to be "on call' at all times during a trip, even if they were off of their eight-hour protective shift (as were the agents who went out the night of November 21). Secret Service regulations further stated that "violations or slight disregard" for this rule "will be cause for removal from the Service."[20]

But Secret Service Chief James Rowley testified before the Warren Commission that a Secret Service investigation of the breach of regulations had found that the performance of agents involved was in no way impaired. Rowley asserted that each of the nine agents reported for duty on time, was in full possession of all mental and physical abilities, and performed all duties satisfactorily on November twenty-second. He further claimed that agents' activities the previous night did not, in even the slightest manner, impede any action that might have averted the president's death.

Rowley contended that while under ordinary circumstances some disciplinary action would have been taken against the offending agents, in this case it was not appropriate because it would be unfair to agents and their families: it would create the impression that the breach of conduct contributed to the assassination which, according to Rowley, it did

not. The latter claim was based primarily upon the finding that none of
the nine agents were in a position to have performed any action that
might have saved the president, since none were in the president's car
but only in the follow-up car. Rowley told the Commission that the agents
involved were aware of the seriousness of their breach of conduct and
would not do it again.

At minimum, it would seem to have been appropriate to banish the
offending agents from any protective assignments for the remainder of
their careers. Moreover, Chief Rowley's assertion that the agents' conduct the previous night did not in the slightest way prevent them from
taking any action that might have averted the tragedy seems to ignore the
fact that, for whatever reasons or contributing factors, the performance of
the Secret Service follow-up car, in which four of these agents were
riding, seems to have been less than effective. While there were eight
agents in the follow-up car and only four had stayed out late, Rowley's
blanket assertion that the late-night activity did not in the slightest manner impede performance fails to specifically account for the causes of the
lack of reaction by agents in the follow-up car.

As a post-assassination Secret Service document describes, all agents
in the convertible follow-up car are instructed to "watch their routes for
signs of trouble, scanning not only the crowds but the windows and roofs
of buildings, overpasses and crossings" from their positions on the running boards and inside the car.[21] Chief Justice Earl Warren sharply questioned Rowley about the fact that agents did not spot a rifle or a sniper
before the shooting, since one witness claimed to have seen a man with a
rifle in the depository window before the shooting; and another witness,
Press photographer Bob Jackson, saw a rifle in a depository window
moments after the shooting. Said Warren:

> Now other people, as they went along there, even some people
> in the crowds, saw a man with a rifle up in this building from
> which the president was shot. Now don't you think that if a
> man went to bed reasonably early, and hadn't been drinking
> the night before, he would be more alert to see those things as
> a Secret Service agent, than if they stayed up until three or
> four or five o'clock in the morning, going to beatnik joints and
> doing some drinking along the way?[22]

The follow-up car normally stayed within five feet of the presidential
limousine, except at high speed. This was done so that "agents in the

follow-up car can get to the president as quickly as possible" in case of trouble.[23] On Main Street in Dallas, when the motorcycle escort for the presidential limousine got snarled in traffic and dropped back, an agent from the follow-up car "ran up and got on the rear portion of the presidential automobile to be close to Mrs. Kennedy in the event that someone attempted to grab her from the crowd or throw something in the car."[24]

As can be seen from frame 238 of the Zapruder film, the follow-up car was very close to the presidential limousine when the first shot was fired—as close as two to three feet behind, though the distance appears to have increased as the shooting unfolded. At least one agent in the follow-up car heard what he thought was the crack of rifle fire; another asserted that he was close enough to see a bullet hit the President's back.[25] The president clearly reacted to the first shot, clutching his throat with both hands and moving forward before slumping to his left. White House staff member Dave Powers, riding in the follow-up car, was close enough to hear the impact of the bullet that hit the president's head—"the sickening sound of a grapefruit splattering against the side of a wall."[26]

Yet, during the approximately six to seven seconds of gunfire, the agents in the follow-up car seemed relatively immobilized. At least two drew guns while the shooting was in progress, but none reached the presidential limousine until Agent Hill climbed aboard and pushed Mrs. Kennedy back into the car, after the final shot had struck the president in the head.

There is no way to know whether any agent could possibly have reached the president, in the few seconds available, in time to cover him or to somehow screen him from the final, fatal bullet that struck him in the head. For one thing, the presidential limousine was moving at 11.2 m.p.h. This is slow for a vehicle but is still fast enough to require that someone trying to catch up with it must run to get there. Another problem was that the presidential limousine appears to have drifted farther ahead of the follow-up car during the shooting.

At the time of the first shot, the follow-up car was clearly two to there feet behind; at the last shot, before the presidential limousine accelerated, the distance between it and the follow-up car had extended to 15 to 20 feet. This in itself constitutes a failure to follow procedure since the follow-up car was supposed to stay about five feet from the presidential limousine, except at high speeds when it would be impractical to do so.

It is very difficult to determine which among a series of possible factors actually contributed to a particular action not being performed—

inadequate training (at least two agents in the follow-up car thought that they were hearing firecrackers instead of gunfire), lack of precipitating clues, fatigue. But is also difficult to conclude validly that a particular factor had no impact whatsoever, especially when the amount of time available for any particular action is very much dependent upon the reaction time of the individuals involved.

The motorcade formed at Love Field, proceeded through downtown Dallas on Main Street, then turned onto Houston Street and finally onto Elm, passing the Texas School Book Depository. Leading the motorcade were Dallas Police motorcycles followed by the pilot car, a police car that preceded the motorcade by a quarter of a mile and looked for trouble in the form of demonstrators or traffic jams. Then came the "lead car" in the motorcade, an unmarked police car occupied by police and Secret Service agents. Next was the presidential limousine, driven by Secret Service agent William Greer. Beside Greer was Agent Roy Kellerman. Seated behind the two agents were Governor and Mrs. Connally; the president and Mrs. Kennedy were in the third seat. No agents were on the running boards. The presidential follow-up car was next. It carried eight agents and had shotguns and automatic weapons concealed in compartments between the seats. There were two agents riding on each running board; four, inside the open car (along with two White House staff members). Vice-President Johnson's limousine was next, followed by his follow-up car.

The trip through the Dallas suburbs to Main Street had gone well. The president ordered the motorcade to stop on two occasions: once so that he could respond to a sign asking him to shake hands, a second time to speak to a nun and a group of small children. Contrary to the rock-throwing crowd that had confronted Adlai Stevenson, there were no serious incidents prior to the shooting. On Main Street a boy ran into the street and chased the presidential limousine, but he was easily dissuaded by agents.[27]

Of all the locations along the route, Dealy Plaza (Elm Street) had to rank as one of the most dangerous in terms of possible sniper fire. There were several multistory buildings, including the book depository, which commanded a view of Elm Street. When the president's car turned left from Houston onto one-way Elm Street, it slowed down significantly, thereby enhancing any marksman's chances for success. The turn was a sharp one, a 120-degree hairpin turn requiring that cars, especially an elongated limousine, reduce speed to navigate it—right in front of the depository.

Nor could the president's car suddenly speed up after making the turn. Elm Street is one way and has three lanes. There are no breakdown lanes or fences or grassy areas between the street and the fairly broad sidewalks. Thus it was an excellent location for spectators to see the president close up. But Elm Street is also relatively short, so it would have been a conspicuous slight to the crowd to suddenly speed up after making the turn, to rush toward the Stemmons Freeway just ahead. The president's car slowed for the turn and continued down Elm at a very slow pace, making it an easier target. Instead of the 20 to 30 miles per hour which the Secret Service liked to maintain, the presidential limousine moved at only 11.2 miles per hour.*

Just before the limousine made its turn onto Elm, Mrs. Connally remarked, "Mr. President, you can't say Dallas doesn't love you." Moments later, the seven most traumatic seconds in the history of the United States Secret Service began.[28] There was a crack of gunfire. Kennedy clutched his throat with both hands. Agent Kellerman, riding in the front seat next to the driver, heard the president say, "My God, I'm hit." Driver William Greer thought that the sound had come from a motorcycle backfire. He looked back at the president then turned forward again, but took no evasive action.

Agent Greer had had no special training in evasive driving, no specialized driving experience.[29] Secret Service procedures in operation at this time did not allow Greer to accelerate or take evasive action on his own initiative: he was supposed to wait for a command from his colleague seated next to him, Agent Kellerman. But there was no action of any kind taken by either agent during the six to seven seconds that limousine rolled down Elm Street at a snail's pace.

Driver Greer turned and looked back at the president a second time just as the last shot struck Kennedy in the head, thrusting him violently backward and causing a ghastly explosion of blood and brain matter. Then Kellerman blurted, "Let's get out of here, we're hit." Greer accelerated. But it was too late.

It is at least possible that if the limousine had accelerated or taken evasive action during the several seconds between the time the first shot hit the president and the time the last shot struck him in the head that the last shot might have missed Kennedy's head. It is very likely that

---

* The limousine's speed can be precisely calculated from the Zapruder film (the movie of the assassination taken by Dallas businessman Abraham Zapruder with his eight millimeter home movie camera).

Kennedy would have survived the wounds inflicted upon him prior to the head shot. If the president had been pulled down or covered during the interval between the first and last shots, it is possible that he might have survived the attack, although Governor and Mrs. Connally separated Kennedy from the agents in the presidential limousine.

The reactions of at least one agent in the vice-presidential detail seem to have been much quicker and more effective. Agent Rufus Youngblood rode in the front seat of Lyndon Johnson's limousine, next to the driver. As Youngblood recalled:

> As we were beginning to go down this incline [Elm Street sloped downward], all of a sudden there was an explosive noise. I quickly observed unnatural movement of crowds, like ducking or scattering, and quick movements in the presidential follow-up car. So I turned around and hit the vice-president on the shoulder and hollered, get down, and then looked around again and saw more of this movement, and so I proceeded to go to the back seat and get on top of him.[30]

The vice-presidential car had only two seats, not three, so that agent Youngblood could get to Johnson without climbing over an intervening seat as Kennedy's agents would have had to do in order to get to the president. But it is Youngblood's quick reaction that must be contrasted with agents in the presidential limousine. According to both Lyndon Johnson and agent Clifton C. Carter, who observed Youngblood's actions from the vice presidential follow-up car, Youngblood was in the rear seat before the second shot was fired.[31]

The question raised most frequently concerning the Service's failure to keep the president alive was how did the Secret Service miss Oswald? The Service was criticized because Oswald was not in its files, either on its list of 400 dangerous persons or in its general files on more than 40,000 U.S. citizens. The Secret Service searched its protective research files and found no dangerous persons in the Dallas area, though there were two in Houston. The Warren Report described the protective research section as "a very small group of twelve specialists and three clerks."[32]

The Service did make a special effort to identify the individuals who had participated in the rock-throwing incident involving Adlai Stevenson. Agents worked with Dallas police, who found an informant willing to identify the ringleaders of the demonstration by viewing a television film of the incident. The Secret Service then made still pictures of these ringleaders and distributed the pictures to agents and police who would be stationed at Love Field and at the Trade Mart.[33] None of the potential troublemakers were spotted.

In addition, the Stevenson incident prompted the Service to pay "special attention to extremist groups known to be active in the Dallas area." Still, there was nothing in Oswald's record which should have caused the Secret Service to enter him into their files or onto the "watch list." He had not threatened the president, been convicted of a violent crime, or joined a group who "believes in assassination as a political weapon."[34]

The real question was why Oswald was not brought to the attention of the Secret Service by the FBI, which did have a file on him and knew that he was in Dallas. Oswald had defected to the Soviet Union in 1959 and stayed more than two years before returning to the United States, where he became affiliated with several political groups including the pro-Castro Fair Play for Cuba Committee (FPCC), the Socialist Workers Party, and the American Civil Liberties Union. None of the groups joined by Oswald was considered violent nor did any of them use assassination as a political weapon. The FBI's interest in Oswald was a potential subversive, a security risk, not as a violence-prone potential assassin.

However, the Bureau did interview Oswald on several occasions after his return from the Soviet Union and was monitoring him to see if he joined the Communist party, which would have made him particularly subversive in the eyes of the Bureau. Oswald did not join the Communist party.

Dallas FBI Agent James Hosty had interviewed both Oswald and his wife Marina. Oswald resented these interviews and had allegedly written a note to Hosty—the contents of which are not known for certain—warning him not to annoy Marina Oswald. The note was destroyed by Agent Hosty shortly after the assassination.[35] If the note was at all threatening, then this would appear to strengthen the argument that Oswald should have been reported to the Service. If it was not, then Oswald really did not deserve to be reported simply on the basis that he seemed to be a leftist and a potential subversive.

If the Bureau made a practice of reporting suspected subversives to the Secret Service, the latter's files would be overwhelmed. The Secret Service told the Warren Commission that federal agencies were supposed to report "any and all information that they come in contact with that would indicate danger to the president." The handbook given to FBI agents in 1963 required the reporting of specific manifestations of a "threat" against the president, his family, the vice-president or the

president-elect. Thus it is not at all clear, except with the benefit of hindsight, that the Bureau erred in not reporting Oswald to the Secret Service.

Dallas police documents repositing in Warren Commission files show
that despite the public attention focused on the Secret Service and FBI's
failure to identify Oswald as a potentially dangerous person, the real
failure to discover both Oswald and an extremist group in Dallas lay with
the Dallas police. Even though the Service's protective research section
had files on more than 40,000 persons, the Secret Service was very dependent upon local police for "identifying" and "neutralizing" potentially
dangerous persons in the area to be visited by the president.[36] Documents
reveal that operational responsibility for identifying and investigating in-
digenous groups and individuals who might constitute a threat or embarrassment to President Kennedy fell to a 20-man unit of the Dallas Police
Department—the Criminal Intelligence Section, headed by Lieutenant
Jack Revill.

The Criminal Intelligence Section investigated 14 groups in the
Dallas area, including the KKK, the Black Muslims, and the local Nazi
party.[37] Investigations extended not only to group members but to persons in any way affiliated with the groups or friendly with group
members. Members of target groups were placed "under surveillance to
determine associations and movements."[38] As its name would imply, the
police Criminal Intelligence Section had a clandestine capability, as a
police memo describes:

> This Section [Criminal Intelligence] had previously [before
> beginning to work on protective research for Kennedy's visit]
> been successful in infiltrating a number of these organizations;
> therefore, the activities, personalities and future plans of these
> groups were known.[39]

The Criminal Intelligence Section made two glaring errors in protective intelligence gathering. One was the omission of Lee Harvey Oswald.
Unlike the FBI, whose written instructions to agents called for reporting
persons who made threats against the president, the Criminal Intelligence
Section had a broader mission of identifying persons who *might* threaten
or embarrass the president. A list of 400 names was compiled.[40] So broad-
ly was the net cast that four dozen persons who belonged to the Young
Peoples Socialist League were placed on the list simply because of the
left-wing nature of their group. Yet Oswald, whose defection to the Soviet

Union as a self-pronounced Marxist had been covered in the local press, was not included.

The Criminal Intelligence Section evidently missed a very specific opportunity to catch Oswald in its data net: he joined one of the 14 groups under surveillance—the American Civil Liberties Union (ACLU). In the rightest-skewed spectrum of Dallas politics in 1963, the ACLU was targeted because, according to a police memo: "This organization is known to have defended communist causes in many cases and has also opposed laws which are detrimental to the communist cause."[41]

Oswald and his wife and two children had been staying at the home of Ruth and Michael Paine. Michael Paine was a member of the ACLU and regularly attended its meetings.[42] Oswald attended an October twenty-fifth meeting of the Dallas ACLU with Michael Paine. Oswald spoke during the meeting and after it broke up, got into a heated argument with a man who defended the free enterprise system against Oswald's leftist remarks.[43] It must be remembered that the ACLU was under surveillance by police on a continuing basis, even before protective-intelligence-gathering for the president's visit had begun. And police monitored the meetings of target groups.

Within a few days of the ACLU meeting, Oswald formally joined the ACLU and opened up a post office box in Dallas. On the postal form, he authorized the receipt of mail for the ACLU and also for the pro-Castro Fair Play for Cuba Committee (FPCC).[44] This was yet another red flag concerning Oswald's apparent leftist or pro-Communist leanings, and again it was missed or ignored by police intelligence.

In addition to missing Oswald, there was another glaring error in the protective work performed by the police Criminal Intelligence Section. Because of the Stevenson incident, the Secret Service was especially interested in "extremist groups" in the Dallas area, and it was always seeking out intelligence on any group that used assassination as a political weapon. Yet the police intelligence unit failed to report such a group to the Secret Service.

For several weeks prior to the assassination, the Dallas chapter of Alpha-66 was holding meetings in a house on Harlendale Street in Dallas.[45] Alpha-66 was perhaps the most militant, and violent, of all anti-Castro groups. It was composed of Cuban exiles, many of whom had fought in the ill-fated Bay of Pigs Invasion. Alpha-66 was basically a commando group that launched missions against Castro's Cuba from the United States coast—missions involving both sabotage and assassination.[46]

Before the JFK assassination, the Treasury Department's Bureau of Alcohol, Tobacco and Firearms (ATF) had been investigating the owner of a Dallas gun shop regarding illegal arms sales. ATF learned that Alpha-66 had attempted to purchase bazookas and machine guns and, according to the gun shop owner, the group had a large cache of arms somewhere in Dallas.[47] The Bureau of Alcohol, Tobacco and Firearms did not report this to the Secret Service.

The presence of a well-informed group of commandoes such as Alpha-66 would have been viewed by the Service as potentially very threatening to the president, for the group was hostile toward Kennedy. JFK had refused to provide U.S. air cover for the Bay of Pigs invasion and many exiles held him personally responsible for their disastrous defeat at the hands of Castro's army. Kennedy had also forbade Cuban exile groups from launching raids against Castro from U.S. soil and had publicly criticized Alpha-66 for violating this ban, to which the national head of Alpha-66 replied: "We are going to attack again and again."[48]

When the Dallas Alpha-66 did come to the belated attention of the Secret Service, after the assassination, an FBI informant in Dallas reported that the head of the Dallas chapter, Manuel Rodriguez, "was known to be violently anti-President Kennedy."[49] According to another Warren Commission document that was accidently released in 1976 while it was still classified, Rodriguez was "apparently a survivor of the Bay of Pigs episode."[50]

Although the police Criminal Intelligence Section apparently missed Alpha-66 and its leader, another local law-enforcement unit with less intelligence-gathering capacity, the Dallas County Sheriff's Office, stumbled onto Alpha-66. At 8:00 A.M. the day after the assassination, the Sheriff's Office passed along a hot tip to the Secret Service: Oswald had been meeting in a house on Harlendale Street with a group which the Sheriff's Office assumed to be the pro-Castro Fair Play for Cuba Committee.[51] The group reportedly met there for several weeks, up to either a few days before the assassination or the day after.[52] But the group meeting at this house was actually Alpha-66.[53]

The confusion appears to have resulted from the fact that Manuel Rodriguez, the head of the Dallas chapter, bore a resemblance to Lee Harvey Oswald. This was independently confirmed by the FBI. The Bureau checked into a report that Oswald had been in Oklahoma on November 17, accompanied by several Cubans, and discovered that the Oklahoma witnesses had seen Rodriguez, not Oswald.[54] According to an FBI memorandum sign by J. Edgar Hoover, Rodriguez was five feet nine inches, 145 pounds, with brown hair.[55] Oswald's autopsy report listed him as five feet, nine inches, 150 pounds, with brown hair.

The police Criminal Intelligence Section's inability to find or report Alpha-66 is all the more inexplicable because of a tape recording that surfaced in 1978 during the reinvestigation of the JFK case conducted by the House of Representatives Select Committee on Assassinations, 1976-78. The tape had been secretly recorded at a meeting of the Dallas John Birch Society the month before the assassination. At that meeting, an anti-Castro exile and survivor of the Bay of Pigs, though not a member of Alpha-66, denounced Kennedy:

> Get him out. Get him out. The quicker, the sooner the better. He's doing all kinds of deals. Mr. Kennedy is kissing Mr. Kruschev. I wouldn't be surprised if he had kissed Castro too. I wouldn't even call him 'President' Kennedy. He stinks. We are waiting for Kennedy the twenty-second [November], buddy. We're going to see him one way or the other. We're going to give him the works when he gets in Dallas.[56]

As with the ACLU, the John Birch Society was one of those groups being monitored by the Criminal Intelligence Section, and it was surely one of the groups that deserved special attention in the effort to pay particular attention to "extremist" groups in the wake of the Stevenson episode. Kennedy was very unpopular among Birchers, to say the least, because of his alleged softness on communism and his civil rights policies.

The above speech should have been taken as at least an intent to *embarrass* the president if not as a threat. In either case, it should have precipitated increased efforts to discover and monitor any anti-Castro groups in Dallas. Although police documents indicate that they attended meetings of the target groups, the Criminal Intelligence Section either missed the speech against Kennedy or failed to act on it. One police memorandum states that the Birch Society "is an active extremist group" in Dallas and that an "effort was made to determine if this group was planning any demonstration which might be of an embarrassing nature [to the president]. It was determined that no such action was planned."[57]

The Criminal Intelligence Section's failure to discover or report the anti-Castroite's assertion that "we're going to give him the works when he gets in Dallas" or to discover or report the presence of Alpha-66 and its allegedly "violently anti-Kennedy" leader, can be said to have had a detrimental impact upon Kennedy's chances for survival even if no threat from any anti-Castro group ever materialized. The Service had received word of a previous plot to assassinate President Kennedy which was allegedly hatched by an unspecified group of Cuban exiles. The plan was to ram *Air Force One* with a small plane as the president approached Miami.[58] Kennedy's itinerary was changed and no threat materialized. But, given the Service's *modus operandi*, this previous intelligence would have caused it to be very wary of the presence of any exile group, especially a commando group such as Alpha-66. Had the presence of Alpha-66 been detected and reported, the Secret Service might have been able to convince the president to accept additional protective measures, or agents might have operated with a keener sense of impending danger.

The rich documentary record of the Secret Service's performance during the organization's most tragic incident reveals that the failure most often attributed to it—the inability to identify Oswald as a potentially dangerous person—was, in fact, not a Secret Service failure at all. But failures in the gathering of protective intelligence did occur. The Criminal Intelligence Section of the Dallas Police Department had the best opportunity and the best reason to discover both Oswald and Alpha-66, but neither was reported to the Service. Even if Oswald had been reported, there was nothing in his background that would have caused the Service to search him out specifically as a dangerous person to be interviewed or detained; but the reporting of Alpha-66 surely would have caused the Service to red-flag the trip as especially dangerous.

In terms of protective performance during the shooting, though political priorities had predetermined much of the situation—an open car with no agents allowed on the running boards—there appear to have been missed opportunities for immediate evasive and protective action that might *have* contributed to saving the President's life.

The extensive post-assassination criticism and analysis produced improved protective methods and technology. Despite its rather glossy presentations to the Warren Commission, the organization was probably keenly aware of the strengths and weaknesses of its performance.

NOTES

1. Warren Commission, "Memorandum of Conference," March 13, 1964, 3 pages.

2. Sam Anson, *They've Killed the President* (New York: Bantam, 1975), p. 17.

3. Anthony Summers, *Conspiracy* (New York: McGraw-Hill, 1980), p. 1.

4. U.S. Congress, "Report of the Select Committee on Assassinations," 1979, pp. 35–36.

5. *Report of the Warren Commission on the Assassination of President Kennedy* (New York: Bantam, 1964), p. 29.

6. Warren Commission document no. 3, part 1, December 18, 1963 memorandum from Treasury Secretary Douglas Dillon to Earl Warren, section III.

7. U.S. Congress, *Report of the Select Committee on Assassination*, p. 182.

8. Warren Commission exhibit no. 3, p. 2A; exhibit 12, items 8, 9.

9. *Ibid.*; Warren Commission Report, p. 31.

10. G. Robert Blakey and Richard Billings, *The Plot to Kill the President* (New York: Times Books, 1981), p. 5.

11. Warren Commission Report, p. 29.

12. *Rowley Report*, section (a) "Activities of Secret Service in Washington and Dallas, I: Advance Men," Warren Commission file no. 22, "Records Relating to the Protection of the President."

13. Warren Commission Report, p. 41.

14. *Ibid.*, p. 41.

15. Warren Commission document no. 3, exhibit 12 to Report of the U.S. Secret Service on the Assassination of President Kennedy. The description of advance preparations is taken from Warren Commission document no. 3, section B1 a, pp. 7–14.

16. *Ibid.*, document no. 3, Dillon memorandum.

17. *Ibid.*, document no. 3, B 1 a.

18. *Ibid.*, document no. 3, exhibit 12.

19. Warren Commission Report, p. 426–27.

20. *Ibid.*, p. 427.

21. Warren Commission document no. 3, B 1 a.

22. New York *Times, The Witnesses: Highlights of the Hearings Before the Warren Commission on the Assassination of President Kennedy* (New York: Bantam, 1964), p. 534.

23. *Ibid.*, p. 40, testimony of Clinton J. Hill.

24. *Ibid.*

25. Anson, *They've Killed the President*, p. 24.

26. New York *Times, The Witnesses*, p. 39.

27. Warren Commission Report, p. 47–48.

28. This account is reconstructed from the statements of Secret Service agents given to the Secret Service and residing in Warren Commission file no. 22, "Records Relating to the Protection of the President," and from the Zapruder film, a copy of which is possessed by the author.

29. Warren Commission Report, p. 29.

30. *Ibid.*, p. 64–65.

31. *Ibid.*, p. 64–65.

32. *Ibid,*, p. 429.

33. Warren Commission document no. 3, section 1 a 5, 6, 7.

34. Warren Commission Report, p. 430.

35. *Ibid,*, pp. 186–88; p. 377; Warren Commission documents 205, 385; Summers, *Conspiracy*, p. 396.

36. Warren Commission document no. 3, Dillon memorandum.

37. Dallas police document in Warren Commission file no. 22, "Records Relating to the Protection of the President," Document: "Criminal Intelligence Section Preparation for the Visit of John F. Kennedy to Dallas on November 22, 1963," signed by W. P. Gannaway, Captain, Special Services Bureau, February 5, 1964, p. 1. (Hereafter referred to as Criminal Intelligence Section preparation document.)

38. *Ibid.*

39. *Ibid.*

40. *Ibid.*

41. *Ibid.*, report of Detective W. W. Biggis.

42. Hearings before the President's Commission on the Assassination of President John F. Kennedy (Warren Commission), (New York: McGraw-Hill, 1964), vol. II, pp. 408–12, testimony of Michael Paine.

43. *Ibid.*

44. Warren Commission Hearings, vol. 22, p. 717.

45. *Ibid.*, vol. 19, p. 534.

46. U.S. Senate, Final Report of the Select Committee to Study Government Operations with Respect to Intelligence (Washington, D.C.: U.S. Government Printing Office, 1976), Book V, pp. 111–15; John F. Kennedy, Public Papers of the Presidents of the United States (Wash., D.C.: U.S. Government Printing Office, 1963), for April 1, 1963.

47. Warren Commission document 853 a, #, p. 2, Protective Research Section assessment of Manuel Rodriguez, Jan. 14–17, 1964.

48. U.S. House of Representatives, *Report of the Select Committee on Assassinations*, p. 135.

49. Warren Commission document 10850, FBI document no. 10–511740, p. 1.

50. Warren Commission document: Memorandum of April 16, 1964, Griffin to Slawson, subject: "Interview with Frank Ellsworth.

51. Warren Commission Hearings, vol. 19, p. 534 (report of Deputy Sheriff Buddy Walthers, Nov. 23, 1963).

52. Summers, *Conspiracy*, p. 417.

53. *Ibid.*

54. Warren Commission document no. 23, pp. 4–5.

55. Warren Commission document no. 835B, FBI profile of March 9, 1964.

56. Summers, *Conspiracy*, pp. 427–28.

57. Criminal Intelligence Section preparation document.

58. N.C. Livingstone and James Kelly, "Could the President Survive a Real-Life James Bond Movie?," *Washingtonian*, Sept., 1981, p. 174.

10

THE ATTEMPTED ASSASSINATION OF PRESIDENT REAGAN

We didn't have that opportunity that day [that the president was wounded], but it is one human being looking into the eyes of another that is the best detector.

Secret Service Agent Jerry Parr, Head of Reagan's protective detail

On March 30, 1981 President Ronald Reagan was scheduled to give a speech at the Washington Hilton Hotel to 4,000 members of the Building and Construction Trades Union. The itinerary called for a motorcade from the White House to the Hilton, arriving at 1:50 P.M. The president would then enter the hotel, deliver a brief speech, exit the hotel into a waiting limousine and arrive back at the White House by 2:30.[1]

Such trips to the Hilton to deliver short speeches to various groups had become very "standard" events for the Secret Service and the White House staff. The president had been making these appearances every other week for the past several months. The Service's advance preparation work included meetings with hotel and union officials to work out security procedures. In addition, agent Mary Ann Gordon drove over the motorcade routes to and from the Hilton, accompanied by a representative of the Washington, D.C. police department. She coordinated the participation of Washington, D.C. police and U.S. Park Police who would secure the motorcade route and see to traffic control. Communications frequencies to be used by police and Secret Service were agreed upon. At a Secret Service briefing of participating police, a system for issuing and checking IDs and color-coded pins was set up. Agent Gordon called the Washington, D.C. Highway and Traffic Department to make sure that there would be no construction along the motorcade route. She then distributed to all security personnel a memo describing the motorcade route.

The Service conducted an advanced check of the Hilton hotel, scrutinizing it for security problems. Agents were assigned to guard key areas (hallways, doorways) while the president was inside. Other agents "walked through" the president's routes inside the hotel. The names of union officials who would greet the president and of hotel employees were obtained and checked against the Service's dangerous person files.

Just before the president's arrival, a countersniper team was positioned at an undisclosed location outside the hotel. Technicians from the Service's Technical Security Division conducted "sweeps" of the ballroom where the speech was to be given and of the arrival site outside, searching for explosive devices (sought out by a canine team) or anything else in the environment that might harm the president.

Reagan was to enter and exit the hotel via the VIP entrance facing onto T Street. From an overall security perspective, this seemed like a very safe location. The distance from the hotel door to the street where the limousine would be parked was relatively short by hotel standards — 25 to 30 feet. This reduced the time of the President's exposure. The roof and windows of the Hilton were blocked from a view of the doorway by a high, cliff-like concrete wall that shielded the doorway from the main hotel. The eight-story building across the street had sealed windows and its roof would be covered by the countersniper team. Thus, for a big city location, the Hilton VIP entrance seemed relatively safe from sniper fire. The street and sidewalk area outside the doorway were quite small so that there was no room for a large crowd to gather.

The crowd who would witness the president's speech inside the Hilton was subjected to very strict security. Herein lies the paradox of security precautions taken for this event: The crowd inside was given much more scrutiny than the crowd outside. Entrances to the ballroom where the speech would be given were sealed and guarded. Spectators could enter only through two checkpoints. "Explosive ordinance disposal personnel" were stationed at each checkpoint to inspect handbags and briefcases. At a separate entrance and checkpoint set up for the press, cameras and press equipment were inspected for explosives.

Outside the hotel a rope barrier was set up to keep the crowds from getting too close to the president and from blocking the entrance, but the crowd itself was not searched for bombs or guns, nor was it screened for credentials. According to the Treasury Department's report on the attempted assassination, this was because "the area had not been designated a 'press area',"[2] implying that the press would have been screened more carefully than the general public.

Inside the hotel, agents noticed that members of the press corps were "straying outside of the designated press area." The agents quickly undertook steps to correct the situation and kept the press people within their preassigned area.[3] Outside, however, John W. Hinckley would be able to join the ranks of the press corps and get within 20 feet of the president. The inside crowd was screened more carefully even though it would not get as close to the president as the outside crowd.

The Service decided against establishing in advance a press area outside the Hilton. If such an area had been designated, then, by standard procedure, Secret Service agents and White House press people would have controlled access to the area by screening credentials. But agents felt that establishing a press area would have been "impractical" because it might have blocked access to the hotel.[4]

The Treasury Department report stated that the Hilton trip was uncomplicated, security-wise, because it was to begin and end in the most secure of all locations — the White House. The Hilton was also a location that the president and other protectees visited frequently. The report concluded:

> While the agents conducting the advance for the President's March 30 visit to the Hilton handled their responsibilities capably, their preparation did not address certain details which were included in the standard procedure for an advance. This may be understandable, since the procedures were developed for environments outside of Washington, D.C. and do not take account of the fact that trips in the Capitol have become routine.[5]

While it may be true that the Service tends to regard trips within the Capitol city as safer and more routine — and it therefore has a more relaxed attitude toward security — such an attitude could easily erode effective security, for it might also be manifested during trips outside the Washington area that also seem safe because of their location and/or routine nature (trips to President Reagan's Santa Barbara ranch, for example). There also seems to have been a double standard regarding security inside the hotel versus security outside, even though both were part of the same local, routine trip. The prescreened, elite group inside was subjected to more security than the completely unknown group outside, even though the outside group would get closer to the President.

Protective intelligence gathering for trips within the Capitol area is done by the Service's Washington, D.C. field office. Field office agents checked with the protective research section at Secret Service headquarters in order to identify dangerous persons who might be in the area and to check lists of hotel guests and employees against Secret Service files. Agent Timothy McCarthy of the field office checked with headquarters and discovered no problems.

John W. Hinckley was not in Secret Service files. He had been arrested at the Nashville, Tennessee airport on October 9, 1980 as he attempted to board a plane while carrying three pistols. Then candidate Ronald Reagan had just cancelled a planned trip to Nashville; President Carter was in Nashville at the time of Hinckley's arrest.

It has been argued that Nashville police or the FBI should have reported Hinckley to the Secret Service. But there was no direct threat involved, and inclusion in Secret Service files of everyone arrested for a firearms violation in any city where a president or candidate was visiting at the time would overwhelm the Service's files. Since the Service could not possibly interview or monitor all such persons, there was probably no way in which agents would have been looking for Hinckley on March 30, 1981 even if the Nashville arrest had been reported to the Service.* It has also been suggested that the Nashville incident should have caused Hinckley to be spotted as a stalker, but one arrest in proximity to a president does not a stalker make.

President Reagan's motorcade to the Hilton and his arrival were uneventful. He proceeded inside to a "holding room" where he was to have his picture taken with union leaders. Then he went to the ballroom to deliver a 20-minute speech, under the watchful eyes of agents who scanned the audience of 4,000 looking for potential problems. There were none.

Outside the hotel, the press had congregated between the parked presidential limousine and the follow-up car. An agent moved the press out of this area so that the vehicles could get into position for the return trip. The agents standing around the limousine scanned the crowd across T Street and on the hotel side of the street as well, looking for signs of trouble. The president exited the hotel through the same VIP door used

---

*A more complete discussion of this problem of protective intelligence appears in Chapter 6.

for his entrance.[6] Agents took up positions around the waiting limousine. Agents Parr and Shaddick walked just behind Mr. Reagan. In front of him were members of the White House staff (Press Secretary James Brady, Deputy Chief of Staff Michael Deaver, and a military aide) and more agents.

Mr. Reagan moved directly toward the waiting limousine. Agent Shaddick was forced to move around a White House staff member in order to maintain his position to the right rear of the president and in close proximity to him. Shaddick recovered his position before the shooting.

Agent Timothy McCarthy opened the door of the limousine so that the president could enter. There were shouts of "Mr. President" from the crowd. Reagan waved as be began to enter the limousine. Shots rang out from behind the rope barrier, only 15 to 20 feet from the president. Six shots were fired in two seconds.

Though the shots sounded like firecrackers to some bystanders, Secret Service agents reacted instantly, in contrast to the JFK assassination when some agents thought that the shots were firecrackers and looked around without taking action. At the sound of the shots, Agent Jerry Parr immediately pushed the president toward the back seat of the limousine and began to cover him. Agent Shaddick pushed Parr and the president into the limousine as agent Timothy McCarthy turned toward the source of gunfire and spread his arms and legs to shield the president. Shaddick closed the door to the limousine and ordered the driver to leave the scene. The limousine dodged a stalled police car and sped away, evacuating the president within ten seconds of the first shot.

President Reagan was struck by one of the six shots, which ricocheted off of the side of the limousine, passed through the opening between the open door and the body of the vehicle, and penetrated under his left arm. One bullet struck Press Secretary James Brady in the head. He fell to the pavement, bleeding profusely. Agent Timothy McCarthy, who had turned toward the gunfire to screen the President, was hit in the chest. Another bullet hit D.C. policeman Thomas Delahanty in the neck. One ricocheted off of the limousine and broke a window across the street from the hotel.

The first person to reach the assailant was Alfred Antenucci, a bystander who jumped Hinckley from behind as the last shot was fired. Agent D. V. McCarthy was the first law enforcement person to reach Hinckley, diving on him as he continued to squeeze the trigger of the empty gun. Two D.C. policemen quickly wrestled the weapon from Hinckley's hand.

No Secret Service agent saw the assailant draw the weapon prior to the shots. Once the shooting began, several agents drew pistols and automatic weapons and scanned the crowd for other assailants. Agents covered the limousine's escape with their Uzi machine guns drawn. No shots were fired by either agents or police.

Agents remaining at the scene radioed that there had been an attack on the president. They then kept the crowd back, away from the wounded, and tried to preserve the evidence. One agent took the weapon; another handcuffed the assailant.

Meanwhile, in the presidential limousine, Agent Parr got off of President Reagan and helped him to a sitting position. Parr asked the president if he was all right and Mr. Reagan responded affirmatively. Parr quickly examined the president. He checked the back of Mr. Reagan's coat for wounds and ran his hands inside the coat. Parr found nothing and ordered the driver to proceed to the White House.

Thirty seconds later, the president complained that he was having trouble breathing and he had a sharp pain in his chest. Reagan thought that he might have broken a rib. Parr then noticed blood in the president's mouth and ordered the driver to "go to George Washington Hospital, fast!"

Agent Mary Ann Gordon, riding in the follow-up car, tried to radio the D.C. police to obtain their help in clearing a route to the hospital. She could not get through: police frequencies were jammed by the heavy radio traffic precipitated by the shooting. Gordon ordered her car to pass the presidential limousine so that it could run interference en route to the hospital. When the president's car suddenly changed direction and turned onto Pennsylvania Avenue to get to the hospital, the lead car in the motorcade and four escorting motorcycles failed to make the turn and were separated from the limousine.

Agents who had heard Parr's radio transmission (about getting to the hospital, fast) radioed the hospital that the motorcade would arrive there and that there were injuries. But hospital personnel were not told specifically that the president had been injured. Agent Parr did not broadcast that because he feared that everyone monitoring his frequency would then know that the president had been hurt: Parr did not want to breach communications security. The hospital readied its emergency room to treat the unspecified "injured."

In one Secret Service transmission to the hospital, there was no request for a stretcher to be waiting to carry "the injured" inside. Another transmission did request a stretcher.[7] Yet there was no stretcher waiting for the president when he arrived. The trauma room was ready, however. Only three minutes after the shooting, the president was at the hospital. Agents Parr and Shaddick helped Reagan as he wobbled into the hospital. His knees began to buckle and the agents and two paramedics carried the president to the emergency room where he was placed on a cart and immediately taken to the trauma room. Only upon removing Reagan's clothes did the medical personnel realize that he had been wounded.

Mr. Reagan and Officer Delahanty recovered fully from their wounds. Press Secretary James Brady suffered extensive brain damage. The rapidity with which the shots were fired (six in two seconds) made it difficult for the FBI to determine the exact sequence of the wounds. The Bureau concluded that Reagan was hit after he had been doubled over by Agent Parr, who was pushing him into the limousine.[8]

The bullets used were called devastators and were particularly lethal. An empty box of devastator bullets was found in Hinckley's Washington, D.C. hotel room. These bullets contained an aluminum cap which, when detonated, would explode. This caused the bullet to fragment and tear through the victim much like shrapnel.[9] The bullet that struck James Brady in the head apparently exploded; the one that hit the president did not.

Doctors at George Washington Hospital had decided not to remove the bullet from policeman Delahanty's neck until they were informed that it was an exploding bullet. Thus it had to be removed, for as FBI Agent Roger Young described: "These bullets could explode at any time. Anything can make them go off, like heat or pressure or impact." When the doctors removed the bullet from the president's lung, they did not know at the time that they were dealing with a bullet that could explode at any moment.[10]

Shortly after the shooting, Agent Jerry Parr, the head of Reagan's protective detail, told an interviewer: "I have a feeling — I've always felt this, and it's what agents know — that the eyes are windows to the soul. If you look at the agents working around the president when he is shaking hands, they'll be looking at faces, eyes, hands. Those are very critical."[11] Although none of the Secret Service agents or police noticed Hinckley before he began to fire, two of the military personnel who had driven cars in the presidential motorcade and who were waiting for the president to exit the Hilton noticed the strange behavior of an individual in the crowd. The man who manifested "erratic behavior" was not John W. Hinckley. It was a man whom agents recognized immediately because they had interviewed him on several previous occasions and had determined that he presented no danger to the president.[12]

As for the man in the crowd who *was* a danger to the president, Hinckley was noticed by John M. Dodson, a Pinkerton Detective Agency employee who was watching the crowd from a seventh-floor window across the street from the Hilton. According to Dodson, Hinckley was conspicuous because he kept turning his body from side to side. "The best description was fidgety," said Dodson.[13]

Walter C. Rogers, an Associated Press reporter, had also noticed Hinckley before the shooting. Rogers claims that Hinckley was hostile to the group of reporters whose uncredentialed ranks he had joined.[14] ABC television cameraman Henry M. Brown stated that he complained directly to a Secret Service agent about people "penetrating" the police line (the rope barrier) and creating crowded conditions for the press which made it difficult to work.[15] Agents took no action, probably because the area was not defined by the Secret Service as a press area: therefore, there was no reason to exclude the public. Another bystander outside the Hilton, iron worker Samuel Lafta, claimed that one police officer stared at Hinckley several times but did not approach him.[16]

A major flaw in Secret Service protection occurred after the shooting. No Secret Service agents or Uniformed Division officers were posted at George Washington Hospital when the president first arrived there.[17] Some additional agents were dispatched to the hospital from the Washington field office but this was approximately a half hour after the president had arrived, and the reinforcements were not sufficient to secure the hospital effectively. There was no advance detail to secure the entrance to the hospital, the halls, or the emergency room. Agents arriving with the president escorted him inside and then had to set up security at the hospital.

Technical Security Division personnel arrived at the hospital in time to run security checks of the environments in the operating room, the recovery room, and the intensive care area, but not in time to check the emergency room where the president went upon arrival. Canine teams (to sniff out explosives) and countersniper teams did not arrive until later that evening.[18]

Fortunately, the dearth of security at the hospital had no negative consequences for the president's safety — in this particular case. But, under different circumstances, it could have been disastrous, even fatal. At the time that the president was taken to the hospital, minutes after the shooting, the extent and nature of the attack were not known. There could have been a hit squad following the presidential motorcade to the hospital or other assailants waiting for him there.

According to the Service's priorities, all agents should give first priority to the safety of the president. This takes precedence over helping wounded bystanders, capturing assailants, or preserving evidence. When the president arrived at the hospital, not only was there no advance protection but he was being protected by only a portion of his original protective detail. Several agents had remained behind at the scene of the shooting. The president's protection was spread perilously thin.

Agent Gerald Bechtle, who was acting as Assistant Director of Protective Operations, sent instructions to the agents at the Hilton that members of the president's original security detail should remain at the crime scene in order to implement what Bechtle understood to be an "interum federal presence," as described in the Service's 1979 memorandum of understanding with the FBI.[19] Yet the Secret Service's first priority has always been the safety of the president. The 1979 agreement with the FBI was more concerned with delegating full investigative responsibility for assassination and attempted-assassination cases to the Bureau rather than the Service, by requiring that any evidence gathered by the Service should be immediately turned over to the FBI. The agreement was never meant to intrude upon the first priority status of the Service's protective mission, which in this case dictated that all agents should have escorted the president to the hospital (in case of a second attack along the way or at the hospital). The concept of "interum federal presence" was primarily designed to limit the Service's investigative role vis-à-vis the FBI, not to require the Service to remain at the crime scene to protect evidence and to help the FBI conduct its investigation.

Some agents seemed to interpret the 1979 agreement as requiring the Service to stay at the crime scene even after the FBI had arrived. Secret Service agents stayed on to give interviews to FBI agents. The failure of Secret Service headquarters to properly interpret "interum federal presence" in accord with protective priorities could have had serious consequences under less fortuitous circumstances.

Neither Secret Service headquarters nor the Washington field office thought to assess the level of security at the hospital and to dispatch the additional agents needed to provide effective protection. The Washington field office has primary responsibility for trips within the Washington, D.C. area. Advance preparations and intelligence gathering for the Hilton visit were handled by field office agents.[20] Through Secret Service headquarters was brought into the crisis immediately after the shooting, the Washington field office continued to play a major role.

The Washington field office had a major protective responsibility for the Hilton trip, but it became heavily involved in investigative and law-enforcement activities in the aftermath of the shooting, even though protection at the hospital did not reach an adequate level until hours after the president's arrival. One request for reinforcements made by agents at the hospital to the Washington field office could not get through, apparently because the field office circuits were glutted (in part, because of the field office's investigative and law-enforcement involvements).[21] The field office did not get in touch with the hospital in order to determine the adequacy of protection or the need for additional personnel.

As the Treasury Department report describes: "Most of the attention of supervisory Washington field office personnel was directed to the arrangements concerning the custody of Hinckley; the transmittal of information derived from Hinckley's personal effects."[22] The field office responded to a request from Agent Ramsey, who was at the Hilton. Ramsey's request was probably based on orders he had received from Secret Service headquarters concerning the establishment of an "interum federal presence." He requested that the Washington field office send additional agents to the Hilton to help the FBI with its investigation. The field office dispatched two agents to help the FBI.[23] They arrived at the crime scene at a little after 2:30—about the same time that President Reagan arrived at the hospital with no advance protection and with a diminished protective detail accompanying him.

Very shortly after the president had left the Hilton, two of the agents in his protective detail went with John W. Hinckley as he was taken to police headquarters. Upon arriving at the police station, one agent "covered" Hinckley as he was taken from the car to a cell. The two Secret Service agents then searched the suspect for weapons and informed him of his rights. One agent stood guard outside Hinckley's cell.

The second agent then phoned the Washington field office. Unlike the agent who called the field office from George Washington Hospital, the agent who was escorting Hinckley did get through and requested that additional agents be sent to the police station. The Washington field office complied, dispatching three agents to Hinckley's cell block. These agents stayed while the suspect was being interrogated, helped transfer him from the police station to an FBI office—he was transported in a Secret Service armored car—and attended a second interrogation at the FBI office.[24] Agents quickly reported the substance of these interrogations to the Service's Washington field office.

The field office continued its involvement in the investigation well into the evening. Agent Carlton Spriggs determined from Hinckley's personal effects that he was registered at the Park Central Hotel. This was relayed to the field office which sent two agents to search the room, along with FBI agents (at 5:45 P.M.).

Throughout the first hour of the crisis, Secret Service headquarters assumed that if additional agents were needed at the hospital, agents in Reagan's original protective detail would call for them. While a small number of additional agents arrived at the hospital during the afternoon, the crisis managers at Secret Service headquarters had no specific data concerning the level of protection at the hospital, nor did they make any systematic attempt to obtain such data. As the Treasury report describes:

> In effect, the headquarters crisis managers followed the implica-
> tions of existing procedures and assumed that presidential
> detail personnel on site, and the Washington field office person-
> nel sent there shortly afterward,* would request whatever
> assistance was necessary. The requests they received from the
> hospital site were few and took some period of time to fulfill; as
> a consquence, the number of Service personnel at the hospital
> did not reach a level substantially greater than the security that
> had been established at the Hilton prior to the shooting until
> late in the afternoon of March 30.[25]

Part of the reason that few requests for assistance were received from the hopsital site may have been that communications facilities at the hospital were inadequate. George Washington Hospital was considered by the Service to be the primary emergency hospital for trips in the downtown area; but the White House Communications Agency did not consider it the primary hospital for medical treatment of the president. A military hospital had been selected for that role. Because of this, com-munications at George Washington Hospital were very limited until addi-tional equipment was brought in, within fifteen minutes of the president's arrival.[26]

There were communications problems at the Treasury Department as well as the hospital. Treasury's Telecommunications Center first heard of the shooting when one of the operators heard about it from a friend. On her own initiative, the operator immediately began to notify the of-ficials on Treasury's emergency notification list. The officer on duty at

---

* Two agents were sent by the Washington field office about one half hour after the shooting, but this was not sufficient and was not linked to any systematic assessment of security needs.

the Treasury Department Watch Office first heard of the attempted assassination when the news appeared on the press wire.[27] It would be preferable for Treasury's emergency communications systems to obtain immediate information from an authoritative, primary source within the Secret Service or the Treasury Department.

Another problem was that vital data which should have been immediately at hand was not. The president's medical records were not on file at the hospital nor were they carried along in his limousine. The Service had conducted a survey of George Washington Hospital in July 1980, but the report, including a "security survey," was not in the possession of agents in the presidential detail. It did not get to them until the crisis had passed.[28]

The Service's report on George Washington Hospital contained a security checklist but did not contain a security plan for the placement of guards or the establishment of a "command post." Although the information in the report would have been helpful in planning security, it did not constitute a security plan. The hospital had its own "hospital disaster plan" which was activated by the hospital administrator. It called for limiting access to the hospital and thus was helpful to the Service, but it was not an effective game plan for presidential protection.

The agents who arrived at the hospital with the president, with no advance detail to help them and with their numbers diminished by posting agents at the crime scene, were faced with the simultaneous tasks of protecting the president and designing security.[29] This made the need for instant reinforcements all the more acute.

Yet another procedural lapse concerned the protection of the vice-president. The Service had no written procedure or policy in place that would automatically increase the protection afforded the vice-president in the event of an attack on the president.[30] It would make sense to do so, not only because the vice-president is next in line to the presidency but also because any attack on the president might be part of a broader attempt to assassinate several top officials, as was the case in the Lincoln assassination. Moreover, there is no way to instantly determine that an attack on the president is a totally isolated event and not a broader conspiracy.

Agents in the vice-presidential detail did take special precautions. When Mr. Bush's plane landed in Austin, Texas to refuel, the vice-president stayed aboard and agents sealed off all entrances and took out their automatic weapons. On the other hand, the refueling stop in Austin had been scheduled well in advance. As the Treasury Department report observes: "It is unclear whether the Service made a special check to determine whether trouble might be anticipated at this stop."[31] Clearly, the Service should always assume the worst—that a coordinated attack on the president and vice-president might be unfolding. The appropriate response to such an assumption would be to thoroughly check out the Austin landing site and to greatly increase security before landing there, or to divert to another refueling site (since the Austin stop was scheduled in advance and might therefore be the site of a planned attack).

John W. Hinckley, a deeply disturbed young man who had developed a fantasized love affair with actress Jodie Foster, was found not guilty by reason of insanity. This was the third unsuccessful presidential assassination attempt in six years. The Secret Service had urged Mr. Reagan not to pause and chat with the press during his exits. "Wave and move, Mr. President," agents had urged.[32] Outside the Hilton the president had done just that, and he got shot anyway. How did it happen?

Effective security would seem to dictate that the area outside the Hilton should not have afforded unrestricted access in such close proximity to the president (15 to 20 feet). Either the area should have been designated a press area and credentials should have been checked or an unrestricted area should have been set up at a greater distance from the president. The fact that this particular sidewalk area was in Washington, D.C. would seem to have no logical bearing on the design of effective security.

In the aftermath of the shooting, security was tightened. The president began to exit through parking garages instead of out on the street. The press was kept at much greater distance, which meant fewer opportunities to ask questions of the president.[33] Decoy limousines were used on subsequent trips to the Hilton to confuse bystanders as to where the president would exit. Because of the map and newspapers found among Hinckley's possessions, it was decided that advance publicity concerning the president's agenda had aided the assailant. The practice of releasing the president's daily itinerary was discontinued by the White House.

It is also evident, however, that there was much more than the Secret Service's exit-security procedures that needed repair. Agents guarding the president performed flawlessly in evacuating him within ten seconds of the shooting; but from then on, the crisis seemed to expose one flawed procedure after another—flaws that had no negative impact on the outcome only because the case involved a single attack by a lone assailant rather than multiple attacks by numerous assailants. Presumably and hopefully, the problems of inadequate communications, of not having the appropriate information on hand when it was needed, and of failing to provide appropriate levels of protection to the president and vice-president while helping the FBI and while guarding the assailant, have been solved.

NOTES

1. U.S. Dept. of the Treasury, "Management Review of the Performance of the U.S. Department of the Treasury in Connection with the March 30, 1981 Assassination Attempt on President Ronald Reagan" (Washington, D.C.: Treasury Department, 1981). This account is based upon pp. 7–12, 43–49.

2. *Ibid.*, p. 47.

3. *Ibid.*

4. *Ibid.*, p. 49.

5. *Ibid.*

6. *Ibid.*, this account is taken from pages 7–12, 55–61, 68–70.

7. *Ibid.*, pp. 1, 59.

8. *Time*, April 13, 1981, p. 38.

9. Philip Taubman, "Explosive Bullet Struck Reagan, FBI Discovers," New York *Times*, April 13, 1981, p. A1.

10. *Ibid.*

11. Norman Black, "Agent Talks About Reagan Shooting," Bryan, Texas *Eagle*, April 30, 1983, p. 1.

12. U.S. Treasury Dept., "Treasury Report," p. 48.

13. Richard D. Lyons, "Witnesses to Shooting Recall Suspect Acting 'Fidgety' and 'Hostile,' New York *Times*, March 31, 1981, p. 1.

14. *Ibid.*

15. Benjamin Taylor, "A Scene of Violence and Confusion," Boston *Globe*, March 31, 1981, p. 2.

16. Lyons, "Witnesses to Shooting."

17. U.S. Dept. of the Treasury, "Management Review of the Performance of the U.S. Department of the Treasury in Connection with the March 30, 1981 Assassination Attempt on President Ronald Reagan" pp. 21–22, 63–66.

18. *Ibid.*, p. 64.

19. *Ibid.*, p. 21.

20. *Ibid.*, p. 42.

21. *Ibid.*, p. 64.

22. *Ibid.*, p. 21.

23. *Ibid.*, pp. 69–70.

24. *Ibid.*, pp. 70–71.
25. *Ibid.*, p. 22.
26. *Ibid.*, p. 6.
27. *Ibid.*, p. 88.
28. *Ibid.*, p. 66.
29. *Ibid.*, p. 63.
30. *Ibid.*, p. 73.
31. *Ibid.*
32. "Can the Risk Be Cut?," *Newsweek*, Oct. 6, 1975, p. 19.
33. Lou Cannon, "One Year Later, Shot Still Echoes," Boston *Globe*, March 30, 1982, pp. 8–9.

11
CONCLUSION

The United States Secret Service is a highly professional, merit-based organization with good morale, a positive public image, and excellent Congressional relations. Yet it is fundamentally a dual-mission agency and, in a very real sense, has a schizoid organization identity. Its investigative mission of pursuing counterfeiters and forgers is performed in as close to apolitical fashion as is possible within a federal agency. But the mission for which it is most renowned, protection, is performed not in the arena of law-enforcement bureaucracy (as is the investigative mission) but in the political arena. There, in the caldron of presidential politics, most facets of the Service's work are highly politicized.

Agents doing protective work are very professional and some dimensions of their work are beyond political influence. For example, the Service surely protects Democrats and Republicans with equal vigor. Still, there can be no doubt that political expectations regarding the accessibility of political leaders — expectations held by politicians and the public alike — coupled with the fact that protection is voluntary on the part of the protectee, result in the politicization of much of the protective mission. This produces decreased effectiveness of protection and increased risks to political leaders, though such risks may be viewed as a necessary sacrifice for an open democratic system in which politicians are accessible to the polity.

After recognizing the profound influence of politics upon protection, and recognizing that the impact is negative in terms of maximizing protection, the question remains as to whether protection is "sufficient" within the constraints of the American democratic process. Even within such constraints, there are improvements in protective methods and

197

procedures that can increase the quality of protection. And this can be done without wholesale changes in our political culture that would de-emphasize personal contact between politicians and voters.

The effectiveness of Secret Service protection has increased markedly since the assassination of John F. Kennedy. But the threats faced have escalated, if not in number then surely in technological sophistication. The question arises as to whether the Secret Service's improvements in protective methods have kept pace with the increased severity of threats. Put another way, has the Service made innovative changes in its methods that are designed to meet the threats of the terrorist age or has it drifted along with a "more-of-the-same" response (using more resources to beef up the implementation of existing methods rather than changing the methods themselves)? This is difficult to answer because of the secrecy involved.

Former Assistant Secret Service Director James P. Kelly, writing with N. C. Livingstone in 1981, asserts that the Service is losing the race to modernize its methods fast enough to keep up with newer, more-deadly threats:[1]

> It is true that nearly all attempts on the lives of U.S. presidents have been by single gunmen, but the Secret Service's orientation nonetheless is reminiscent of the French General Staff in 1939: prepared to fight the previous war rather than the next one.
>
> The whole orientation of the Secret Service must be changed to anticipate the threat posed by terrorists. This will require novel strategies comparable to those developed by the crash program launched after President Kennedy's assassination.

Yet, the Secret Service is not oblivious to the terrorist age. It has formed a CAT (counterterrorist assault team) unit within the White House protective detail. This elite unit of agents is trained specifically to combat terrorist attacks. Whether Kelly and Livingstone exaggerate the gap between protective methods and threats, or whether there is really no gap at all, there are still improvements that need to be made, as is made evident by the numerous and glaring inadequacies of methods, procedures and communications manifested during the attempted assassination of President Reagan in March 1981.

In addition to methods and procedures, there is one suggestion that emerges from the organizational analysis of the Secret Service presented in previous chapters. The Service's status as a dual-mission organization with personnel and resources shared between the protective mission and the mission of chasing counterfeiters and forgers should be thoroughly evaluated by outside consultants, in order to determine its impact upon the effectiveness of protection. Though the Secret Service claims that the dual training of its agents and the rotating duty assignments between investigative and protective work produce more effective agents who are well-rounded in their skills, this impression needs to be systematically analyzed. The Secret Service claims that it would be "impractical" to have personnel trained exclusively in protective work, but this assumes a dual-mission organization with existing limitations of money and personnel.

Priorities and the allocation of resources could be changed: the "impractical" might become practical if it were discovered that protection would be much better served by a single-mission organizational structure. The notion that the quality of protection is enhanced by having well-rounded agents is easily rebutted by the notion that effectiveness is reduced because organizational resources are spread too thin. If ever a bureaucratic entity had a single, salient characteristic whose impact upon performance was in need of thorough and detached analysis, it is the Secret Service's status as a dual-mission agency. Such analysis may or may not confirm the Service's impression that the quality of protection is enhanced by its present structure.

Though improvements in protective methods and possible improvements in organizational structure are important to the quality of protection, it is the values and attitudes of our political culture that have the most impact. To what degree does the public believe that Secret Service protection is necessary, and at what cost in terms of both money and reduced access to political leaders? While there seems to be a consensus that some form of protection is necessary, there exists considerable debate as to whether present levels are inadequate, adequate, or excessive.

In this sense, the protective mission is subject to the same kind of debate — based on differing value priorities and different assumptions about risk — that exists regarding national defense. It all depends upon how the problem of protection is defined and what priority is assigned to providing the scarce resources needed to solve the problem. Just as a certain set of statistics about numbers of nuclear warheads is viewed by some as outrageous overkill and by others as dangerous vulnerability, the protective mission can be viewed from two sharply contrasting perspectives.

From one perspective, there have been 39 presidents of the United States and nearly one quarter (nine) have been shot at by assassins. Four were killed. Given the present level of terrorist activity and the escalating technology of assassination, the need for protection is greater than ever. Secret Service's very presence can be a deterrent to attack.

Presidential protection can be regarded as a form of national defense, as it was viewed by many U.S. officials when a Libyan hit squad had allegedly been sent to assassinate President Reagan. The psychological and political cost to the country that results from losing a president can be viewed as far too great not to devote increased resources to protection. When viewed as national defense, protection of political leaders is relatively inexpensive. The annual budget for the entire Secret Service (both protective and investigative expenditures) is under $200 million — the approximate price of 15 new fighter planes. In an era in which private security firms garner huge sums for protecting heads of corporations and movie stars, taxpayers must be willing to protect their top officials, even at an increased cost.[2]

From an opposing view, the Secret Service's protective mission is not of crucial importance to the U.S. political system. In the 20 years since the assassination of John F. Kennedy, there have been only three assassination attempts (two on Ford, one on Reagan) with no deaths and only one wounding.

Writing in the *New Republic* in 1981 (prior to the attempted assassination of President Reagan), Stephen Chapman argues against the growth of the protective mission.[3]

> It [the Secret Service] is one of those agencies set up with a reasonable idea in mind, but which over the years has grown into something its creators would barely recognize. It exists purely for the benefit of a very small class of favored people, who have grown quite accustomed to this special treatment and who would raise an unholy howl if anyone ever tried to withdraw it. It has grown rapidly in recent years, not for any outwardly logical reason but due mostly to the bureaucratic urge to expand. It could be cut back with no great loss to the citizenry or any grave danger to the Republic.
>
> In all the years of the great Secret Service boom, there have been no major attempts on the lives of presidential family members, or on former presidents, or on their families. On a list of people most likely to get shot at, most of these

individuals (one can think of exceptions) would not rank very high. It is not surprising, for example, that John Lennon was a more tempting target for some lunatic than Rosalynn Carter.

Secret Service agents are viewed by their detractors as high-priced political factotums who, at taxpayers expense, enhance the imperial image and ego satisfaction of presidents and politicians by standing around, opening doors, guarding private homes, and keeping toublesome reporters at bay.

In the final analysis, it is not simply the debate between Secret Service supporters and critics or between protective hawks and doves that will determine the future of the protective mission: it is primarily the norms of our political culture. If the public expectation continues to be that politicians should be physically accessible, at least to some degree, and if the old-fashioned, press-the-flesh style of politics appears to promote electoral success, then politicians will continue to view political contact as having a higher priority than protection. There is, however, another possibility. Perceptions of an escalating terrorist threat, whether accurate or distorted, may alter our political norms toward a higher priority for protection, and may do so more rapidly and to a greater degree than the normal evolution of our domestic political culture would ever have permitted.

NOTES

1. N. C. Livingstone and James P. Kelly, "Could the President Survive a Real-Life James Bond Movie?" *Washingtonian*, September, 1981, pp. 168–77, at p. 177.

2. Robert Charm, "There Are Numbers in Safety," Boston *Globe*, June 11, 1982, p. 30.

3. Stephen Chapman, "The Secret Service's Biggest Secret," *The New Republic*, Jan. 24, 1981, pp. 18–21.

BIBLIOGRAPHY

Anson, Sam. *They've Killed the President.* New York: Bantam, 1975.

Clarke, James W. *American Assassins: The Darker Side of Politics.* Princeton, N.J.: Princeton University Press, 1982.

Crotty, William J. (ed.). *Assassins and the Political Order.* New York: Harper & Row, 1971.

Donner, Frank. *The Age of Surveillance.* New York: Vintage Books, 1981.
Dorman, Michael. *The Secret Service Story.* New York: Delacourt Press, 1967.

Janke, Peter. *Guerrilla and Terrorist Organizations: A World Directory and Bibliography.* New York: Macmillan, 1983.

Kirkham, James B. *et al.* (eds.). *Assassination and Political Violence.* New York: Bantam, 1970.

Lesberg, Sandy. *Assassinations in Our Time,* London: Peebles Press and Bobbs-Merrill, 1976.

McKinley, James. *Assassination in America,* New York: Harper & Row, 1977.
Montana, Patrick J. and George S. Roukis. *Managing Terrorism: Strategies for the Corporate Executive.* Westport, Conn.: Quorum Books, 1983.

Neal, Harry. *The Secret Service in Action.* New York: Elsevier-Nelson, 1980.

Rhodri, Jeffreys-Jones. *American Intelligence.* New York: The Free Press, 1977.

Wise, David. *The Espionage Establishment.* New York: Random House, 1967.

Youngblood, Rufus. *Twenty Years in the Secret Service: My Life with Five Presidents.* New York: Simon and Schuster, 1973.

ARTICLES

"Can the Risk Be Cut?" *Newsweek,* April 13, 1981, pp. 18–21.
Chapman, Stephen. "The Secret Service's Biggest Secret." *New Republic,* Jan. 24, 1981, pp. 18–21.
Clines, Francis X. "Culling the Secret Service's 400 List." New York *Times,* May 8, 1981, p. 51.

"Did the Secret Service Drop Its Guard?" *U.S. News & World Report,* April 13, 1981, p. 27–29.

Freedman, Lawrence Z. "The Assassination Syndrome." *Saturday Evening Post,* July/August 1981, pp. 66–68.

"Guarding the President: The Job Gets Tougher." *U.S. News & World Report,* Oct. 2, 1978, pp. 76–79.

"Guarding the President — A Rugged Job." *U.S. News & World Report,* Dec. 10, 1979, p. 63.

Hassel, Conrad V. "The Political Assassin." *Journal of Police Science and Administration,* 4 (Dec. 1974) 399–402.

Kaiser, Robert Blair. "Presidential Candidates Disagree on Value of Secret Service Watch." New York *Times,* Feb. 10, 1980, p. 1.
Kaplan, John. "The Assassins." *Stanford Law Review,* 59 (May 1967) 1110–51.
Kurtz, Howie. "Executive Protection Racket." *Washington Monthly,* October 1978, pp. 47–50.

Leeper, E.M. "Could the Secret Service Predict Violent Behavior?" *News Report,* National Academy of Sciences, Jan. 1982, pp. 14–19.
Livingstone, N. C. "From JFK to Reagan: What the Secret Service Thinks of Presidents They Protect." *The Washingtonian,* Sept. 1981, pp. 170–71.
———. "Taming Terrorism: In Search of a New U.S. Policy." *International Security Review,* Spring 1982, pp. 17–34.
——— and James Kelly. "Could the President Survive a Real-Life James Bond Movie?" *Washingtonian,* Sept. 1981, pp. 168–76.

Melanson, Philip. "Secret Service Survives on a Prayer." San Antonio *Express-News,* Aug. 14, 1983, p. 7H.
Mohr, Charles, "For the Secret Service, a Hail of Bullets Disrupts 'Routine Duty' with President." New York *Times,* March 31, 1981, p. A2.

Robinson, Wilse G. "A Study of Political Assassinations," *American Journal of Psychiatry,* 121 (May 1965) 1060–64.

Slomich, Sidney J. and Robert E. Kantor. "Social Psychopathology of Political Assassination." *Bulletin of Atomic Scientists,* 25 (March 1969), p. 9–12.
Sullivan, Joseph F. "Security Forces Prepare for Ford Visit to Newark." New York *Times,* Oct. 2, 1975, p. 83.

Tays, Dwight L. "Presidential Reactions to Security: A Longitudinal Analysis." *Presidential Studies Quarterly,* Fall 1980, pp. 600–9.

PUBLIC DOCUMENTS

Central Intelligence Agency. *International Terrorism in 1979.* Springfield, Va.: National Technical Information Service, 1979.

Report of the Warren Commission on the Assassination of President Kennedy. Washington, D.C.: U.S. Gov't. Printing Office, 1964.

U.S. Congress, House. *Report of the Select Committee on Assassinations.* Washington, D.C.: U.S. Gov't. Printing Office, 1979.

U.S. Congress, Senate. Select Committee on Government Operations with Respect to Intelligence. Alleged Assassination Plots Involving Foreign Leaders. Washington, D.C.: U.S. Gov't. Printing Office, 1975.

––––––. Select Committee on Government Operations with Respect to Intelligence. *The Investigation of the Assassination of President John F. Kennedy: Performance of Intelligence Agencies.* Washington, D.C.: U.S. Gov't. Printing Office, 1976.

U.S. Secret Service. *A Brief History of Presidential Protection.* National Archives, Warren Commission files, Record Group #22, Records Relating to the Protection of the President. Washington, D.C.: U.S. Secret Service, 1964.

––––––. *Election Year 1980.* Washington, D.C.: U.S. Secret Service, 1980.

––––––. *Excerpts From the History of the United States Secret Service.* Washington, D.C.: U.S. Treasury Department.

––––––. *Rowley Report.* National Archives, Warren Commission file #22, Records Relating to the Protection of the President. Washington, D.C.: 1964.

––––––. *The Secret Service Story.* Washington, D.C.

––––––. *Special Agent.* Washington, D.C.

––––––. *Training Manual.* National Archives, Warren Commission files, Record Group #22, Records Relating to the Protection of the President. Washington, D.C., 1954.

U.S. Treasury Department. *Management Review on the Performance of the U.S. Department of the Treasury in Connection with the March 30, 1981 Assassination Attempt on President Ronald Reagan.* Washington, D.C., 1981.

INDEX

forgery, 12, 15, 19, 30, 32
Fort Detrick, Md., 84
Foster, Jodie, 78, 194
Frankel, Max, 145
Freedman, Dr. Lawrence Z., 77
Freedom of Information Act (FOIA), 109, 148, 161
Fromme, Lynette "Squeaky," 61-63, 78, 113
Fullbright, William, 162
Gaddafi, Muammar, 85
Garfield, James A., 8, 53
Gaudet, Edwin, 67-68
General Accounting Office (GAO), 153
Germany, 11, 12
Giarrusso, Clarence, 67
Good, Sandra, 62
Gordon, Agent Mary Ann, 45, 182-183, 187
Grammer, Billy, 57
Grant, Ulysses S., 4
Greer, Agent William, 170, 171
Guiteau, Charles J., 8, 53

H

Haldeman, H. R., 155, 157
Halpern, Charles R., 145
handguns, 75
Harding, Warren G., 12, 13, 152
Hazen, William P., 6
Hearst, Patricia, 64
Hearst, William Randolph, 64, 66
Herman, Joseph, 145
Hill, Agent Clinton J., 41, 133-134, 156
Hinckley, John W., Jr., 63, 78, 80, 105; behavior before shooting, 188-189; and Reagan assassination attempt, 183-184, 185, 186, 187, 191, 194-195; and Secret Service files, 113-115 (*see also* Reagan assassination attempt)

Hirohito, Emperor, 83
Hoover, Herbert, 13, 14, 92
Hoover, J. Edgar, 14, 15, 26, 147, 176-177
Hosty, James, 173
House of Representatives Select Committee on Assassinations, 177
Humphry, Hubert H., 56, 60, 141

I

Institute for Defense Analysis, 89
Interior, Department of, 40
Internal Revenue Service (IRS), 40, 43, 147
International Security Review, 83

J

Jackson, Andrew, 7-8, 53, 86
Jackson, Robert, 168
Japanese Red Army, 83
Jeffreys-Jones, Rhodri, 7
John Birch Society, 177
John Paul II, Pope, 82
Johnson, Andrew, 2-3
Johnson, Lady Bird, 23, 120
Johnson, Lyndon B., 59, 126, 127, 129-130, 131, 133-134, 139, 141, 142, 150, 151, 170, 172
Johnson, Marion, 161
Jones, Paul, 68

K

Kellerman, Agent Roy, 170, 171
Kelly, James P., 84, 153, 198
Kennedy, Ethel, 69
Kennedy, Jacqueline, 156, 169
Kennedy, John F., 39, 153; attitude toward protection, 124, 125, 127,

129, 131, 162; and Cuban exiles, 177; (*see also* Alpha-66); and Cuban policies, 175–176; (*see also* assassination of John F. Kennedy)

Kennedy, Robert F., 33, 49, 55, 133

Kennedy, Senator Edward M., 34, 35 142; attack on, 69

Kerbegovic, Muharen (the "Alphabet Bomber"), 85, 86

Kerner Commission, 77

King, Martin Luther, Jr., 49, 55, 133

Knight, H. Stuart, 44, 80, 128, 132, 142, 148

Kotch, Dr. Paul, 75

Ku Klux Klan (KKK), 4, 174

Kurtz, Howie, 30

L

Lafta, Samuel, 189

Lawrence, Richard, 8, 53, 85, 86

Lawson, Agent Winston G., 164

Lennon, John, 201

Levi, Edward, 109

Libyan Assassination Team, 85, 119

Lincoln, Abraham, 2, 8; assassination of, 2, 3, 53

Livingstone, N. C., 84, 153, 189

Lodge, Henry Cabot, 9

lone assassin, 74–75, 82, 84, 86, 194–195; dissimilarities among, 78–79; "profile" of 76–78, 80–81 (*see also* dangerous persons, loner)

loner: concept of, 79–80 (*see also* dangerous persons, loner)

M

Malcolm X, 49

Malony, James J., 15

Mankiewicz, Frank, 139

Mansfield, Mike, 140

Manson, Charles, 62, 63

Marcos, Ferdinand, Mrs., 49

Margolis, Jane, 144

McBride, Judge Thomas J., 62–63

McCarthy, Agent D. V., 186

McCarthy, Agent Timothy J., 105, 132, 186

McClellan, General George B., 2

McCullough, William P., 3

McGovern, George, 56, 139

McKinley, William, 6, 7, 8, 9, 10, 53, 54, 86, 160

McMillan, Judge James B., 151

Meese, Edwin, 34

Merchant, Jack, 64

Merryman, Clyde, 58

military intelligence, 112, 147

MINARET (CIA project), 149

Mona Lisa, 15

Mondale, Walter, 45, 102–103, 141

Moore, Sara Jane, 27, 64–66, 81, 113

Moran, William H., 15

Moro, Aldo, 82

Muskie, Edmund, 56

N

National Aeronautics and Space Administration (NASA), 116

National Archieves, 161

National Academy of Sciences, 75, 116

National Parks Service, 40, 150; rangers, 95

National Rifle Association (NRA), 26, 76

National Security Agency (NSA), 111, 112, 147, 150

Nazi Party, 174

New Republic, 200

New York *Times*, 100, 145

Nixon, Donald, 151
Nixon, Richard M., 44, 56, 103, 139, 141, 143, 149, 155; attitude toward protection, 131, 132, 157; and Manson family, 62; political uses of Secret Service, 150, 151, 152; security improvements on home of, 153-154; stalked by Arthur Bremer, 59-60; and Uniformed Division of Secret Service, 30

O

O'Brien, Charles, 76
Ochberg, Dr. Frank, 41, 107-108
O'Donnell, Kenneth, 124, 162, 163
Office of Management and Budget (OMB), 40
Office of the Director of Defense Research and Engineering, 88-89
Office of Science and Technology, 88
O'Shea, Jack, 65
Oswald, Lee Harvey, 78, 79, 113; and protective-intelligence gathering for Dallas trip, 171-174, 175, 176, 178 (see also assassination of John F. Kennedy)
Oswald, Marina, 173

P

Paine, Michael, 175
Paine, Ruth, 175
Parr, Agent Jerry, 137-138, 182, 186, 187, 188
Pearson, Drew, 166
Pierce, Laurens, 60-61
Pinkerton, Allan, 2, 6
Plummer, Chester M., Jr., 70
Pogash, Carol, 66
Pontius, Ron, 64

Powers, Dave, 169
presidential politics and protection, 138-144, 157-158 (see also assassination of John F. Kennedy: political plans for Dallas trip)
presidential protection, 90-92, 94-95, 106, 107, 166; advance procedures for, 98-99, 101-102, 111-113, 115-116, 118-119, 182-185 (see also assassination of John F. Kennedy: Secret Service advance work, Reagan assassination attempt: advance security); and attacks, 104-106, 138-139, 140 (see also assassination of John F. Kennedy: the shooting, Reagan assassination attempt: the shooting); early history of, 7-11, 13, 14, 15; and psychological orientations of presidents, 128-129, 130-134, 157-158; and travel, 98, 99-100, 102-104 (see also protective methods)
Privacy Act, 109, 148
privacy of protectees, 126-128, 130
protective methods, 74, 85, 88, 94, 96, 98-101, 102, 103-106, 111-112, 117-118, 120-121, 165-166, 168, 171-172, 189-190, 193-195; and "safe zone," 101, 103, 106-107; technology of, 88-90, 92-95, 96, 97-98, 146 (see also assassination of John F. Kennedy: performance of agents, Reagan assassination attempt: the shooting)

R

Rand Corporation, 89
Ramsey, Agent Steven, 191

211

Ray, James Earl, 113
Rayburn, Sam, 156
Research Analysis Corporation, 89
Reagan assassination attempt, 63, 69, 80, 105, 138, 148, 198; advance security, 182-184, 194-195; arrival at Hilton Hotel, 185-186; bullets, 186-187; communications problems, 192-193; medical and security data, 193; protective intelligence, 185; role of Secret Service Washington, D.C. field office, 190-192; security at hospital, 189-190, 191-192, 193; security tightened after shooting, 194-195; the shooting, 186-187; trip to hospital, 187-188; vice-presidential protection, 193-194
Reagan, Ronald, 94, 102, 103, 105, 126, 152; attitude toward protection, 131-132; use of bulletproof protection, 100, 101; and Libyan assassination team, 85, 119; secrecy regarding travel, 102; Secret Service guards home of, 6, 154 (see also Reagan assassination attempt)
Revill, Jack, 174
Robertson, Nan, 145
Rodriguez, Manuel, 176-177
Rogers, Walter C., 189
Roosevelt, Eleanor, 128
Roosevelt, Franklin D., 14, 15, 127, 131, 147, 151; attempted assassination of, 54; tricks played on Secret Service agents, 129
Roosevelt, Theodore, 8, 9, 10, 35, 91; attempted assassination of, 53-54, 87
Rossides, Eugene T., 59
Rowley, James (Secret Service Director), 145, 157; and John F. Kennedy assassination, 160, 167-168

Ruby, Jack, 49
Ryan, Hugh, 70-71

S

Sadat, Anwar, 82, 103
St. Elizabeth's Hospital, 96, 97
Schlesinger, Arthur Jr., 162
Secret Service: Advisory Committee on, 34; alleged mismanagement by, 6; budget, 38, 39-40, 108, 200; candidate protection , 34-35, 39-40, 55, 57, 125-126, 141-142, 143-144; canine unit, 28, 189; communications division, 24; and Congress, 5-6, 10, 11, 12, 13, 14, 25, 33, 42, 146, 147, 148, 150; and Constitutional rights, 144, 145-146, 147-148, 150, 151, 152; counterintelligence role, 7, 11, 12; counterterrorist assault team (CAT), 85, 198; crisis procedures, 105-106; debate about usefulness of, 200-201; director of, 18, 25, 44, 137; dual-mission status of, 199; espionage role, 7, 14; Executive Protection Service (now the Uniformed Division), 27-28 29, 30; field offices, 23, 46, 109; files on U.S. citizens, 23, 61, 63, 65, 81, 111, 112-113, 114-117, 145-146, 148-150, 172-173, 174, 183, 185; headquarters, 21, 23, 26-27; intelligence gathering, 11, 12, 14, 147-150, 151; investigative role, 10, 11, 12-13, 14, 21, 22, 197 [and threat cases, 66, 67-68, 145]; legal counsel for, 25; Liaison Division, 24; and local police, 147; Office of Administration, 25; Office of Inspection, 25; Office of Investigations, 19-22;

Office of Protective Operations, 23, 27; Office of Protective Research, 21, 23, 24, 109, 111, 172; Office of Public Affairs, 25, 26–27; organizational development of, 1, 3, 5, 6, 13; organizational structure of, 18–22, 38; personal use of by presidents, 152–153, 157; personnel levels, 38–39, 40; political influences upon, 138, 139, 145, 151, 154–155, 197; political neutrality of, 137–138; political uses of by presidents, 149–152, 157; and presidents' private homes, 153–155; protection of ex-presidents, 39; protective intelligence gathering, 86, 108–120, 147, 148, 165 (*see also* assassination of John F. Kennedy: intelligence gathering for Dallas trip; intelligence role of Dallas police, Reagan assassination attempt: protective intelligence); protective mission, 32–35, 47, 55–56, 138, 149, 197–198, 199, 201; protective subdivisions, 23–24; relations with press, 143–144, 145, 151–152; Technical Development and Planning Division, 24; Technical Security Division, 23–24, 183, 189; and Treasury Department, 25–26; Treasury Security Force, 22; Uniformed Division (formerly Executive Protection Service) 22, 28–30, 41, 42, 43, 95, 96, 97, 108; Watch Office, 110–111; White House detail, 44–45, 67, 151 [pressures upon, 155–158; Washington, D.C. field office, 19 (*see also* protective methods, presidential protection, Secret Service agents)

Secret Service agents: critics view of, 200–201; killed in line of duty, 70–71; reactions of, 106–108, 121; recruitment of, 43–44; salaries, 44; stress and fatigue, 40–41, 107–108, 144–145; training of, 43, 45–51, 169–170, 171; tricks played on, 129–130; women, 44, 45 (*see also* assassination of John F. Kennedy: performance of agents, Reagan assassination attempt, Secret Service)
Sepple, Oliver, 64
Shaddick, Agent Ray, 186, 188
Shah of Iran, 84
Shigenobu, Fusaka, 83
Shrank, John, 54, 85, 86
Snow, Robert, 40, 46
Socialist Workers Party, 173
Sorrels, Agent Forrest, 163, 164
Spanish-American War, 6, 7, 11
Spriggs, Agent Carleton, 191
STAR Reports, 88–90
Starling, Col. Edmund, 131
Sterling, Claire, 82
Stevenson, Adlai, 161–162, 173, 177
Stout, Agent Stewart, 55
Symbionese Liberation Army (SLA) 64

T

Taft, William Howard, 11
Tate, Sharon, 62
Taylor, Agent Robert H., 157
Tays, Dwight L., 130, 131
Teapot Dome, 12
Teflon bullet, 75–76, 85
terrorism, 29, 74–75, 76, 86, 198; growth of 81–82, 83, 84; possible terrorist attacks, 83–85; in U.S., 83 (*see also* weapons availability and technology)

Zapruder, Abraham, 171
Zapruder film, 49, 169
Zarvos, Agent Nicholas, 58

ABOUT THE AUTHOR

PHILIP H. MELANSON is Professor of Political Science and department head at Southeastern Massachusetts University.

Dr. Melanson has published widely in the area of political science. His articles and reviews have appeared in the *American Political Science Review, Comparative Political Studies, Political Methodology, Politics and Society, Polity, Public Policy, Transaction/Society,* as well as in *The Nation* and in various newspapers and magazines. He is the author of *Political Science and Political Knowledge* (Public Affairs Press, 1975) and the editor of *Knowledge, Politics and Public Policy* (Winthrop Publishers, 1973).

Dr. Melanson holds a B.A., M.A., and Ph.D. from the University of Connecticut.